PARAGRAPHS ON TRANSLATION

D0870339

DÉPARTEMENT D'ÉTUDES LANGAGIÈRES

DÉPARTEMENT D'ÉTUDES LANGAGIÈRES

MULTILINGUAL MATTERS

About Translation
   PETER NEWMARK
Attitudes and Language
   COLIN BAKER
Computers in Applied Linguistics
   M. C. PENNINGTON and V. STEVENS (eds)
Fluency and Accuracy
   HECTOR HAMMERLY
Language Education for Intercultural Communication
   D. AGER, G. MUSKENS and S. WRIGHT (eds)
Linguistic and Communicative Competence
   CHRISTINA BRATT-PAULSTON
A Practical Guide for Translators
   GEOFFREY SAMUELSSON-BROWN
Tasks and Language Learning
   GRAHAM CROOKES and SUSAN M. GASS (eds)
Tasks in a Pedagogical Context
   GRAHAM CROOKES and SUSAN M. GASS (eds)

Acheté à Melbourne

XIVe Congrès de la FIT

Février 1996

Please contact us for the latest book information:
Multilingual Matters Ltd,
Frankfurt Lodge, Clevedon Hall, Victoria Road,
Clevedon, Avon BS21 7SJ, England

TOPICS IN TRANSLATION 1

PARAGRAPHS ON TRANSLATION

PETER NEWMARK

MULTILINGUAL MATTERS LTD
Clevedon • Philadelphia • Adelaide

FOR MY SON MATT

Library of Congress Cataloging in Publication Data

Newmark, Peter
Paragraphs on Translation/Peter Newmark
p. cm.
1. Translating and interpreting. I. Title.
P306.N473   1993
418'.02–dc20

British Library Cataloguing in Publication Data

A CIP catalogue record for this book is available from the British Library.

ISBN 1-85359-192-0 (hbk)
ISBN 1-85359-191-2 (pbk)

Multilingual Matters Ltd

UK: Frankfurt Lodge, Clevedon Hall, Victoria Road, Clevedon BS21 7SJ.
USA: 1900 Frost Road, Suite 101, Bristol, PA 19007, USA.
Australia: P.O. Box 6025, 83 Gilles Street, Adelaide, SA 5000, Australia.

Copyright © 1993 Peter Newmark.

Reprinted with minor revisions, 1995

Printed and bound in Great Britain by the Longdunn Press, Bristol.

CONTENTS

v

More on French Economic Translation • Notes on the Translation of
Quotations • Adapting Metaphors as a Translation Procedure • Titles •
Translating Poetic Discourse • The Thin Line of Values • The Eternal
Unfindable • Of Course.

INTRODUCTION

The following chapters are the first of a series of *Paragraphs on Translation* which I began contributing once every two months to *The Linguist*, the journal of the Institute of Linguists, in September 1989, and which I am likely to continue as long as I go on teaching. The format of sections and paragraphs appeals to me, since it gives me the freedom (and indeed the 'space'!) to discuss any topic as succinctly as I like. I think that more or less self-contained paragraphs have an impact that is missing in chapters of prescribed length.

I have written these *Paragraphs* for various groups of readers: first for translators, students and teachers of translation, and even for translation theorists; secondly for language teachers, linguists and educationalists; thirdly for public administrators, politicians, directors of townhalls, airlines, hospitals, museums, theatres, art galleries, etc; and most importantly for the general and educated reader, who is continuously and increasingly affected by translation in the streets, in the supermarkets, in public buildings, in planes and trains, in information and tourist offices, to an extent that has never occurred before.

The content of the book can be categorized as follows:

1. Translation of erotic language, which is *sui generis*.

2. Straight translation topics such as quotations, back translation, repetition, keywords, the sounds of words, symbols, phrasal words, short stories, plays, economic and legal texts, where my purpose is to assist translators by setting out options, quoting translation examples and making recommendations; I had intended to include these topics in a revised edition of my *Textbook of Translation*, but this would have made the book intolerably long. I regret that there is little here on technical translation, which I have not taught in recent years, and nothing on machine translation, which is of great importance, but where I am only an interested observer.

3. Translation theory. I have produced some correlative comparative propositions which partially supersede my distinction between 'semantic' and 'communicative' translation; have defined and insisted on the medial factors in translation; and have discussed the responsibilities of the translator. I do not write to provoke, but what I write on these themes is often tentative and controversial. However, I write only what I feel as well as think, and am possibly an unusually serious writer.

4. Translation, foreign language teaching and linguistics.

5. Translation as a topic of public interest. This includes the national importance of translation in public life, not only as a professional

activity, but also as a product in the form of public notices in public places, of instruction manuals, of traffic signs, of goods labeling, of airline literature and announcements etc as an essential means of communication not only for visitors and tourists, but also for all the linguistic communities of a country.

6. Critical discussion of translation periodicals, conference proceedings, and recently published books. I have endeavoured to focus on particular points and examples rather than to write general reviews.

7. The book has three sub-texts:

(a) Political. I am committed to some human, animal and environmental rights, many of them generally, some not yet generally accepted. All of these rights are reflected in an attitude to language and a treatment of translation method. Translation is too important as a discipline and as a practice to be morally neutral or non-political. However there are many texts where universal rights have a slight or no role (except as regards sexist language), and it is counter-productive to harp on them.

(b) Artistic. I love certain musical works, poems, plays, fiction and paintings, and I want, rather too concisely, to convey this love to any readers I have. I admit that the connection between the works and translation is sometimes rather tenuous and artificial. For instance, I have not the slightest interest in the title of Goya's most impressive masterpiece; nevertheless, the Prado should produce an authoritative translation of *The Third of May*. As an excuse, I can always have recourse to Ramon Jakobson's and George Steiner's thesis that virtually any mental process is translation, though I do not personally subscribe to this thesis.

(c) Linguistic. I am absorbed and fascinated by language, and I attempt to make a small contribution towards its understanding and appreciation.

These paragraphs then cover a wide field. They are designed to be of general interest, but many sections should be specially useful and suggestive to particular groups of readers.

I have made as few alterations as possible to the original articles (converted to chapters) as they appeared in *The Linguist*. Some items provoked a lot of controversy, as well as favourable and unfavourable reactions, and this correspondence and my replies can be read in the journal. I have modified some of my ideas in the course of the two years, and the chapters are therefore sequenced chronologically. The Contents list gives the section titles and all the book's main topics.

I have made some personal acknowledgements in the course of the book, and as previously, I particularly thank my main informants and most searching critics, Pauline, Elizabeth and Matthew Newmark.

I
MAY 1989

Introduction

The purpose of this introduction is to provide a framework for the paragraphs that follow in this and subsequent chapters, as I have modified my ideas about translation and changed my terminology in the course of these twenty years.

I think there are primarily two methods of full translation. Full, as opposed to 'partial' or 'functional' translation, accounts for every detail of a source language text. The first method, which I call 'semantic' translation, is used to translate all authoritative texts, that is texts where the content and the style, the matter and the manner, the thought and the words in their structures are all equally important. Authoritative texts include serious imaginative literature, ex-cathedra statements, any text that the translator considers to be well written and true; but an authoritative text may also be badly written since authority derives either from the status of the text's source or from the intention to express the author's personality and feelings, as in a work of art.

Authoritative texts are translated at the author's level, to reproduce a maximum degree of the SL contextual meaning in the target language; they follow TL natural usage when they use 'social' language, viz. common SL syntactic structures, punctuation, sentence lengths, colloquialisms, standard metaphors, connectives, and collocations, accepted technical, institutional and cultural terms; when they use 'personal' language, viz. unusual syntactic structures, neologisms of form or meaning, original metaphors and collocations, unusual sentence-lengths and punctuation, the 'personal' language has to be preserved, usually through literal translation. Usually, authoritative texts keep within the source language culture, but the translator may make concessions in the reader's favour on minor points of meaning.

The second method of 'full' translation I call 'communicative' translation. This consistently follows natural usage at the level of the intended readership, and is used for all non-authoritative texts. The translation has to be well written, whether the original is or not, but linguistically and culturally it may have to be adapted to suit the comprehension of the readership.

I am assuming that in principle one can reach a measure of agreement about standards of good writing, which is covered by Swift's 'proper words in proper places', as well as a close correspondence between thought and language, and the absence of cliché, tautology and inflated jargon. Translations of non-authoritative texts should be

1

clear, neat and elegant, but keep the tone and flavour of the original. The style of authoritative texts should, in translation, follow that of their authors.

Both methods of translation aim to be accurate and concise within their different bounds. The more authoritative a text, the closer must be its translation.

The paragraphs that follow are concerned with translation problems stemming from examples. Briefly, a translation problem arises from a stretch of text of any length which is not readily amenable to literal or word for word translation. Therefore there will be a choice of translation procedures, depending on the relevant contextual criteria. Even after arriving at a preferred solution, there may well be approximately synonymous solutions of equal merit; much translation is a compromise between one solution and another; a juggling act, a toss up, a tightrope; it is often subject to a change of mind within any space of time on the translator's or reader's or critic's part. For this reason alone, the concept of translation equivalence, while it is useful operationally, cannot be defined without a series of provisos and qualifications. But in this or that instance, it can be profitably discussed, and this is what I shall try to do.

On Technical Translation

In a technical text, one wants to use terms used by experts, either practitioners or academies, always assuming that the readership is correspondingly expert. Nothing wrong with translating *spéléologue* as 'caver', *la rivière souterraine* as 'the river cave' or *le système des circulations souterraines* as 'the drainage' for practitioners; 'speleologist', 'underground river' and 'underground water flow system' for academics. The first versions are narrower and more concrete than the second.

 Again, *concrétion* is more precise than 'formation', and although 'concretion' is a perfectly valid English word, 'formation' is justified if it is more commonly used by experts, and is likely to be well understood in its context. In an informative technical text, the translation's function is to give the information clearly, neatly and elegantly (that is its 'literary' quality), preferably in professional language (technical and ordinary). It need not give all the information explicit in the original, provided it is implicit in the translation, and that the reader is likely to grasp it.

The German Titular *Zum/Zur*

'On', 'about', 'concerning' . . . ? The only full translation of this invaluable preposition is 'A contribution towards . . .'

On (*Zur!*) Lexical Translation

Whilst more objects, processes and qualities have generally accepted one to one word equivalents in two languages than linguists normally admit, few of these equivalents have the same status in the two languages; often one (*Erscheinung*, phenomenon) is less frequently used, therefore narrower in range of meaning, than the other (*phénomène*). Again, the mere fact that many objects have the same functions but different dimensions and composition in two cultures (handicrafts as opposed to mass production) means that the equivalence is linguistic rather than referential. Qualities (adjectives, adverbs, adjectival nouns) being the expression of mental judgements, will have fewer equivalents; thus *original* (F) is usually 'original' but in other contexts will be 'eccentric', 'novel' or 'odd'. *Affinité* (F) normally translates as 'affinity', but being more common than its English equivalent, it may be 'kinship' or 'close conformity'.

General Words

It's a truism that general or 'hold-all' words sometimes deviate from apparently straightforward literal translation. Thus *qualité* is often 'property', 'qualification', 'position'; *'phénomène'* may be 'factor', and even 'structure' (any language) is not sacred (*structure d'accueil*, 'reception facilities') in translation. Sometimes, (*dans l'optique de ce livre*) a word with no one-to-one equivalent such as 'scope' can be used to replace the more obvious 'point of view', 'perspective', 'viewpoint', 'orientation', etc. At others, a buzz-word such as 'address' (cf. 'perceive'), as in *avant de traiter de ce problème*, tedious as it has become, may replace 'deal with' or 'handle' (informal), 'treat' (unusual collocation), or 'discuss' (too strong).

Connectives

Languages tend to clutter the beginnings of sentences with clichés which the translator can conveniently break down: *il convient donc d'examiner* . . . 'we must now examine'. *On comprend aisément pourquoi*, which, if taken seriously, becomes: 'It is easy to understand why'; as a cliché, it is 'naturally', or it can be not translated. *D'une part* . . . *d'autre part* usually indicates merely 'both . . . and', or 'first . . . secondly'; *il est certain que*, 'admittedly'; *ce qui veut dire que*, 'in effect'. *Il faut donc avoir recours au sirop de chloral* . . . 'we may therefore prescribe a chloral hydrate syrup'. *Il ne faut pas méconnaître également l'alcoholisme de certains toxicomanes* . . . 'Further, alcoholism in some addicts should not be overlooked'.

Metalanguage

How to translate, in a Masonic brochure, '*Étymologiquement, connaître c'est: naître avec?*' To begin with, the statement is not true: *connaître* derives from Latin *noscere*, to know, not from *nascere*, to be born. (Compare English connoisseur with French *connaisseur* — the

French spelling changed in 1835!) Metalingual statements can only be translated literally, if the linguistic forms correspond with their meanings in both languages.

If a metalingual statement is not important in its context, its translation can often be omitted. In the sentence above, where the idea is important but the text is not authoritative, any sentence emphasising the importance of thorough knowledge may be adequate. If the text were authoritative, the sentence should be translated literally (it makes an emotive point), but the etymological error must be indicated in a translator's note, either at the bottom of the page or in square brackets afterwards in the text.

Vestiges of the Bac

French and Italian writers often leave traces of their *philo* examinations in their writing. English has no equivalent. A phrase such as *en bonne épistémologie* can be translated as 'strictly speaking', as it means little more. Compare *manichéisme*, a 'black or white approach'.

Jargon

Ailleurs cependant l'évolution se fera peu à peu vers une extension des articulations touchées et réalisera le deuxième grand tableau.

The extract is from a study of articular chondrocalcinosis, an inflammation caused by calcium deposits in a cartilage, which can be diagnosed from a succession of three clinical patterns, of which the first is pseudogout and the second a type of pseudorheumatism.

The SL extract is an egregious instance of jargon combining empty verbs and verb-nouns such as can be found literally translatable and translated in any 'developed' (i.e. much contacted) language: 'Elsewhere however the development will occur gradually towards an extension of the affected articulations and will realise the second main pattern'.

This gobbledegook could be recast along these lines: 'In other cases, where the joints gradually become increasingly affected, the second clinical pattern (pseudorheumatism) will be observed.'

Modulations and Other Procedures

Cette revue des principaux mécanismes financiers comporterait une lacune s'il ne s'y ajoutait, en raison de sa brûlante actualité, ce qu'on appelle communément le mécanisme de l'inflation.

'This review of the main financial mechanisms would be incomplete if it did not include, as this is a controversial and topical issue, a discussion of what is usually called the inflation mechanism.'

The above translation example demonstrates a number of points:
1. Modulation (*comporterait une lacune*; 'would be incomplete'). The English is weaker but smoother than a literal translation ('would contain a gap').

2. Inclusion and equivalence. Whilst *se composer de* and 'consist of' denote equivalence; *comporter*, *comprendre*, 'comprise' denote inclusion or equivalence; *contenir*, *englober*, *renfermer*, *embrasser* denote only inclusion. *Entre autres* and *u.a.* (G), being more formal than 'among other things' can often be translated with their verbs as 'include'.

3. Transposition. *Brûlante actualité*. The cliché transposition would be 'highly topical', but *brûlant* can mean 'urgent', 'delicate', 'controversial', 'passionate', 'fascinating', 'risky'.

4. Metalingualism. *Ce qu'on appelle* is a 'red light' word. You have to check that what it refers to applies in the TL as well as in the SL. Here it does.

5. Literal translation. Note my predisposition towards literal translation if I'm in doubt, if there's nothing plainly better, if that's what the author transparently wrote. (*Cette revue* . . . etc.)

Additional Information

Where additional information is peripheral to the main sense of a text but is a matter of interest to the TL reader, it should be incorporated in the TL text rather than footnoted. Thus in the following sarcastic extract from a piece on mental illness:

'un administrateur d'un grade élevé — inspiré sans doute par le récit des noyades de Carrier dans le guide Michelin — imaginait récemment des bateaux à fond ouvrant propres à immerger les nombreux malades incurables et improductifs,'

the parenthesised passage would be obscure to the reader in a close translation, but could be rendered as:

'A senior administrative official, doubtless inspired by the story of Carrier's mass drowning counter-revolutionary rebels in the Loire in 1793–4, recently devised the idea of boats with opening bottoms for drowning the numerous incurable patients . . .'

(The historical information is available in the *Encyclopaedia Britannica* as well as the *Michelin* guide to Britanny.)

Contrast as a Semantic Indicator in a Text

In the following extract from *Le système bancaire français* by G. Rouyer and A. Choinel (PUF, *Que sais-je?*, 1981):

marché va alors se dédoubler; d'un côté, des grandes entreprises (risques faibles, volumes importants, conditions limées, relations techniques), d'autre, des PME (plus grande fragilité, faibles volumes, meilleures marges, contacts personnalisés), some of the collocations could hardly be understood or translated unless one bears in mind that the first set of four are positive, the second negative, and that they parallel each other. The translator is obliged both to point and clarify these oppositions, e.g.:

'The market then began to split, on the one hand into large companies (low risks, large quantities, easy terms, mechanised communications); on the other, into small and medium-sized firms (greater risks, smaller quantities, wider margins, personal contacts).' The French is bizarre (*limées*, lit. 'filed down', *relations techniques* '*technical relations'; meilleures marges*, 'better margins') and jargonised (*personnalisés*). *Volumes* may refer specifically to trade figures or turnovers, but 'quantities' leaves it sufficiently general. The passage indicates the use of contrasts (which may be extreme or narrow, and may relate to dimensions, qualities or attitudes, favourable or unfavourable, derogatory or approving), as a pointer in text linguistics, but this dialectical progression is rarely mentioned in the literature, not even the copious texts from the Karl Marx University in Leipzig.

In the next paragraph, the contrast remains but the balance is shifted in favour of the PMEs. Again, the translator could clarify contrasts and strengthen emphases:

Constatant l'inégale rentabilité des opérations proposées par les grandes entreprises et la difficulté de s'extraire de pools de financement de groupes lourdement engagés, les banques entendent davantage jouer la carte des PME en allégeant formules d'intervention et processus de décision en matière de crédit.

'Noting that the large companies proposed to engage in operations which brought in rather variable profits, and that they found it difficult to extricate themselves from financing pools of heavily committed investor groups, the banks tended increasingly to favour the small and medium-sized companies by modifying their intervention and decision-making procedures when they gave credit'.

Knowledge of text-linguistics, in particular the general tendency to a dialectic, to move between thesis and antithesis and an occasional synthesis, determining each language unit's role in this movement, as I have illustrated in the preceding paragraphs, is an important component in a translator's approach to a text. It in no way dispenses with the lexical, grammatical and referential problems that have to be solved at the particular and specific points of the text. The problems of coherence and cohesion coincide when the meanings of sentence-joins such as *alors* and *d'autre part* are to be determined.

II
JULY 1989

Translation
Translation is always possible, more or less. Usually, in one place or another, it calls on priorities, compensations, compromises.

The Prevailing Wind
The prevailing wind amongst writers on translation rather than translators is reader- and target language oriented. Thus Vermeer writes of the 'dethronement' of the original, but the airline magazines are filled with unnecessarily close parallel texts. Chau declares that 'fidelity is a legacy of our servile past' but readers and customers usually want accurate translations. Admittedly much diffuse and badly organised information is transmitted as effectively through gist or summary or abstract as through a full recast well written translation, but if the details are important, the translation is what the reader wants.

As the market, the customer, the client, the consumer, start monopolising translation, and reducing meaning to message, content to function, my instinct revolts, I incline to the other pole. I see translation as a linguistic literary moral weapon for exposing linguistic or literary or cultural bad writing, as a weapon against obscurantist mumbo-jumbo, (post-structuralist, pseudo-literary, elitist,) and in a long tradition of enlightenment. Where others turn away from the original, I want, through translation, either to enforce its strength, or to deculturalise it in the cool wind of common sense, to show it up, to lay it bare in its shallowness and poverty of expression. A scrap example from a Cadiz tourist brochure: 'There is singing all over the place whilst the wine flows in a great frenzy of joy and happiness'.

The Translation of Key Words
Raymond Williams, in his superb *Keywords* (second edition 1983, Flamingo/Fontana) curiously never defines the term. For the purpose of translation, I would define it as a conceptual term which covers a significant part or the whole of a text, and which normally recurs several times; it stands out from the text, so that it tends to be context-free. In principle, the translator finds a single TL equivalent for any SL key word, and repeats it whenever it is used. When there is no one-to-one equivalent and the term is partly transparent and partly misleading, it is sometimes transferred for an educated readership: thus the 17th Century *gloire*, meaning public national State honour or prestige, as opposed to personal honour (*honneur*) so brilliantly

savaged in Corneille, may be reproduced at each mention in the SL text. The difficulty may come when a key word in the SL text has several even apparently contrary senses, and the translator has to translate differently at each mention. Keywords, and the different senses of the same key word (not uncommon in Chinese) are often best discussed in a translator's preface.

The Frequency Quandary

Sometimes a translator is obsessed as much by doubts about frequency of use as about precision of meaning: *La réforme Reagan continuera certainement à exercer son effet de contagion.* 'The Reagan reforms will certainly go on having an influential/strong/contagious effect/strong attraction'. Sometimes 'semantic' translation is a relief after 'communicative' translation; it reproduces what the author actually wrote. Otherwise, 'the Reagan reforms will continue to catch on?'

Dilemmas of Register

La rémuneration de l'actionnaire est, par nature, aléatoire. 'The shareholder's remuneration is essentially uncertain'. Meaning is abated because the semantic equivalent of *aléatoire* here, 'chancy', is too colloquial. 'Uncertain' is semantically inadequate, and 'governed by/dependent on/subject to/chance' too heavy.

Latinisms and Register

The main argument for preserving Latinisms in English is that they are concise (Latin is almost as synthetic as Russian) and useful in a formal register. Thus *a fortiori* is stronger than 'all the more so' and shorter than 'for similar and more convincing reasons'.

Vogue English

Trendy British English is seeing a generalisation of financial terms (portfolios, takeovers, mergers) and their acronymic spawn (oiks, dinkies, yids) and a secularisation of religious terms (mission, vision). Translators have to be aware of language trends — whether they conform or resist may as usual depend on a hundred contexts.

Holdall Words

One of the quirks of languages is to include a technical as one of the senses of its holdall words: *Objekt*, 'property' (especially in the GDR); *Objektiv*, 'lens'; *Objektträger*, 'slide'; *tempérament*, 'instalment'.

Categorisation

Broadly, there are only two methods of translating, which I refer to as 'semantic' and 'communicative' translation. They have fuzzy edges, overlap and each still often leaves an embarrassingly large choice of translation solutions, in particular for words of quality and assessment, where reference-criteria are merely implied. Recreative translation, used for advertisements, propaganda, adaptations of comedies and poems, is a possible third method, but it includes no verification principle. Since these translation methods cover every text type and all stretches of language, categorisation is needed to explain or justify any translation decision or principle. The term 'categorisation' is misleading, since it implies 'categorical' meaning 'strict' and 'unqualified', when in fact these categorisations are not hard and fast, and merely have a basis of frequency and probability. Thus whilst in general terms, authoritative texts are translated 'semantically' and non-authoritative texts 'communicatively', the principle that the more sacred a text, the more 'semantically' it is translated may cut right across other categorisations. Thus if an advertisement is translated for the purpose of selling the product to the TL customer, the translation will be 'communicative'. If the purpose is linguistic, i.e. to explain SL styles of advertising to the TL readership consisting of advertisers, PR agents etc, the translation must be 'semantic'. Again, whilst serious imaginative literature is in general terms translated 'semantically', there is a wide difference in the way one translates a lyric for oneself or for one reader, where the translation should ideally be reread a hundred times, and the way one translates a serious comedy, which is only heard once, may have a mass of recherché cultural references, and hopefully a large and varied audience. The lyric is perhaps the 'purest' example of 'semantic' translation, expressing meaning through sound as well as words, which includes its own aesthetic versus referential tensions, whilst the comedy will stretch as far as it can towards 'communicative' translation, since if it doesn't raise a laugh or two from its receptors, it fails as a translation. So categorisation and sub-categorisation proceed with qualifications at every stage.

Kamasutra and Alice

How to translate erotic or humorous literature? The ratio of culture to universality in each? It is a verifiable topic.

Symbols

For translation purposes, symbols are objects which represent an idea (a dove, peace), a social group (sickle, peasants), a quality (fur, smooth), an event (red circle, the Revolution) of considerable importance. A symbol may have a virtually universal, a cultural or an individual significance; it is the strongest form of metaphor, whilst a connotation is the weakest. Thus a sword (*épée, Schwert*) used to symbolise power, authority, the masculine principle, warfare — perhaps it still does so in some collective unconsciousnesses. It has however other regional and local connotations which are cultural and which in translation would have to be explained to an uninformed readership.

Other symbols are cultural, say when they represent a basic food or drink in a particular area. Thus how to translate 'the quality of the sausage on the dinner table'? A sausage is a symbol of a basic food in some European countries and N. America, and could therefore be appropriately intertranslated; in Asia and Africa, however, the symbol carries no weight, and would have to be replaced by a common food or dish of varied quality. Note also: 'Capel had difficulty in keeping the kind of staff who prefer champagne to a pint of bitter'; this could be reduced to sense ('require high living standards'). Alternatively, 'bitter' could be replaced by 'beer' or 'wine', and 'champagne' is an international symbol for this kind of readership.

Note that there are symbols of extreme wealth in many language cultures — those of poverty (rags) are universal, those of wealth (Rolls, Jacuzzi) more likely to be cultural and likely to require classifiers for translation. Thus North and South have opposite meanings in Italy and Britain. The sub-class of motivated symbols — icons, indices and symptoms (see John Lyons, *Semantics*, CUP) — have to be treated with similar caution in translation. If an iconic sound such as 'quack' and meeow' denotes a duck and a cat respectively, it can usually be appropriately translated, or transformed if the TL culture does not contain these animals; where indexical language refers to certain social classes (words and accent), there are all the problems of translating dialect. (See my *Textbook* for an inadequate treatment). The colours of the face (purple, white, green etc) are symptoms (connotations) of the moods and emotions of some individuals, whites rather than blacks, and have to be appropriately translated. Colours and animals are always strongly culture-bound, but contiguous cultures often overlap.

Default Translation

I define default translation as translation of a not understood and often not previously found stretch of language where the translator by a process of reduction, of *lucus a non lucendo*, becomes convinced that no other interpretation is possible. Usually it is a question of a single word never previously seen or whose meaning in the context is plainly remote from all its dictionary or encyclopaedia meanings or which is misspelt or miswritten, and after all allowances have been made for irony, nonsense, surrealism, and so on. Default translation is normally notified to the employer and the readership.

Default Translation

Example: *Les jeux de pousse-pousse entre monnaies des pays riches ne changent cependant pas grande-chose à la situation des monnaies du tiers-monde rattachées directement ou non aux grandes devises.* Li translation: 'The rickshaw games between the currencies of the wealthy countries do not much change the situation of the third world currencies that are directly or indirectly connected with the major currencies.' 'Rickshaw' does not make sense literally or connotatively as one country supporting another like a rickshaw. A default translation focussing on the literal meaning of *pousser* would suggest that *pousse-pousse* is a game resembling tiddlywinks. (Names of games may be insufficiently documented in French dictionaries.) Default translation: 'Jostling for position between the currencies of the wealthy countries has little effect on third world currencies which are more or less directly linked to the major monetary systems'.

Die Ewige Wiederkehr (Nietzsche's 'Eternal Recurrence')
Reading Furtwängler on Toscanini must be like listening to any 'targeteer' (TL oriented) on any 'sourcerer' (SL oriented).

The Philo Factor
My impression is that educated French writers are marked all their lives by the *philo* courses they took in their bac. The result is modern Cartesianism. Its strength is in its orderliness, its logic, its structure. Its weakness is its abstractness, its excessive use of holdall words like *phénomène, évolution, mesure, a priori.* Does any other language have so many meanings per word? Take now a scrap example from Raymond Barre: *On appelle flux le mouvement d'une somme d'objets déterminé par un ensemble homogène de décisions; ce mouvement s'effectue de secteur, les secteurs étant les lieux d'entrée et de sortie des flux,* which could be translated as:
'A flow may be defined as the movement, which is determined by a coherent set of decisions, of a certain amount of capital; this movement proceeds from one sector to another, each sector being determined by the point of inflow and of outflow.' Seven words in this short sentence have been particularised in the English.

Creativity
It is one of the many paradoxes of translation that it is nowadays usually claimed to be a creative activity or process, when it appears to be in essence imitative. Novelty, originality, inventiveness, imagination, resourcefulness are usually associated with creativity, as well as activity rather than meditation. However, the process of simulation then imitation, being unnatural (pretending to be someone else, another, *l'autre*) calls on artificial and distorted activity.
At the lowest level, one could claim that all decision-making is creative, and only literal translation is imitative and non-creative. The paradox is that literal translation and transference are sometimes the

most creative elements in translation, since they enrich the target language and subsequently the TL culture, whilst the hermeneutic, an essentially creative approach that grapples with the SL sub-text may be a find, a *trouvaille*, but may be a translator's mistaken hunch.

Translation is for Discussion

These paragraphs are controversial emotive Nietzschean. Translation is the product of paradoxes and oppositions, triadic as well as dyadic, that is, the moral and material facts of the truth as well as the old yawns: the writer and the readership, the word and the text, the two languages, the two cultures. Translation must always admit a plurality of views, be an instrument of democracy, eschew dogmatists and bores.

These paragraphs fail if they do not arouse response and eventually narrow a few gaps.

III
SEPTEMBER 1989

Translating Erotica

I assume that translating erotic literature is one of the oldest professions in the world, though not as profitable or as degrading as the oldest. When asked about this type of translation, I have suggested that where there are choices, the translation should be slightly more rather than slightly less erotic than the original. (The same goes, *pari passu*, for humorous literature.) The erotic instinct is universal rather than cultural, but its direction is influenced by censorship, which may be ideological as well as governmental, and by commercially motivated fashion in clothes. Universally, its goal is the buttocks*, thighs, hips and the genitals rather than busts, legs, shoulder and (even, when compelled) ankles. The belly dance, the black bottom. The essence of the erotic is in surprise, fantasy, vigour, reciprocity and sometimes risk.

I take a few examples from *L'Amour en France au XII siècle* by Georges Duby, a sociological study with an ill concealed erotic undertone. Each example is followed by a 'weak' and my 'strong' translation. *Il lui est interdit de l'échauffer.* 'He was forbidden to warm her up.' ('He was forbidden to arouse and excite her.')

Les prêtres ont planté une croix dans les reins de cette femme.' 'The priests have planted a cross in this woman's loins.' ('. . . have stuck a cross up her crotch.')

Des assauts qui lui répugnaient. 'Overtures she found repugnant.' ('Assaults that repelled her.')

Il est interdit à l'époux et à l'éspouse de s'élancer l'un vers l'autre dans l'ardeur et la véhémence. "Husband and wife were forbidden to be carried away in a transport of love by their intense ardour.' ('. . . to pounce on each other in mutual vehemence and passion.')

Le mariage manquait d'être le lieu de l'élan des corps et remplissait mal la fonction d'apaisement. 'Marriage could not be the place for physical passion and badly performed the function of appeasement.' ('Marriage was not the place for thrusting bodies and so offered no physical relief.')

Ils brûlaient. 'They were consumed with love.' ('They were tormented by lust.')

A post-graduate student doing a thesis on Lanie Goodman's translation of Eugène Carrière's enigmatic *La Moustache* told me she

---

* Note, in order of phonic sensuality: arse/behind/haunches/rear/bottom/ buttocks/rump/croup/backside/hips/tail/back/posterior/derrière/bum/ass.

was worried by the 'bad taste' of the translation of the breathless unpunctuated erotic scene. *Sexe* was translated as 'cock' instead of 'penis'! By the back translation test, 'cock' should be *bitte* and *sexe* (here) the 'genitals', but clinical words won't do in erotic passages, so I think 'cock' (or 'prick') is justified. (*Le coq français* has no sexual connotations.) The student also complained that the verb *baiser* was translated as 'fuck' instead of 'make love'. *Baiser* being the all-time unmentionable word at French lessons in English classrooms (up to 198?), it's essential to translate it as 'fuck' or 'screw' or even 'lay'. Goodman actually jibs at 'cunt' for the female *sexe*, and prudishly replaces it with 'vagina'. But the book is well translated.

I take it as axiomatic that the translation of a good erotic scene should be fresh, earthy and surprising. The Germanic monosyllables help. Nothing is so offturning as a familiar blue passage or painting (except the Rokeby Venus?): read or seen too often! Erotic literature, as opposed to pornography, should be well-written, suggestive and revealing about its characters as well as sexually.

Privacy

A long time ago someone said that Russian had no word for 'privacy', as though this was another sinister symptom of a communist state. (Compare Reagan's misguided reference to no Russian word for 'freedom'.) In fact, I doubt if any language has a comprehensive one word equivalent for 'privacy'. The Spanish *intimidad* and to a lesser extent the French *intimité* fit in some contexts, but they are evidently more 'intimate' than 'privacy' in others. 'Privacy' has important components of personal solitude, tranquility, freedom from interruption and interference, the reverse of publicity and the media. The word in this conceptual sense ('I want privacy') is, *pace* the text linguists, fairly context-free and easier to contrast negatively than to define positively, though it has no antonym.

Translating Latin

The translator should not assume that an educated English reader understands Latin. If she (like me) wants to keep some knowledge of Latin alive, she should use couplets, (i.e. transference plus translation) stressing the more important alternative and subordinating the other. Examples from *L'amour en France au XII siècle:* 'hatred' (*odium*); '*caritas*' or affection; '*a curialis*', a member of the Papal Court'; 'a young soldier (*juvenis miles*). Footnotes in such cases are fussy and unnecessary. For medieval Europe, Latin words can be retained as international key-words, not unlike the Linnaean classifications of plants and animals and the medical grecolatinisms which secure a basis of international comprehension and translatability. In the case of historical terms, the Latin will be lost or forgotten unless it is translated.

Proper Names

Proper names are a translation difficulty in any text. In literature it has to be determined whether the name is real or invented. In non-literary texts, translators have to ask themselves what if any additional explanatory or classificatory information has to be supplied for the TL readership. Thus: 'Cleveland' — Ohio port *or* NE England county (from 1974) *or* NE England region *or* an American president.

The Semantics of Sounds

Analysing the meanings of sounds is more popular amongst poets than linguists or semanticists, let alone phoneticians and phonologists. Language is claimed to be arbitrary, and animal cries are differently recorded in many languages, though the difference is not that great. Rimbaud in his sonnet memorably defined the meanings of the basic vowel sounds. Grammont in his brilliant treatise (*Petit Traité de Versification française*) barely distinguishes the meanings of the plosive stops (p, b, t, d, k, g); but voiced sounds seem blurred, unvoiced abrupt, t's the sharpest, k's the most forceful sounds in language. Anyone brave enough to interpret phonemes is usually confronted but not confounded by numerous exceptions.

The meanings of sounds derive from the spontaneous cries of humans and animals and the noise of the wind and the rain, reflected in pleasure, pain, anger, fear, tranquility, and other spontaneous emotions. These are universal sound elements, and translators who are writers have to be aware of them.

Revisers

I believe that all commissioners of translations (publishers, agencies, companies, individual clients) and particularly freelance translators must recognise that all translations have to be revised by a third party, and that the necessary cost of this revision must be included in the calculation of the fee. The days of the lone freelance translator could be over, though commercial and legal translators should still take out indemnity insurance. It is ironical that whilst forty years ago the name of the translator of a book was often omitted, and even now say Garzanti (of all publishers) puts it in tiny letters on the back of the title page (my protest, about my own book has received no reply), the name of any reviser of a translation is never mentioned, unless it is some consecrated husband-and-wife team. The contribution of the reviser should be credited in any published work, but the final responsibility for it remains with the translator.

If a translation is not revised, the result can be horrendous. It's a matter not only of linguistic and referential mistakes but of slip misprints and above all inadvertent omissions, which to make. Some time ago I was engaged in advising translator, a careful and competent linguist, who had made a small number of mistakes and omissions in translating a contract. The agent said it was fine. Then the client said it was mistake-ridden and substandard, incompetent and inadequate, and refused to pay the agent. Then the agent refused to pay the translator, alleging he had lost business not only from the client, but from other local firms, since the client had reported the case to the local chamber of commerce. As I see it, the agent should pay the translator and the client should pay the agent, setting off a sum for the correction of the errors, for which the agent is responsible. But that may not be how the law works. The costs may or may not be considerable, and the distress is already enormous.

No profession is as vulnerable and exposed as that of translators, if they work on their own, except that of surgeons, who, though they head a team, cannot have their work revised.

Some Notes on Legal Translation

Legal translations, like legal documents, have to be flawless, not only referentially but linguistically, unlike any other type of translation. Anything less is unsatisfactory. Terms of art have to be translated by their exact equivalents, and if these do not exist, they have to be transferred and closely defined (Thus in French, *common law*, may in context have to be transferred and distinguished from *droit coutumier*). Non-legal words, which usually constitute the bulk of any legal text, have to be precisely accounted for, and emphases preserved.

My impression is that legal language and terminology are more orderly than the terms of other branches of knowledge, particularly medicine, the most ancient and the most chaotic. Lawyers often have to define their terms before they use them, especially in the case of contracts. (Lawyers are linguists; doctors and engineers are not.)

Pitfalls are innumerable. An *entrepreneur* (F) may be an entrepreneur, but he's more likely to be a 'contractor'. A term such as *association* (F) has many legal meanings when it has collocates such as *momentanée* (joint venture, in Belgium), *en participation* (partnerships of various kinds), *syndicale* (property owners' syndicate), *de malfaiteurs* ('criminal conspiracy'), whilst 'association' (E) has technical meanings in psychology, chemistry and ecology, sometimes unhelpfully obscured by a lack of collocates. But even in legal texts, when terms such as *association, définitif* (definitive, not final), *société, structure* etc are used non-technically, as ordinary language, and without collocates (note *structure d'accueil*, 'reception facilities') they should be translated literally.

A semi-legal collocation may have several meanings: *tomber dans le domaine public*: 'come out of copyright', 'become government property', 'fall within the public domain' (no longer secret).

The essence of legal language is not spoken but written language, not 'how would you say it?' or 'would you hear a lawyer say that?' but 'would you see that in a legal document?' *Pétrole* may be called 'oil' or 'crude', but in a legal or scientific document it is 'petroleum'. Many of the 'targeteer's' normal ideas of style go by the board in legal translation. An *annexe* (F) is an 'annex' (E), not an 'appendix'; a *juxtaposition* (F) is a 'juxtaposition', not an 'association'. Such correspondences may not apply in the case of collocations. But normally, literal translation comes into its own. In fact, there are little differences of meaning in these examples, but clients will frequently try to exaggerate them. (I use the coinages 'targeteer' for a target language-oriented translator, 'sourcerer' for a source-language oriented translator. Both terms are 'translations' of Ladmiral's *ciblistes* and *sourciers* respectively.)

For the lay person, legal language is a minefield. Who would think that *à la diligence du ministre* is not 'at the insistence' but 'at the request' or 'on the initiative of the minister'?

Abstracting
Abstracting is becoming an increasingly important part of the translator's work. Abstracts are of two kinds: (a) straightforward résumés of the original; (b) abstracts for a particular kind of reader or readership, where the emphasis may be on description or function, causes or results, details or generalisation, the sequence of the events or the present position, dates or approximations, etc. Some would say that (a) do not exist, and indeed it is all a matter of degree.

A Word on Metaphor
May Snell-Hornby, in her remarkable *Translation Studies: an integrated approach* (Benjamins; Amsterdam; 1988), which I warmly recommend, states that the metaphor 'sea', as in 'a sea of faces', implies 'potential movement', whilst *Meer* expresses 'endless monotony'. I think that this distinction is somewhat personal, and that the main sense of the universal not cultural metaphor 'sea' is 'vastness' or 'large numbers', both in English and German, and that the 'large numbers' could apply to roofs as well as faces.

The Soviet translation theorist Aleksandr Švejcer, in his wide ranging book, *Übersetzung und Linguistik* (translated by C. Cartellieri and Manfred Heine, adapted by Albrecht Neubert with Brigitta Schrade; Akademie Verlag, Berlin, 1987) is still insisting that the metaphor/simile 'summer's day' in Shakespeare's eighteenth sonnet, 'Shall I compare thee to a summer's day?', when translated into Arabic, should be rendered as, for example, 'a spring day'. If so, what does one do with 'the darling buds of May?' (But Svejcer shows no interest in poetry.) I have already rehearsed the arguments why 'summer's day' should be preserved in a close translation: not because it's a universal metaphor (it's not), but because that's what Shakespeare wrote, and summer is a central theme of the poem, and it's made abundantly clear within the poem that the English summer is beautiful, and if it's not the Arabic reader must do some homework and find out, and if he reads it again and again he'll appreciate it better than an English reader, and that will be 'dynamic equivalence' (Nida) with a vengeance.

Translating Humour

The essence of humour is incongruity and freshness. If you see a lot of men wearing top hats and white shirts in England, you might, or might not, laugh. But not in Israel. That is culture 'shock'. If you see a lot of people wearing red bulbs on their noses, you might laugh. That is a universal, but a sense of humour is individual as well as universal and/or cultural, and besides, what is humour? Something that makes you giggle or smile or chuckle or roar? If a text is humorous, it must be well written. I suspect that one day the translators will find P.G. Wodehouse, and he will be as popular as Lewis Carroll.

IV

NOVEMBER 1989

Similes

Similes are the poor cousins of metaphors. Unlike metaphors, they are not *ipso facto* a lie, but they have none of the power and the incisiveness of metaphors. Their purpose is to describe approximately, to illustrate, and often to decorate. Normally, they present no translation problems, and are translated literally in any type of text, however improbable or bizarre they may be. As they state a supposition rather than a fact, the translator has no cause to intervene, unless, in a scientific text, they are misleading. Otherwise, 'His skin was like silk' — *Seine Haut war wie Seide* — may be silly, but that's all there is to it.

The main translation problem is to decide when a similar is a simile, and when it is a metaphor. In the case of epithets like 'silky' ('smooth' or 'like silk') or 'silvery' ('clear, ringing' or 'like silver') where the target language has a near-perfect equivalent, the ambiguity can remain or be resolved by the collocate, but other adjectives like 'furry' (*à poil, en peluche, entartré chargé, pâteux*) may force a decision on the translator. A genitive such as 'a master's' may raise similar problems, as it may indicate ownership or physical or figurative association.

Demise of Translation?

I think it would be clearer if the writers busily engaged in redefining translation would desist and simply point out that whilst the essence remains the same, the scope of the activity has widened and translators also have to perform all kinds of paraphrasing, gisting, abstracting, summarising, sifting jobs that derive from translating.

Ironically, at a time when translation becomes everywhere more conspicuous, essential and pervasive, some writers are claiming that the concept is out of date. The idea of truth, accuracy and fidelity which is the core of translating is to be swamped, swallowed up in a vague mass mess of 'intercultural communication' or 'intersemiotic events' which are to be concocted *ad hoc* to satisfy a targeted readership with its own requirements and tastes. Just because in some instances, a readership which has little in common with the original readership does have to be targeted, and in others a close translation is superfluous, as the original text is so diffuse or trivial, or in others the original is so morally or factually inaccurate it has to be corrected or annotated when it is translated, it is misguided to abandon the word translation which has in any case always had a large number of readily available quasi-synonyms, many of them dangerously vague (go into, render, turn, adapt, betray, mean, etc.) as well as itself having at least fourteen figurative or technical meanings.

Seen from Catalonia, Quebec, Slovakia, Wales, India, etc, any attempt to 'dislocate' translation would be destabilising to the constitution of these countries and regions, and would injure the self-respect and pride of a large number of their citizens, since mandatory translation is not only the basis of their laws, but of all their public writings, their communications, their notices, their street signs, their instructions, their advertisements.

Personification
All languages tend to personify concepts, but why time? Is it to stress drama? *La période qui nous occupe n'a laissé seulement des écrits normatifs.* ('In the period we are concerned with, we have not merely been left with prescriptive documents.')

Gloire
Corneille and De Gaulle had a great sense of *gloire*, but for all intents and purposes, outside the standard collocations, this concept boils down to 'reputation' rather than the emotive 'fame'.

Senior
Ironic that this loaded Latin word dissolved into *seigneur*, 'sir', *signore, señor*, leaving its English sense of age and rank to be translated as *ancien* or *anziano* and debased as 'senior citizen'. In German (*Senioren*), it at least has no ageist connotations.

There is Always a Reason
In Claudio Magris's *Danubio, L'io si dilata e si contrae come una medusa* is translated as 'The ego dilates and contracts like a Portuguese man of war.' (*Danube*. Tr. Patrick Creagh.) A medusa is a jellyfish, and it seems strange that it wasn't translated as such. However, a 'Portuguese man of war' is 'a large jellyfish with long poisonous tentacles hanging below its floating body', so the translation is perfectly legitimate. But what about the poor untargeted English reader, chasing mythical Portuguese battleships?

The Targeted Readership
The present Government uses the term 'targeted' to show that it limits its charity to those that need it, apart from beggars and the cardboard city, and does not waste it on the idle of the former welfare state. This somewhat narrow (two senses) concept of 'targeted' is sometimes applied to the readership of a translation in blanket terms.
When a document is translated for one person, it is strictly targeted.

Medical papers in academic journals are targeted at specialists, but authors may or may not and translators may or may not have GPs, nurses and students in mind. Some authors and translators may want to educate the readership rather beyond the strict function of their stories. (Remember the long scientific chapter 'Researches' (*Forschungen*) in *The Magic Mountain?* I wonder who ever reads it.)

Vermeer, Chau, Nord, Reiss, Kussmaul, Hönig conceive their 'degree of differentiation' (Hönig and Kussmaul's pretentious pseudo-scientific term) narrowly — all that the readership is allowed to read — their targeted readership gets no chance to learn anything but the 'message', as they, the translators, not the authors determine it. Vermeer claims that Thomas Mann consciously wrote for a cultured readership. I doubt it. I think Mann wrote to educate his readers a little, and hoped they would take the trouble to turn to dictionaries and encyclopaedias when they read him. Mann taught me and I revere him. I don't want 'any degree of differentiation' coming between me and an author.

The duller, the more passive a readership, the more it has to be targeted.

Words, Music and Translation

It has been said that poetry is untranslatable, against all the facts. It has not yet been said that *lieder* are untranslatable. In a sense, sung words are the least translatable of all words. Words accompanied by music, better, music accompanied by words is the densest and most precise vector of meaning. If Pamina sings: 'the truth' instead of '*die Wahrheit*' (for me the greatest and most astonishing moment in all opera, or Tamino sings 'Perhaps' instead of *Vielleicht* (the most yearning), it is indeed a lame translation, but since the music is so much more powerful than the words, the semantic loss is not great. Surtitles (libretto translations synchronically screened for the audience), though sometimes too comically literal, in theory get the best of both worlds, and are certainly here to stay. For *lieder*, whether you know German or not, I think a useful preparation is checking 'communicative' against a word for word translation. As for all art, the words will only gain in semantic force with repeated hearings.

Collocations

Collocations may override even meanings of powerful concepts. Thus *la nature et la culture* becomes 'nature and nurture'.

Frequency

The 'frequency rule' may override particular meanings. Thus *la règle infrangible* becomes 'the inviolable rule'.

Translating Universal Humour
Universal humour is simple, surprising, gentle, childlike if not childish, always perfectly translatable, even if the translation is not perfect, may allow alternatives. The most obvious examples can be found in the most universal of all great works — wait for it — Mozart's *Magic Flute* (surprise, surprise, do I still have a reader, let alone a readership?), not only in the spoken dialogue but also the recitative, not only in Papageno and Papagena but also in the three Ladies and Monostatos:
Nein, nein! Das kann nicht sein. Ich schütze ihn allein. 'No, no! That won't do, I'll protect him on my own (by myself).' (The rhymes are lost, but it's just as funny.)
Furcht eben nicht, nur eiskalt läufts mir über den Rücken. (Not really afraid. I just have icy shivers running down my spine.)
Pfui Papageno! Sei ein Mann! — Ich wollt ich wär ein Mädchen. Disgusting, Papageno! Be a man! I just wish I were a girl.
Jetzt such ich die Mutter auf, weil die Tochter mir nicht beschieden ist. 'Now I'll sort out the mother, as the daughter's obviously not for me.'
Wie alt bist du denn? Achtzehn Jahre und zwei Minuten. 'How old are you then? Eighteen years and two minutes.' (The funniest and most perceptively critical joke.)
Ich werde dir immer treu sein (für sich), so lange ich keine schönere sehe. I'll always be true to you, (aside) till I see someone prettier.
(Note also the pun about Papageno suspended on a rope, his fate in suspense. *Spannen, in Spannung* might produce a parallel pun.)
Note all these jokes are virtually non-cultural, rather childish. I shall not explain the humour, and I suggest those who don't understand it should do their homework by reading as well as seeing/listening to this funniest, most serious of masterpieces.

The Emphatic Present
The emphatic present (and past) tense appears to be unique to English, and is often overlooked by translators into English (as is the progressive present). Its purpose is to emphasize or affirm, sometimes ironically; it is conversational and informal in register. (*Komm doch herein!* 'Do come in'.)

Books and Papers
Up to the end of the last war, translations of books must have greatly outnumbered those of papers — poems, business correspondence, treaties mainly made up the latter. Now the proportion of papers has increased enormously; hence the rise of the staff translator, who only translates or summarises papers.
But to conclude, on the basis of no statistics, that the number of

'sacred' texts to be translated is rapidly diminishing, is misguided. There is, for instance, a vast backlog of Hong Kong laws and regulations waiting to be translated. EC documents, including applications from outside for specially favoured status, have to be flawlessly translated.

There Must Always be a Happy Solution!
Unfortunately, this is not so. One goes on breaking one's head. (*Kopfzerbrechen.*) One thinks of a million alternatives. One puts the problem away to return to it. One hopes one will wake up screaming in the night with the right solution. But maybe there just isn't one — there is a gap in the target language's lexical resources. One has to make a choice between 'adequate' equivalence or innovation, often through literal translation, which always runs the risk of a giggling reception. ('How ludicrous! No one would ever say that.')

Puns and the Possibility of Translation
I take my example from Thomas Bernhard's superb late play *Der Theatermacher (The Scene Maker, The Play Actor, The Song and Dance Maker?*, now translated as *The Showman*) which is running at the Burgtheater in Vienna: *Dein einziger Reiz ist dein Hustenreiz.* (Lit. 'Your only attraction is the irritation in your throat'.) The pun is on *Reiz*, meaning 'attraction', 'stimulus', 'lure', 'appeal', 'charm', and since this is dialogue, it is not reproducible. One is left with the typical choice between a semi-pun and a forcible rendering of the sense, say
'Your only charm is charming up coughs.'
'All you can do well is cough.'
'All you ever manage successfully is to cough.'
'Your only attraction is the tickle in your throat.'
I suspect the last is the best (please improve), but Bernhard's wit is lost. It is perhaps adequate, not equivalent. In a library version, I would explain the pun with the help of a literal translation.

Belated Acknowledgements
In my last piece on 'translating erotic literature', I could have mentioned that Anne Boyer was writing a thesis on Lanie Goodman's translation of Eugène Carrière's *La Moustache*, and that Jane Dunnett has done a fine translation of Georges Duby's *L'Amour en France au XII siècle.* (I was her 'translator's reader'.)
Grosso modo, they produced the more 'tasteful', I produced stronger versions of the examples.

Blurbs for Translators
Book jackets, so lavish with praise and biographies of authors, should always include at least a note about their translators.

Cultural Humour?

Notice on rear-window of car: *Entschuldigen Sie, dass ich so dicht vor Ihnen herfahre.* ('I do apologise for driving so closely in front of you.') Cars span the world and are barely cultural any more. Irony and understatement may or may not be appreciated more by the educated than the uncouth. In any event if this joke is to be effective (make the reader chuckle (not laugh), reflect and keep his/her distance), the proposition has to be closely translated, but the personal comment (*Stellungnahme*) can be varied to make it as persuasive as possible. ('I sincerely apologise', 'I am so sorry', 'Please do forgive me', 'Do excuse me', etc, etc.)

Translating Wilde

Rainer Kohlmayer's *Bunbury, oder, Es ist wichtig, Ernst zu sein*, his new translation of *The Importance of Being Earnest* (Reclam 1988) is first-rate. It has a brief and perceptive 'afterword' (Auden's translation of *Nachwort*). Kohlmayer takes it for granted that a translator must keep to the original, making no cuts and rendering the puns and the difficult passages (*Stellen*). He points out that most German translator-adapters of Wilde have been stimulated to 'creativity' by for instance translating mild colloquialisms ('Good heavens!') into barrack-room slang (*Himmelsarsch- und -Zwirn*). Kohlmayher is engaged in an analysis of how Wilde's plays were adapted in Germany in the Nazi period, which should be a more enlightening essay in reception theory than the models which describe but fail to evaluate by comparing the adaptation with the originals. Nazi racialist theatre (*Thingspiel, Völkisches Theater*) started with a bang but collapsed in about 1936. After that, the theatre became a haven for the 'non-political' middle-classes, and the force of most plays, German and foreign, was emasculated in the Gründgens period.

The Importance of Close Translation

I take the case of Catalonia (*Catalunya, Cataluña*). An official pamphlet states that it is a small country in NE Spain, with an 'extension' of 32,000 sq. km., which is now an Autonomous Community (*Einheit*) within the Spanish State (*Staatsverband*) with its own government (*Generalitat*, the Catalan term — the Castilian term *Generalidad* is not transferred).

The two languages, Castilian and Catalan largely overlap lexically but the morphology and the function-words are different, as well as some collocations (*Bones vacances* (Cat); *felices vacaciones* (Cast). Thousands of people are employed to translate between the two languages, and the translations are almost but not quite literal. The work must be exceptionally tedious (reading the two versions is even more so), but for all official texts close translation is essential — there is no place for creativity. This is an obvious opportunity for MT, but it will have to be efficient, since for a long time it may be more cost-effective to translate manually than to post-edit after MT. In Catalonia there is also a vast amount of publicity and tourist material that appears in up to seven languages — Cat, Cast, E, G, F, Du and It. Here again, provided that the original is well written and the publicity is not idiosyncratic or gimmicky, there is a good case for accurate translation, if only on the ground of cost-effectiveness. Much of the translation in this area appears excellent, the main mistakes being misspellings and misprints. The delirious mistakes of the Italian brochures are sadly missing. Occasionally a translator overdoes it by introducing her own opening — 'The Costa Brava, the Rugged Coast, has brought world-wide fame to each and every one of its villages, from Port-Bou to Blanes'. A general problem is to what extent the exaggerations of the original (*confèrent un caractère sans pareil*, 'give a unique touch') — are to be reproduced. 'From these phantasmagoric places the Jews of Gerona extended their huge prestige and spread their mastery as far as remote horizons'. The humane spirit of this brochure outweighs its linguistic defects.

Lastly, the importance of close translation can be conspicuously illustrated in the labelling of products in the supermarkets of Europe and beyond, say the contents, preparation and instructions for use. ('Do not overcharge; *nicht wiederaufladbar; non ricaricare; ne pas recharger.*) If the author were 'dethroned' here, and a new text created, the result would be unfortunate. Maybe the aim in some translation should be to increase its universal and decrease its cultural elements.

Der erste deutsche Arbeiter — und Bauernstaat
Absurd of the BBC to go on referring to *Bauern* as 'peasants'! But it's difficult. 'Industrial and agricultural workers?' 'Workers on the land and in the factories?'

Keine Gewalt!
No force? No violence? The wonderful chant of Leipzig's passive resistance is not going to be forgotten.

V
JANUARY 1990

When I recently participated in an enormous translation conference in Trieste on *Autori in Confronto*, a discussion of the many translations of Umberto Eco's *Il Nome della Rosa* and Claudio Magris's *Danubio*, I introduced my paper by stating my attitude towards translation. My contribution was written as a programmatic challenge to the influential theory that the study of translations should be descriptive rather than evaluative; that translations should be regarded as target language oriented to the extent of being virtually detached from their originals; that they should be considered primarily in terms of their function within the literature of the target language, and that if the original is to be studied at all, it should be in terms of transcultural communication, or of intercultural transfer, ignoring all truth values or standards of good writing, even in the case of a serious text, literary or non-literary, rejecting it as a 'criticism of life', as Matthew Arnold put it, concerned with humanity.

I have reacted against this theory. I believe that translation critics should have their own *tertium comparationis*, a third factor of comparison, which consists of values drawn from the growing documentation of universal human rights which transcend national cultures (to which the translating profession continues to subscribe), and their reflection in truthful and personally conscientious writing. I assume that close translation is a weapon, and that the factual and moral flaws in a text, once translated and therefore more or less deculturalised and exposed, will become plainer, often ludicrous, in another language, and that goes for journalism and the media as well as the lies of much romantic literature and the detailed triviality and heartless dryness of much of the analytical literature that preceded it in the 18th Century, as well as the products of their present-day 'epigones', (a word more common in German and Italian than in English), their inferior followers, their uninspired imitators. When a text is closely translated, it is divorced from its source language literary, linguistic and cultural norms; its weaknesses are shown up, its strengths more difficult to assert. It is bare, removed from its natural habitat.

Cavo Assilario (It)
Axillary hollow? Axillary cavity? Axillary cable (howler)? It's merely the homely armpit, technically, the axilla.

Dit (F)
Dans la société dite féodale. Not necessarily 'the society known as/

referred to as feudal', but simply 'feudal society'. *Dite* gives it a little emphasis, as though the term were slightly unfamiliar, should be better known but not enough to spell it out. (Similarly, *sog.* (G), *cosidetto* (It).

Erotic Language Again

An erotic translator should bear in mind that both *Beine* ('legs') and *ventre* ('belly' in belly dance) may well be 'euphemisms' (what a word) for 'behind'. In earlier English, 'ankles' too. Note also that new erotic words like 'bonk' should not be transferred as they initially have no erotic charge in a foreign language. Could a *bitte* (F) ever turn a non-French person on? Strange idea.

Retenir (F)

Retenir like *assurer* or *Anlage* is one of those maddening words that have too many meanings, and the dictionaries fail to stress the most typical ones, which I think are 'accept', 'consider' and 'take into account' (a proposal, an argument, a project). The *Dictionnaire du français contemporain*, which is excellent and often neglected, gives fifteen meanings, but not 'consider', 'discuss' or 'accept'. The Collins-Robert gives twelve meanings, ignores 'take into account', and places 'accept' last. The *Dictionnaire du français contemporain* gives a good summary of my sheaf of meanings: *estimer, digne d'attention, de réflexion, d'étude.*

Some Notes on (French) Economic Translation

I think the basis of a good economic textbook often resembles the bones of a human skeleton, where the main features are duplicated in strong oppositions or contrasts, and there are clear divisions and subdivisions. (Compare the 'Text' of Roget's great *Thesaurus*.) This is particularly so in a 'science' like economics, whose only purpose is to promote the welfare of humanity, but whose content is fundamentally mathematical, a constant balance or up and down of assets and liabilities, profit and loss, credit and debit, income and expenditure, exports and imports, input and output, etc.

It is these oppositions, and often the hierarchies which they head, that translators have to search for and preserve, say in Denise Flouzat's challenging and nicely written *Economie contemporaine: Cette analyse a permis de préciser l'équilibre de parfaite concurrence de longue periode; celui-ci sera atteint au plan de chaque producteur quand il aura déterminé une capacité productive telle qu'il y aura disparition du profit moyen (profit considéré comme anormal). Autrement dit, l'entrepreneur cessera d'investir quand l'investissement additionnel entraînera l'égalisation entre le prix (recette moyenne) et le coût moyen. Tant que le profit moyen subsistera, d'autres entreprises investiront et, suscitant une concurrence accrue, feront baisser les prix jusqu' au niveau où le coût moyen est minimal.* (t. I,p.484). This is clear, but the cartesianism is dizzy-making. In the following version I make 'changes' only to bring out the contrasts: 'In this analysis, the equilibrium of perfect competition over a long period is demonstrated. A producer achieves this equilibrium when s/he establishes a productive capacity at the point where average profit disappears, and the profit is therefore considered 'abnormal'. In other words, an entrepreneur gives up investing when additional investment causes prices (average receipts) and average costs to become equal. As long as there continues to be average profit, other companies continue to invest, and as they invite increased competition, they bring down prices to the point where average costs are minimal.'

Grammatically, there are few problems in economic texts; one misses the syntactically contorted and lexically overblown sentences of the French medical press. What is sometimes perplexing is the abrupt use of an adjective or a past or present participle (e.g. *Étendu à une large population, il réflète mal . . .*) in the first position of a sentence, which can represent any kind of adverbial clause (when, if, because, although, whilst etc), where the context may not indicate what is intended. However, it is effectively used here: *Difficile déjà au plan national, l'utilisation des indices de prix de détail pour établir des comparaisons internationales est très discutable, car les structures de consommation diffèrent d'un pays à l'autre.* ('The use of retail price indices is difficult enough (=déjà) on a national level, but when international comparisons are being made, it becomes extremely questionable, as consumer structures differ from one country to another.')

Lexically, an economic text consists of ordinary language, descriptive economic language, and standard (*consacré*) economic and institutional terms. As I see it, a translator is free to simplify or improve the ordinary or economic language, but the standard terms have where possible to be preserved in aspic (!), thus: *L'indice des prix de gros qui comporte des décompositions* (why not *ventilations*, one of my favourite words?) *par catégories de produits . . .* 'The wholesale price index, which is broken down in product categories' . . . *Des révisions de cet indice doivent intervenir périodiquement . . .* 'The index has to be revised periodically.' (I blow the syntax, the stresses and the order (i.e. the FSP), but the lexis is sacred.)

EC standard terms are immediately intertranslated, and the Commission produces invaluable French glossaries, but I have not seen any for German or other languages. Terms restricted to one country, such as 'junk bonds' (fortunately), *'en pension'*, 'market maker' (*teneur du marché*), 'at the money', 'back up lines' (see *La Banque et les nouveaux instruments financiers*, Revue Banque, 18 rue Lafayette, 75009 Paris), 'greenback' (when used technically; otherwise *billet vert*), are often transferred and defined, depending on the knowledge *or* the interest of the putative readership. Some terms begin as descriptive before they become standard terms, e.g. *les besoins de financement du secteur public*, 'public sector borrowing requirement', with the help of an acronym (PSBR). In other cases, a metaphor such as *circuit monétaire* is continuously used, so that it may be best to translate it literally, enclosed in inverted commas, to denote its strangeness in an English text.

Loose 'stylish' use of synonyms in economic language has to be avoided: *un abaissement uniforme du taux de l'impôt sur le revenu des personnes physiques* has to be 'a uniform', not an 'equal', a 'unified', nor a 'homogeneous' 'reduction in the rate of personal income tax'. (*Sur les personnes morales* would presumably be 'corporation tax' in a wider sense than *sur les sociétés*.) However *politiques inflationnistes* is ambiguous: if it means 'policies that will cause inflation', it is 'inflationary'; if it means 'policies that favour inflation', it is 'inflationist'.

The End of Junk German?

For forty years the official language of the GDR was a language of slogans and clichés. Take one of the last scrap sentences of Honecker's in *Neues Deutschland* (14.10.89): 'What is at stake is the continuation of the unity of economic and social policy, economic efficiency and its use for all, democratic cooperation (*Miteinander*) and committed collaboration (*Mitarbeit*), a decent range of products for the population of the GDR and pay according to performance, the media close to life (*lebensverbundene Medien*), opportunities for travel and a healthy environment'. Perhaps a ghost-writer added the last two items, but soon afterwards, the worn needle gave out.

A few weeks later, the *ND* became another paper, adopted a different simpler language, and published a moving appeal for a 'socialist alternative' drafted by the dissident Christa Wolf, signed by, among others Stefan Heym, whom, like Nietzsche, the GDR refused to publish; it warned that sooner or later, the Federal Republic would swallow (pocket, occupy, *vereinnahmen*) the country. Too late?

Armature

A strange word, hovering in several languages between the technical and the general or the figurative. Mozart's piano concertos are the armature of his works or *oeuvre*.

The Categorisation of Translation Mistakes

When evaluating a translation, one can look at it globally or analytically — both procedures are useful and complement each other. Analytically, one may describe mistakes as *either* misleading *or* 'nuanced'. There are I think two types of misleading mistakes: (a) referential — that is, misstatements of fact, e.g. if *conseil d'administration* ('board of directors') is translated as 'management committee' (*comité de gestion* or *de direction*), or *100m* as '50 yards' (b) linguistic, e.g. if *cote* (rating) is translated as 'coast' or *aura promis* as 'might have promised'. The degree of seriousness of these mistakes is a function of their functional *or* intrinsic importance in the text.

The 'nuanced' mistakes are (a) stylistic, i.e. mistakes of usage or of register, where inappropriate language is used for a particular topic or occasion, where in a formal text say *l'histoire a le don de vous surprendre* is translated as 'history gets up to all kinds of surprising tricks' or *surtout* as 'above all' or *s'efforcer* as 'strive to' (it's too personal, too emotional); (b) lexical, where unnecessary synonyms or paraphrase is used, e.g. when *hausses attendues* is translated as 'anticipated' or 'foreseen' or 'predicted' rather than 'expected rises'. I think these errors should be avoided, but they only become mistakes in authoritative or expressive texts; errors relate to 'meaning', mistakes to 'message'; errors may be personal, harmless, make little difference either way (not to the author, not to the reader), are sometimes in the taste area. Personally, I prefer the truth, what the author wrote, unless there's some rational argument against it — that's my *avis préjudiciel* my pre-judical opinion. *Pravda vitezi* (Cz. truth prevails), but it takes a long time.

Phrasal Words

Not surprisingly, many translators are not aware of the functions of phrasal words. They are (a) less formal (but sometimes neutral, as in 'go out') (b) less pompous (c) more forceful, than their non-phrasal equivalents. They are often missing in foreign language to English bi- or multi-lingual dictionaries, and their functions are rarely stated even in good monolingual dictionaries like the *Collins English* or the *Cobuild*. The particles of phrasal words are often intensifiers, emphasising thoroughness or completion ('use up', 'sleep in', 'pick out'). Phrasal nouns (often collocated with 'empty' verbs) are rarer but more powerful than phrasal verbs ('It's a cop-out'). English phrasal verbs show up semantic gaps in most foreign languages, and therefore they are invaluable to a translator into English and frustrating to a translator from English. (Compare German (Nietzsche's use) and Russian's prefixed verbs, which have some analogous functions, but not their prevailing informality; note also that many phrasal verbs, but not nouns, are polysemous.)

Potentially, phrasal verbs are either physical/behavioural ('put on clothes') or mental/emotional ('put on an air of'), and often have three or four additional meanings in both categories. ('Put on' has nine.) They respond to a popular social need for simple colloquial or informal language, and in a climate of more or less real democracy, meet less prejudice than say fifty years ago. They meld with and restore the basic monosyllabic and analytical, as opposed to synthetic character of English, but also with the constant media and coterie vogue for 'in' words. As they pullulate, they remain a continual translation problem. Note that phrasal nouns, which started only in this mid-century, are also increasing, always subsequent to their verbs. Creagh uses phrasal verbs with exceptional skill. Take: *una serie di violenze abbellite da un sentimentale kitsch* (186) as 'a series of acts of violence tarted up with sentimental kitsch (175). *Le case squillano . . . il liberty ha aperto i suoi rubinetti . . . Una sinagoga pare uscita da un Disneyland . . . Il canale scorre* (431): 'The houses shriek out . . . Art Nouveau has turned all the taps on . . . A synagogue appears to have popped out of Disneyland (323) . . . *The canal runs on, runs on* (401). Creagh gives a negative sense to *abbellito*, since it collocates with *kitsch*; he reproduces the onomatopoeia of *squillano*, emphasising it with the intensifying particle; *aperto* is given its appropriate idiomatic translation; 'pop out' is beautifully suggestive of Disneyland. The 'runs on, runs on' is evocative as the canal flows out into the Black Sea and the close of the book.

Phrasal verbs were frowned on and disapproved of as slang, vulgar, lower class in the 18th, 19th and far into the 20th Century by the educational hegemony. They did not follow the Latin exemplars, and if passivized, or present in a relative clause ('nonsense with which I shall not up put' — Churchill), they led to the proscribed practice of ending a sentence with a preposition.

Note that the most commonly used phrasal verbs (say 'get rid of') become less formal in the course of time, but they may retain their forceful value, and can be used in 'neutral' contexts that are statements of fact.

Grammar and Stress

Unless it is exceedingly complex, grammar is not usually a major problem in translation. Patrick Creagh the translator of Claudio Magris's *Danubio* neatly splits some long sentences and paragraphs. What is striking in this work is Italian's flexibility in word-order (unmatched in English), where any component of a sentence can be stressed without need of passives or relative clauses. Creagh often seems unaware of the relation between word-order and stress:

1. *Questa gioia Stifter la cerca nella monotonia.* (136)
'Stifter seeks for (!) this joy in monotony. (129)'
Possibly: 'This is the joy that Stifter looks for in monotony.'
2. *Preoccupato della comparsa, nel loro tranquillo orizzonte, di Goethe.* (138)
'As he was concerned at the appearance of Goethe over their tranquil horizon.' (132)

Perhaps: 'Preoccupied as he was by the appearance, over their tranquil horizon, of Goethe.' Creagh misses the emphasis on Goethe in contrast to 'their tranquil horizon'.

3. *Moriva un' altra volta, e definitivamente, la vecchia Austria.* (211) 'Old Austria died again, this time for ever.' (198)

The stress has been transferred, perhaps justly, from Austria to 'for ever', skilfully reinforced by 'this time'. Alternatively: 'Death came, this time for ever, to the old Austria'. The basic structure: V(imp.) + S which puts the stress (communicative dynamism(CD)), a term in Functional Sentence Perspective, (see numerous papers by J. Firbas) on the subject, is common enough in Italian; in English, prefaced by 'there' or 'then', it is rather quaint and heavy: 'Then died Austria . . .'

4. *Diventando una pure sia straziata rettorica.* (343) 'Turning to rhetoric, however lacerated that rhetoric might be.' (321)

This is neat and illustrates Italian's concise use of participles as well as modal particles like *pure*. Creagh can produce a similar casual and moral effect when he translates *dicendogli che non lo ero* (202) by 'telling him that actually I wasn't (a Jew) (190) and *Era solo una domanda* (202) by 'I was only asking'. Note also that (a) the English passive in *This story was told me by Miklos* (291) (alt. 'This was the story Miklos told me', can neatly keep the emphasis on 'story' in *La storia me l'ha raccontata Miklos* (311); (b) the subject of a passive whether it is new, old or anticipated (e.g. 'The waiter', after a restaurant has been mentioned) information, normally has more stress than any other component of the sentence. The translator into English can therefore use this structure to stress any noun group in an SL sentence, even by ending his sentence with a preposition (say: 'The story had never been thought of (before).'). Another good example of flexible word-order that retains the stress is:

Un battaglione è solo il suo colore (148) translated as: 'You can tell a battalion only by the colour of it.' (141) (Alt. '. . . just by its colour.')

Translation Theory Now

Théories contemporaines de la Traduction by Robert Larose (University of Quebec 1989) is already in its second edition, but appears to have been little noticed here. It is a survey of the literature on the subject in French and English in the last thirty years, is well written and is generous with its quotations from the so-called 'classics' (*sic*) in the field, consisting of Vinay and Darbelnet, Mounin, Nida, Catford, George Steiner, Ladmiral, Delisle, and, surprisingly, me. Unfortunately, the Soviet and the East and West German literature is virtually ignored, and there is not much on the Spanish or the Italian. The book closes with sixteen 'pragmatic' English texts, from which examples are drawn from Larose's rather complicated scheme of 'parameters for the

textological evaluations of translations'. After the heavy doses of
Steiner, I don't know why there is no literary text. I think it's mainly for
theorists, linguists and teachers of translation practice/theory and I
found it absorbing.

Reinforcement of Descriptive Words

Creagh is well aware (intuitively only?) that in Magris's slow moving
book, the language is descriptive/static rather than narrative/dynamic,
rich in adjectives that are likely to have inadequate one to one
equivalents, and must therefore be reinforced with a kind of
componential analysis which distributes subtle meanings over two or
three words, or with compound words, or with the addition of
emphatic relative clasues. I only have space to offer a few brief scrap
examples out of many, thus; *esige abusivamente* (72) 'makes spurious
and unlawful demands' (71); *estremo* (53) 'last ditch' (53); *lindo* (a key
adjective) 'spick and span', 'neat and clean'; *mina dell'odio* (189) 'time-
bomb of hatred' (178); *la grande economia* (206) 'top-notch economics'
(193); *le mie oscurità* (218)'the dark places of myself' (205); *la sessualità
concreta* (220) 'sexuality in the raw' (207); *la genericità della sua
espressione* (222) 'the completely superficial quality of her expression'
(208); *anche fortunati* (222) 'some of whom have had success' (208);
rivela la seduzione dei meccanismi (341) 'reveals how seductive
mechanisms can be' (319); *notte assoluta* (342) 'night in its most
absolute sense' (320); of the death of Celan's parents — the destruction
of the Danubian Jews haunts and pervades the book; *anziani* (402)
'getting on in years' (375); *testamento* (403) 'last will and testament'
(375); *un altro ordine* (13) 'another and different order'; *di neve* (13),
'snow-fresh'; *plumbeo* 'heavy-handed'.

Metaphors

Apart from the main Danube metaphor, Magris makes use of rather
conventional metaphors that are conventionally reflected by Creagh:
thus, *chi vede fuggire la vita* (291) 'those who see their sands running
out' (272); *nel giro* (410) 'in the swim of things' (382); *la prosa del mondo*
(12) 'the world is humdrum' (16), but note *doppio gioco* (401) as 'double
speak' (373). Sense is also turned to standard, but livelier and stronger
metaphor, in *il suo costo altissimo* (295) 'its staggering cost' (276); *si
lodano* (316) 'clapping each other on the back' (296); *ha ripreso vigore*
(327) 'taken on a new lease of life' (307); *aggiornato* (401) 'in the swim'
(brilliant) (373); *ha sgombrato* (428) 'has packed its bags' (398); *a poco
distanza* (410) 'only a stone's throw away' (398); *finito* (11) 'done for'
(15), *ripetendo con lui* (12) 'echoing him' (16); *intelligente* (165) 'bright
spark' (like Creagh!) (156); *beoti* (165) 'muttonheads' (156). But
parabola (223), a standard metaphor, is translated as 'parabola' (210),
an original metaphor.

From this brief sampling, then, I have the impression that Creagh is sharply aware of the power of translating literal by figurative words, which is not usually found in bilingual dictionaries. He frequently, I suspect spontaneously, converts 'sense' to metaphor, in an endeavour to enliven a style that is occasionally turgid. As I see it, this would be misguided if he were translating say Camus or Kafka or the great Triestino, the Jewish Italian Svevo, with their more or less dry deadpan style, but in this less strict writing it is justified. (My guess is also that English language, being less synthetic and more analytical (i.e. having a smaller grammar and a larger number of idioms) as well as less controlled, in spite of the Italian dialects, than Italian, makes use of a larger number of idioms, so that some additional transitions in translation from Italian sense to English idiom are *per se* warranted.)

French Medical Language Revisited

How delightful to return after ten years, if only for three weeks, to the mad world of French medical language. Here are a few snippets:

L'équipe soignante suscite un système de relations (i.e. 'the nurses want the patients to have company' or now 'to form networks').

Ils subissent une situation particulièrement contraignante où ils doivent mobiliser des mécanismes de défense. ('When faced with a particularly frustrating situation, the patients' defence mechanisms have to come into play!)

Le fait même de cette création, la spécificité de la pédiatrie dans ce cadre, et la cooptation réciproque des premiers membres de cette équipe ont favorisé le développement rapide d'une idéologie soignante commune, destinée, au moyen d' un travail d'équipe, à une meilleure maîtrise de la situation ci-dessus définie. ('The team has had to work out a common approach and procedures to control this situation, drawing on their technical resources and special paediatric skills, and also recruiting additional staff.')

Cette approche prend une dimension particulière. ('We had to adopt a particular approach.')

Finally, an extract from the English translation of the abstract: 'In a Service of Pediatric Oncology, after studying what does the patients and their families need, it is possible to set up an organisation of adapted cares.' (sic)

This, at one remove, is the crazy world of Barthes, Baudrillard and Bourdieu, not to mention Foucault, Greimas, Kristeva and Derrida, transferred to the other world of medical literature. Then there 'arrived' André Gorz, who writes plain French, plain language. How long will he last?

VI
MARCH 1990

Universal Culture

Just as there is in principle, a pure universal language that underlies all language (as Benjamin believed), and which all languages aspire to, but did not originate from, so there is a pure universal culture (a contradiction in terms, since cultures are not universal), from which maybe (a sceptical 'maybe') all cultures have fallen (a Christian view) and towards which all cultures are striving. This universal culture is based on respect for human, animal and ecological rights. The translator uses both the universal language of deep structures and non-cultural words, and the universal culture of equal rights as a point of comparison, a *tertium comparationis*, a mental criterion between source and target language texts. Cultures have their good and bad sides, and the bad ones are exposed in the light of the universals by the deculturalising force of close translation.

The Commissariat

How to translate the *Commissariat général au Plan*, when there is no standard translation? I suggest you transfer it for an academic paper and a textbook, adding 'the French national planning office' for the latter, and retaining this English descriptive and functional equivalent (without the transference) for most other text-types. '*Commissariat*' is a false friend, as it is always associated with food supplies in English.

Computer Language

To an outsider, computer language (as opposed to computer languages) is chaotic. As one generation of computers succeeds another, fresh, often exotic terms are introduced for the same or slightly more sophisticated referent. The *Penguin Dictionary* has alternative terms on every page, and Renée Fischer's *Dictionnaire des nouvelles Technologies* often gives four or more translations for one term. Note the revival of the noble word 'architecture' as a technical term, and the disastrous implications of 'to lose'.

Approaching an Economic Text

Many economic texts are built up on a balance between two agents, each represented by a number of key-words; thus you can have, on the one hand, *actif, patrimoine, entrée, recettes, revenu, dépôt, avoirs, crédit* etc., depending sometimes on whether you are looking at them from the lender's or the borrower's point of view; on the other hand, *passif, dette, perte, exigibilités, investissement, placement* etc. Or it may be between *État, gouvernement, budget* and *fonction publique* on the one hand, and, on the other, *Commissariat général au Plan, Commission des Comptes* and *comptes de la nation.* You are pursuing two thin threads, sometimes intertwined sometimes disentangling, going through the whole text.

Evolution

The all-time hold-all word 'evolution' seems to have a record number of equivalents in many languages. Take your pick: course, process, advance progress, progression, change, changes, development, evolution, trend. In this area, 'trend', 'scope', *décalage*, are useful words that expose lexical gaps in other languages. (But *Trend* is a German word.)

Default Translation: An Example

In the text on the Sun, I was unable to find a translation of *éruption* (F) in any bilingual dictionaries. The *Petit Larousse* defines *éruption solaire* as *phénomene de l'activité solaire se manifestant par l'accroissement brutal* (sudden) *et temporaire des émissions de radiations électromagnétiques et de corpuscules d'une région de la chromosphère et provoquant d'importantes perturbations* (significant disturbances) *du champ magnétique terrestre* (the earth's magnetic field). In the *Encyclopaedia Britannica*, 'solar flares' (defined in Collins as 'a brief powerful eruption of intense high-energy radiation from the sun's surface') figured prominently and there was no mention of 'eruption' as a technical term in the article on the sun. I decided that 'solar flare' and 'eruption' must be identical.

A Sidelight on Translation

Translation is concerned with moral and with factual truth. This truth can only be effectively rendered if it is grasped by the reader, and that is the purpose and the end of translation. Should it be grasped readily, or only after some effort? That is a problem of means and occasions.

A Sliding Scale Theory of Translation

I unify my dual theory of semantic and communicative translation with three propositions (two correlations and a rider):

(a) the more important the language of a text, the more closely it should be translated.

This is valid at every rank of the text: the text itself, the chapter, the paragraph, the sentence, the clause, the group (which may coagulate as an idiom, e.g. 'couldn't help laughing'), the collocation that lexically cuts across the group ('defuse a crisis', 'decisively defeat'), the word, the morpheme (e.g. 'pro-', 'pre-', 'nephro-', '-junct-', '-less' — all, *pace*

Halliday, eminently translatable), the punctuation mark (e.g. that French colon); other linguistic units, such as proverbs, metaphors, proper names, institutional terms, familiar alternatives (*gatos* as Madrileños, citizens of Madrid; '*hrad*' as the Czechoslovak presidency'), eponyms (Ceausescu' as 'tyrant'), may be found at one or more of these ranks. Sometimes one word (like 'chaos'?) may be more important than the unit at any other rank of the text. If sound (alliteration) or phonaesthetic effect (rhythm) is of prime importance, that too has to be rendered, or at least compensated.

Conversely, (b) the less important the language of a text or any unit of text at any rank, the less closely that too need be translated, and therefore it may be replaced by the appropriate normal social language: (example: *Se algo puede dar un golpe mas fuerte que los que de Gorbachev, solo es el caos total*. 'Only total chaos could shake the Soviet Union as much as Gorbachev has done.') Or again, the less important the nuances of meaning of the text, the more important the message to be communicated, the more justification for (smoother) undertranslation, which simplifies or clarifies the place (*Stelle*) in the translation.

But (c), and this is the rider, the better written a unit of the text, the more closely it too should be translated, whatever its degree of importance, provided there is identity of purpose between author and translator, as well as a similar type of readership. If the details and nuances are clearly expressed, they should be translated closely, even though they could just as well be paraphrased. There seems no good reason not to reproduce the truth, even when the truth is not particularly important.

The Importance of a Text's Language

These many references require definitions and illustrations of the terms 'importance' and 'close'. 'Importance' superficially depends on the occasion of the translation and the client's criteria, but it may also be imposed on the translator by the values of the text . . . 'Importance' may be defined as language that denotes what is exceptionally valuable, significant, necessary, pertinent or permanent. Further, importance may be conferred on a text or a quotation by the status of whoever is responsible for it — I refer to such a text as 'authoritative'; thus the phrase 'to be or not to be'; *sein oder nicht sein; être ou ne pas être; ser o no ser* (which limits its meaning), or the nouns in the sentence 'Water consists of hydrogen and oxygen', where 'consists of' is not important, since it may be replaced by 'is' (*es de*) or 'is composed of' (*se compone de*), or 'constitutes' (*constitute*) or 'comprises' (*consta de*) or 'is the equivalent of' (*es equivalente a*) etc. in descending order with negligible semantic loss. Similarly, in many contexts, it is not important whether one translates *bien* or *buen* as 'good', 'fine', 'OK', 'excellent', *parfait* etc, provided that the message gets across. Note too that the important factor in a text may not be restricted to words or other linguistic units, but may be tone (urgency), style (harsh), form (chaotic), metaphor (for its concision), or sound-effect (for emphasis), and they may be imposed by the occasion, e.g. by the requirements of clients or readers. Moreover, if the importance of a text lies merely in its means rather than its end, it is a decorative text and the translator may change its meaning to suit the sound, as in Jiři Levy's famous Morgenstern example — 'a weasel sat on an easel', 'a parrot swallowed a carrot', 'a cadger was chasing a badger', etc. The important element of a text is the invariant factor that has to be reproduced without compromise in an exercise that often entails many compromises.

The Closeness of Translation Procedures

Further, the term 'close' has to be defined. The closest translation is transference, where the SL word (*glasnost*) or idiom ('last but not least' in German) or collocation (*dolce vita*) or cultural (*tagliatelle*) or institutional (*Cortes*) term is already more or less rooted in the TL. The more rooted, the more it modifies its pronunciation and its connotations in the direction of the TL, e.g. 'Berlin', 'machismo', — provided the term has not yet changed its meaning. After that, close translation may be grammatical or lexical: grammatical, first when a group or clause is reproduced ('after his arrival', *nach seiner Ankunft*), secondly, when it is rendered by its standard equivalent ('extremely important', *de première importance*), where the emphasis of functional group perspective is changed, however; thirdly, when it is replaced by a more remote grammatical recasting ('which reaches the height of importance'); lexical, beginning with word for word translation — 'large garden', *grosser Garten*, although 'garden' may connote a less formal image in English than in other languages; secondly, an average one to one up to six to six translation, from 'Friday' as *vendredi*, 'measles' as *rougeole*, 'soldier' as *militaire*, sailor as *marin* or *matelot*, up to say *la matrone et la mal mariée* as 'the matron and the mismarried woman' may reach a degree of closeness varying from perfect equivalence through correspondence to adequacy (fruitless to define equivalence, a common academic dead-end pursuit, or to pronounce where equivalence ends and where correspondence, or adequacy, begins); one can however state that the longer the passage, the less close the translation may be, but that the dissimilarity between the generics bowl and *bol* may be greater than that between this English 'bowl' and that French *bol*.

Further translation procedures, roughly in order of closeness, are componential analysis ('murky' street as *rue sombre et sale, calle oscura y sucia*); modulation ('no mean city' as *ciudad soberbia*); descriptive equivalent (*escudilla* as 'hollow dish'); functional equivalent ('knife' as *instrumento cortante*); cultural equivalent (*bachillerato* as 'GCE A level', *paella* as 'stew') — cultural equivalents are usually inaccurate but they are a shorthand, have emotional force, are useful for immediate effect on the receptor, e.g. in the theatre or cinema (dubbing or sub-titling), and they transport the readership uncritically into the TL culture; synonymy, say *difícil problema* for 'awkward' or 'tricky' problem (or *probleme épineux*), which is pretty feeble, but all the *Larousse English-Spanish* gives, and which may, in the context, be all that is necessary; and lastly paraphrase, the loosest translation procedure, which simply irons out the difficulties in any passage by generalising: *por la razón de la sinrazón de un puyazo en el morrillo* ('owing to the injustice of a blow to the back of a bull's neck') as 'why the picador has to do that to the bull's neck'.

A general principle of closeness in translation is that normal or natural social usage must be rendered by its normal, equally frequent equivalent in *any* text; thus, for 'cheers', *merci* or *au revoir* or *à la tienne*; in an authoritative text, both innovation or cliché should be reproduced (both to the same degree of deviation from normal usage in TL as in SL); but they should be replaced by normal usage, neat and unobtrusive, in any non-authoritative text. So if Ms Thatcher proclaims 'The ship of State may founder' or James Joyce writes: 'The figure was that of a broadshouldered deepchested stronglimbed frankeyed freely freckled brawnyhanded hero', the first state has to be rendered by an equally banal phrase, while the second has to be translated almost word for word, with some attempt to reproduce the alliteration. But if both sentences were the work of hacks, you might translate 'The government may founder' and perhaps 'He was exceptionally attractive and well built'.

Creativity in Translation
The creative element in translation is circumscribed. It hovers when the standard translation procedures fail, when translation is 'impossible'. It is the last resource, but for a challenging text, it is not infrequently called on. If it dominates a text, as in Andrew Jenkins's translations in Fritz Paepcke's *Im Übersetzen Leben*, or in Pound, or in many pre-Romantic translations, it becomes an adaptation, an idiosyncratic interpretation which can hardly be verified (or a bad translation). I think an at least approximate verification, where there are correspondences to be assessed through back-translation, is the scientific element in an appraisal of any translation.

It is not difficult to produce group examples of what I mean by creative translation, say in Patrick Creagh's brilliant translation of Claudio Magris's *Danubio: una vera passione* (a true passion) as 'a downright passion'; *diventando una pure sia straziata rettorica* (becoming a rhetoric, even though tortured) as 'turning into rhetoric, however lacerated that rhetoric might be'; *una mina d'odio* (a mine of hatred) as 'a time-bomb of hatred'; *di neve* (of snow) as 'snow fresh';

notte assoluta (absolute night) as 'night in its most absolute sense'; *la prosa de mondo* (the prose of the world) as 'the humdrum world' — the fitness of these creative translations can be better appreciated in a larger context, but you can see they are a kind of deepening, an *approfondissement*, of literal translation, a for once justified attempt to go below the words to the author's thinking.

The argument for creative translation is the obverse of the argument for the strict impossibility of translation — leaving aside the argument that any kind of translation decision, say translating *Gewalt, force, forza* as 'violence' rather than 'force' (German only has one word anyway) to stress brutality (which is a bottom line argument) could trivially be described as creative. Admittedly or minimally, there is no argument for impossibility in translating routine texts. In informative texts, the creative element is limited to fusing the facts with an appropriately elegant and economical style, as often in *The Guardian Weekly's* translations of *Le Monde* articles. In persuasive texts, creativity often lies in converting source language cultural components (forms of address, evaluative expressions, hypocorisms) neatly into their cultural equivalents, say toning down Latin hyperbole *egregio, illuminatissimo, carissimo* to British English understatement ('dear').

However, it is in expressive texts, poetry, stories, sagas, considered to be untranslatable by a succession of Romantic and post-Romantic literary people (from Humboldt through Croce and Ortega y Gasset to Graves and John Weightman), where words represent images and connotations rather than facts, that creativity comes into play, and the play of words becomes creative. I list the most obvious occasions for the need for creativity:

1. Cultural words — objects or activities with connotations, that are specific to one community (koa, for furniture).

2. Transcultural words with similar referents and different connotations — the 'classical' examples are the staples: bread, rice, wine etc.

3. Concept words with different emphases in different communities (liberalism, liberty, obedience, bureaucracy).

4. Peculiar syntactic structures. (Seeing you is good. *Et lui de partir.*)

5. Cultural metaphors, idioms, proverbs, puns, neologisms. They may have to be spelt out in the TL — concision, force, nuances of meaning are lost or compensated.

6. Significant phonaesthetic effects (bauble, pullulate).

7. Words of quality with no one to one equivalent (downright, grand, wonky). This list is not exhaustive, and to a translator it is depressing, but hopefully useful. Yet we all know that more or less, anything that is said in one language can be said in another, and often has to be. All the above seven factors are only a stumbling block when the full meaning is functionlly important, when it is a component of the actual message rather than a marginal nuance. When they are

important, they have to be compensated by overtranslation, which adds further meaning. (Say 'grand' translated as *grandiose* or *magnifique*.) When they are not, a synonym (*maladroit* or *ungeschickt* for 'gauche') or a generic term ('jellyfish' for *medusa*) or a recast nominal group (*à te voir* or *Dich zu sehen* for 'seeing you') may do, and the phonaesthetic effect has to be sacrificed (often, it is merely slightly rhetorical — 'the ragged rascal') — it usually is.

Whilst in principle, the meaning of any word in any language is unique, due to differences in frequency, usage, connotations and lexical gaps in other languages — in context, the great majority of non-cultural words have perfectly satisfactory equivalents in other languages. Their number depends mainly on the degree of contact present and past between the languages therefore the cultures in question.

Creativity in translation starts where imitation stops. The imitative procedures, defined thirty-two years ago by Vinay and Darbelnet as 'direct translation', are transference (*emprunt*), through-translation (*calque*), and literal translation. The other procedures, four of them defined as 'indirect translation' — but there are rather more than those four — are all in one sense or another creative. The wider and the more numerous the choices, the more (in quality and in quantity) creativity is required. Again, if the translator adopts larger units of translation, seeks dynamic equivalents (say substitutes TL culture for SL culture, 'bits and pieces' for *tapas*), unearths the sub-text, the hidden agenda, the *vouloir-dire*, is pre-eminently target-language oriented, s/he is less circumscribed, more creative — and liberty in translation easily turns to licence. Creativity at its most intense is in translating poetry, where there are so many important additional factors: words as images, metre, rhythm, sounds. Inevitably a good translation of a poem is as much a modest introduction to as a recreation of the original. But again, the most successful is the closest, the one that can convincingly transfer the most important components of the source into the target text. The most creative translated poem is one that is most compressed;

Foul yellow mist had filled the whole of space:
Steeling my nerves to play a hero's part,
I coaxed my weary soul with me to pace
The backstreets shaken by each lumbering cart.
(The Seven Old Men, Roy Campbell: 1952)

Un brouillard sale et jaune inondait tout l'espace
Je suivais, roidissant mes nerfs comme un héros
Et discutant avec mon âme déjà lasse,
Le faubourg secoué par les lourds tombereaux.
(Les Sept Vieillards, Charles Baudelaire: 1857))

VII
MAY 1990

Two Typical Translating Traps
1. A collocation that makes almost as good sense as a metaphor as it does as an idiom.

Thus, *Le Plan devient bientôt un placard où l'on enferme Michel Rocard* might mean: 'The national economic Plan was soon to become a cupboard in which Michel Rocard was locked up', but in fact it means 'The Plan was soon to become a prison in which Michel Rocard was put away.' (*Mettre au placard* = put inside, put away).

2. SL word that is normally translated but is a technical term when transferred.

Thus *rapporteur* usually means 'reporter', but may also mean 'rapporteur', a person appointed by a committee to prepare reports of meetings or conferences or carry out an investigation.

The Indispensable Webster
You meet *chimie fine*, and 'fine chemistry' does not exist. A glance at the Webster, and you find 'fine chemicals' (small amounts, usually in a pure state), which fits perfectly in the context.

Terms of Art
Jean Maillot has warned that the same technical terms may have different meanings in different sciences or technologies. Another translating trap is that innocent looking collocations like 'work stations' and 'expert systems' are also technical terms.

Les Aventures du Corps
Words in context may slip easily from the negative to the positive (e.g. 'minor'), process to product (e.g. 'establishment'), the active to the passive. Thus *aventure* (F) may be active ('the adventure') but in the above collocation, is more likely to be passive ('the body and its experiences').

Reading About Translation
Readings in Translation Theory, edited by Andrew Chesterman (1989, pp 200), obtainable from Oy Finn Lectura, Ab Rautatielaisekatu 6, 005200 Helsinki, Finland, consists of a series of extracts from Dryden, Benjamin, George Steiner, Jumpelt, Levy, Jakobson, Vinay and Darbelnet, Catford, Nida, Koller, Reiss, me (*sic*), Neubert, House, Toma and Vermeer, introduced in each case by helpful comments by

Andrew Chesterman. There is a comprehensive and up-to-date bibliography.

The book is to be recommended as prescribed reading in any course in Translation Theory (or such like), as it covers a wide range of literary and non-literary translation topics. The main gaps are Tytler, Snell-Hornby and Krings. It is attractively presented. All extracts are in English.

Discourse Analysis and Translation

Basil Hatim and Ian Mason in their *Discourse and the Translator* (Longmans, 1989) are often more concerned with discourse than with translation. However they produce one fascinating translation example from Rousseau's *Emile* (Book I):

C'est à toi que je m'adresse, tendre et prévoyante mère, qui sus t'écarter de la grande route et garantir l'arbrisseau naissant du choc des opinions humaines! Cultive, arrose la jeune plante avant qu'elle meure; ses fruits feront un jour tes délices. Forme de bonne heure une enceinte autour de l'âme de ton enfant: un autre en peut marquer le circuit, mais toi seule y dois poser la barrière.

This was translated by Barbara Foxley in 1911 as 'Tender, anxious mother, I appeal to you. You can remove this young tree from the highway and shield it from the crushing force of social conventions. Tend and water it ere it dies. One day its fruits will reward your care. From the outset raise a wall round your child's soul; another may sketch the plan, you alone should carry out its execution.'

Apart from one case of 'mismatch' (*sus t'écarter*), the authors accept this translation holus-bolus, and show more interest in its cohesive relations, rhetorical functions, anaphoric references, texture and thematic progression than in its accuracy, to which Rousseau is entitled. It is a tricky passage, and I suggest the following translation: 'Tender and foresighted mother, I appeal to you, who turned from the highway and managed to protect the burgeoning shrub from the clash of human opinions! Tend and water the young plant before it dies; one day its fruits will delight you. Build an enclosure round your child's soul in good time; another may well mark out its course; but you alone must set the bounds.'

This is a rather desperate stab at linguistic and pragmatic accuracy, even retaining the 'rhetorical function'. The last sentence should be compared with Hatim and Mason's suggestion: 'Raise a wall . . . another may sketch the plan, but you alone must be its builder.' Generally, Hatim and Mason, as is the fashion, are so anxious not to be prescriptive and to remain descriptive that they refrain from making envaluations, which would be useful. However, they are not claiming to teach. In one of their concluding remarks they state that 'The ultimate test of translation is: can the consumer of the translated play 'read off' the ideology being signalled?' In context this means: Will (say) the social purpose of *Pygmalion* be understood in translation? This may or may not be 'the ultimate test', but why must it be dressed up like this and, 'applied' say to *Hamlet*, is it not absurd?

Write Idiomatically?

'We ask for your understanding', the Swissair captain was speaking over the intercom, probably letting his German (*Wir bitten um Ihr Verständnis*) interfere with his English. Would not 'Please bear with us', or 'Please make allowances' be more idiomatic or more natural? Maybe, but I prefer the literal translation, which is fresh, accurate and elegant. All this reminds me of Brian Mossop's brilliant article, 'Write idiomatically and translate ideas not words: three defects of the prevailing doctrine of translation', which has somehow strayed into Candace Séguinot's *The Process of Translation*, of which more later. In his attack on 'idiomatic idea-oriented translation (IIT!), Mossop even appears to prefer 'Nasty dog' rather than 'Beware of the dog' as a translation of the 'lawn sign' *Chien méchant*, which I don't. (Note that in France, *Attention au chien!*, conforming to my 'human-animal-ecological' rights hypothesis, appears to me to be becoming more common.)

Mossop criticises IIT on three grounds:

1. It eliminates the option of linguistic innovation in translation.
2. If one translates ideas not words, literal translation is *ipso facto* excluded.
3. If words are ignored, ideas may be distorted and the text mistranslated.

Mossop's examples of linguistic innovations are: modalities (F: terms and conditions of an agreement); gay; animate/animateur (virtually, be the main spring of a club, group, etc — I have also suggested this); file (issue). He points out that English lacks words having the generality of many French ones (but this applies to most languages) and many could (and are) being filled in by naturalisation (e.g. interlocutor).

I have, I hope, quoted and commented enough on this important article to convince 'sourcerers' that Mossop is for them; but 'targeters' will benefit most from him.

The Translation Process

Candace Séguinot has edited an attractive paperback (pp. 98) with the above title, obtainable (at a price?) from H. G. Publications, School of Translation, Glendon College (where she teaches fervently and impressively), York University, 2275 Bayview Avenue, Toronto, Ontario, M4N 3M6 Canada. Four of the articles use scripts or videotapes of translations in progress and the elicitation techniques of think-aloud (*Lautdenken*) protocols to look at the strategies (methods?) that are used by professional translators (Krings, the pioneer here, had used students).

The introduction contains some wild ('We simply don't know much about how to tell students to make use of their learning' — who's 'we'?) and some platitudinous ('as Toury says, (*sic*) translation is an activity directed by a purpose') statements. However Seguinot's long and detailed 'experimental study of a translator's work on a piece about the genesis of the Canadian postal code is, shorn of the jargon, enlightening and helpful. In comparing the source text with its translation, she complements points arising from any product view of translation, e.g. 'Improved logic', where she (prescriptively) points to wrong logical connections in the original:

Le 2e caractère, un chiffre, diminue l'espace géographique, mais surtout identifie un bureau rural si ce caractère est un zéro.

'The second character, a number, narrows the geographic(al) area; (in particular), if it is zero, it indicates a rural post office . . . The translator's corrected typescript is fascinating.

Ray Ellenwood's piece on literary translation convincingly shows how the line: *Toute sèche tu chantes à ravir* converts from 'Desiccated you sing ravishingly' to 'Parched you sing a siren song', respecting the sound effect, the standard collocation and the main sense of the original. The book closes with protocol (complete record) studies by Sonya Tirkonnen-Condit (over-categorised and over-summarised) and Riitta Jaaskelainen, who demonstrates some interesting translation problems, hesitations and decisions. I warmly recommend it.

Ellipses in Collocations

Ellipses in collocations are another translating trap, since they may not be analogous in source and target languages. Thus in *motions et projets, projets* is probably *projets de loi*, and translates as 'bills', not 'plans', and in Séguinot's example above, bureau is '*post office*', not office. Normally the translator has to decide on the basis of frequency of usage as well as context.

The French Historic Infinitive

The French historic infinitive (*infinitif historique*, or more commonly, *infinitif de narration*), often introduced by *Et* and typically followed by a noun or pronoun subject (the subject is sometimes omitted) plus *de* plus infinitive, originating in the 15th century (see the fascinating Grévisse p. 672, but I can't find it in Judge and Healey), is becoming increasingly common in journalism: *Et François Mitterand de citer avec faveur le propos de Wassily Leontieff, prix Nobel d'économie.* 'In fact, Mitterand has given a favourable mention to a statement by Wassily Leontieff, the American Nobel Prize winner for Economics'. Note that the historic infinitive is meant to denote an action starting up suddenly (*qui se déclenche vivement*), and following on another action, but it seems to have calmed down a bit since the great Grévisse of 1936, and being unique (?), is not easy to translate.

The Curse of Dogma in Translation Studies

At the recent AILA (International Association of Applied Linguistics) jamboree, which was notable (?) for the strange absence (scilicet, *entendez*, do I mean boycott?) of the majority of the translatology circuit or non-fraternity, I read a paper with the above title. My targets were six current views of translation:

1. The extreme functionalist theory.
2. The discourse theory, based on text linguists.
3. The culture transfer or interchange theory.
4. The social language theory.
5. The process theory.
6. The 'reception theory' (or 'manipulative') theory.

Now all these theories have their truth and their use, and so have their polar opposites:

1. The essence theory. (You translate the 'words on the page' Leavis) — there's nothing else there (and forget about the message!).
2. The lexicogrammatical theory (as above, in No. 1).
3. The universals theory, relating to culture and language.
4. The individual language theory.
5. The product theory.
6. The theory of translation as a critical weapon, outside of time and age, space and milieu.

All these views can be driven too far: 'and' may mean 'therefore'; 'I read with interest' may mean 'I am sceptical'; there are a dozen ways of formulating: 'Passengers must not cross the lines,'; an Indian academic assures me that 'all ideas and emotions are cultural'. (Many Indians are obsessed with culture). Me, like Goering, I want to reach for my revolver when I hear the word, but it wasn't Goering and it wasn't that kind of culture. As for emotions, they are always universal, never cultural, but they are sometimes culture-laden.

A translator learns most from the typical — the exceptional is merely a warning. Joad's 'It all depends what you mean by . . .' is often a cop-out — the inquirer usually just wants the typical meaning of the word, and *pace* John Sinclair, there almost always is one.

Metaphors Again

The more sustained or complex the SL metaphor, the stronger the argument for retaining the image in the translation, and not reducing it to sense. Thus in the Institute's Translation Diploma, *Quand l'histoire accepte de repasser les plats, mieux vaut en profiter. Pas questions de chipoter, de traîner un manque d'appétit, ni même de manger à la carte. En 1981 les militants socialistes veulent, tout de suite, tout le menu. Entendez tout le programme.* 'When history offers us second helpings, we should make the most of them (alt. not hold back). There is no question of nibbling at our food, or harping on about our lack of appetite, nor even of dining *à la carte.* In 1981, socialist activists wanted the whole menu — immediately! In other words, the whole programme. (Courtesy Amanda McLaren, Richard Nice, me.)

The Last Word

Except in matters of moral and factual truth, which is the bottom line in any translation, there is always room for eclectic thinking and a plurality of views, and none for dogma.

Translating Short Stories

Outside poetry, the short story can be regarded as the most intimate and personal form of writing in imaginative literature. (In contrast, drama and within drama, farce, is the most public form.) Its essence is compactness, simplicity, concentration, cohesion. Its symbolic and connotative power transcends its realism and its denotative effect. As a text to be translated, I think its significant features are:

1. Its structure. Opening and closing sentences and paragraphs are often mutually related, and, together with the title, point to the story's theme and its resolution. Punctuation, paragraphing and capitalization have to be accounted for, if not followed (eg French . . . may indicate a pause, English . . . indicate a passage omitted).

2. Keywords or leitmotifs. Often repeated words, phrases or images to indicate theme. These normally have to be reproduced in the translation.

3. Stylistic markers. Author's typical words or structures, also related to theme (*jagen* in Kafka). These also have to be consistently reproduced.

4. Cultural and universal (encyclopaedic) references. The translator has to decide how many of these he can afford to explain economically within the text.

5. Cultural metaphors. As above.

6. Genre: tale or story, spoken or written mode. But the colloquial (see below) may be bizarre and personal, whilst the written may conform to normal social usage.

7. Tradition. The story may be in line with an established literary tradition. Normally this source language tradition will be preserved in translation, rather than be adapted to a target language tradition. It should enrich the target literature.

8. Collateral works. The translator gains in understanding by reading the author's other work, but is not consciously influenced by it. Some features, such as irony (sometimes) or a sudden switch from concrete to mental (say 'the little girl' meaning 'the thought of the little girl') can be translated neat, without explanation or emphasis.

9. Functional sentence perspective. Given such a compact narrative, it is important to reproduce stresses within the sentences, and to secure their coherent and cohesive links.

Translating a Short Story

Maupassant's *Amour – Trois Pages du Livre d'un Chasseur* (1886) begins as follows:

Je viens de lire dans un fait divers de journal un drame de passion. Il l'a tuée, puis il s'est tué, donc il l'aimait. Qu'importent Il et Elle? Leur amour seul m'importe; et il ne m'intéresse point parce qu'il m'attendrit ou parce qu'il m'étonne, ou parce qu'il m'émeut ou parce qu'il me fait songer, mais parce qu'il me rappelle un souvenir de ma jeunesse, un étrange souvenir de chasse où m'est apparu l'Amour comme apparaissaient aux premiers chrétiens des croix au milieu du ciel. I would translate this approximately as follows:

'I have just read a news item about a tragic love affair. He killed her, then he killed himself, so he loved her. What do He or She matter? Their love alone matters to me; and it doesn't interest me because it moves me to pity or because it amazes me or because it upsets me or because it makes me think, but because it recalls to me a memory of my youth, a strange memory of a shoot when Love appeared to me as crosses appeared to the first Christians in the middle of the sky.'

I have translated almost literally because the lexical items are independent units, the language is concrete, and I have to retain Maupassant's stresses.

Margaret Bourne translated the passage in 1934 as follows:

'Amongst the miscellaneous items in the newspapers, I have just read an account of a tragic love affair, in which a lover killed first his sweetheart and then himself. Their personalities did not concern me. What interested me was the intensity of their passion, not because I was touched, or surprised, or thrilled, or saddened, but because it recalled to me a memory of my youth, a curious shooting incident, which was to me a revelation of love, like those visions of the Cross in the sky which were granted to the early Christians.'

The only justification I can think of for this paraphrase is that the translator thought the story was trivial and poorly written, and that it was her job to rewrite it in good English. Her version omits much of the detail of the original, as well as its abrupt and staccato effect. However, I think it's up to the reader to judge the quality of Maupassant's writing, and my version gives him/her an opportunity to do so.

Maupassant continues: *Je suis né avec tous les instincts et les sens de l'homme primitif, tempérés par des raisonnements et des émotions de civilisé. J'aime la chasse avec passion; et la bête saignante, le sang sur les plumes, le sang sur mes mains, me crispent le coeur à le faire défaillir.*

Again, Margaret Bourne polishes it down and eliminates its starkness: 'By nature I have all the instincts and feelings of primitive man, though modified by the logic and the sensibilities of civilization. I am passionately devoted to shooting and hunting, and when I bring down a bird the blood on its feathers and on my hands thrills my heart so that it almost stops beating.'

The difficulty here is the conceptual language and the faded idiom: 'I was born with all the instincts and the senses of primitive man, tempered by the reasoning and the emotions of a civilized person. I love hunting and shooting passionately: and a blood-soaked bird, with blood on its feathers, and blood on my hands, clutches at my heart so that I almost faint.' The risk of more or less reproducing an old-fashioned metaphor is that many readers will start giggling, but I think it has to be taken.

Lastly, the title, *Amour — Trois pages du livre d'un chasseur* has to be 'Love — Pages from a huntsman's diary', though 'hunter's' is possible; Margaret Bourne's 'sportsman' is old-fashioned linguistically and morally in this sense. It is difficult to decide to what extent 'hunting' and 'sports' include 'shooting'.

In justice, I must add that Margaret Bourne's translating greatly improves later in the story, and her rendering of the anguished, damning conclusion is true and firm.

Lastly, I have to insist that translators today have to ignore the literary fashions of the time, as well as its translation norms, if such now exist, in as far as they are cultural. Admitting that many Renaissance, Restoration and Augustan translations were steeped in contemporary literary conventions, all deriving directly or indirectly from Aristotelian classicism, which were ratified by Tytler with his insistence on propriety and good taste, though at variance with his own enlightened three principles of translation, my guess is that the first examples of close poetic translation, in the modern and scientific sense of the term, were the Tieck and Schlegel Shakespeare translations. Here for the first time, when some of their contemporaries were declaring that translation was impossible, a translation could be seriously and profitably compared with its original, in the light of the truth rather than its literary and cultural conventions.

A Second Short Story

Robbe-Grillet's *La Plage* (1962) has been near-perfectly translated by Barbara Wright (*The Beach*, 1966). The stry is abstract, mathematical, geometrical, universal, without trace of cultural detail (but for three clothing terms), a faint hint of Mondrian or Ben Nicolson. Leitmotifs and stylistic markers merge. I quote the beginning:

Trois enfants marchent le long d'une grève. Ils s'avancent, côte à côte, se tenant par la main. Ils ont sensiblement la même taille, et sans doute aussi le même âge: une douzaine d'années. Three children are walking along a beach. They move forward, side by side, holding hands. They are roughly the same height, and probably the same age too: about twelve.

The story is a perfectly formal work of art, and has its own stillness, movement and power, generalized to the highest degree. This works in favour of a rarely exact translation.

A Third Short Story

Camus' *Les Muets* (1957) was translated by Justin O'Brien in the same year as *'The Silent Men'*, fortunately escaping the hands of Stuart Gilbert. O'Brien, in a useful essay contributed to R.A. Brower's *On Translation*, which is at last again in print, states that 'Absolute verbal accuracy is less desirable than reproducing the tone of voice and rhythm of the original', which I call the targeteer's typically vague getout. Nevertheless it is a good mainly accurate translation: *On était au plein de l'hiver et cependant une journée radieuse se levait sur la ville déjà active. Au bout de la jetée, la mer et le ciel se confondaient dans un même éclat.* Thus O'Brien: 'It was in the dead of winter and yet a radiant sun was rising over the already active city. At the end of the jetty, sea and sky fused in a single dazzling light'. (I would say the translation could not be closer, though I would prefer 'merged' to 'fused'; playing the semantic plus or minus game, 'dead' is an English, *on était* and *éclat* a French plus. I shall not quote the end, since the translation is virtually literal.) O'Brien scrupulously reproduces key words (*jeunesse, vieillir, bonheur, la mer*) and stylistic markers (*lourdement, se buter*) and generalizes one or two technical terms, e.g. *varlope* from 'jointer' to 'plane'. In one case he fails, translating: *Il inspirait généralement la sympathie, comme la plupart des gens que le sport a libérés dans leurs attitudes* ('He generally inspired liking, as do most people on whom sport has had a liberating influence in their manner') as 'He generally aroused liking, as do most people who exude vitality'. It is difficult to judge whether O'Brien simply lost patience with Camus here, and decided to have a fling on his own. Later, he demonstrates a nice creativity in translating: *Parfois, en lui, le mot malheur se formait, mais à peine* as 'Sometimes the word "calamity" took shape in him, but just barely'. The transposition from reflexive verb to process verb ('took') plus product ('shape') is standard. Camus' story, which illustrates that class conflict is rarely manichaeistic, is brilliant.

Metaphors in Economic Texts

A *Revue des Valeurs* ('securities review') article in *Le Monde* opens: *Après avoir soufflé trois semaines, le vent de la baisse, à l'image des bourrasques de l'hiver, s'est éloigné ces derniers jours des rives de la Bourse de Paris, non sans s'être retourné, comme à regret, pour faire encore un peu plier la cote.*

As for all metaphors, there is a choice, in principle, of two translations:

1. 'In the last few days, the wind of price falls (financial decline?), (like the squalls of winter?), after blowing for three weeks, has moved away from the Paris Bourse, but has returned (rather reluctantly?) and slightly brought prices down again.

2. 'After a three weeks decline in prices, the market stabilised, but recently there has been a slight downturn.'

Although the metaphor is prolonged and may be considered picturesque, I think it is rather daft, so I prefer the second version.

Target

Target, a new biannual journal of translation studies, 'focuses on the interrelationships between the position of translating and translations in culture, the norms governing them' (do they govern them?) 'and the modes of performing translation processes under various circumstances'. It is edited by Gideon Toury and José Lambert and published by John Benjamins, Amsterdam. The rather abstract editorial, which has the 'to be sure' stylistic marker of one of the editors, while admitting the pluralism of translation approaches and attempting to give them a 'hierarchical (*sic*) organization', insists on the target-oriented nature, linguistically and culturally, of all translation. Hence the journal's title.

The journal opens appropriately with a piece by Annie Brisset on the Canadian play translators' efforts to establish Québécois rather than metropolitan French as the language of Quebec theatre. Carl James writes on Genre Analysis and recommends that it form part of translation training. He refers to the 'generic status of translation', gives no examples, and hardly makes his case. Wolfgang Lörschner analyses models of the translation process at length, and theorizes without examples. He states: 'The notion of kernel as used by Nida is nowhere defined and remains vague'. In fact, Nida defines it admirably in his Glossary in *The Theory and Practice of Translation*, and unlike Lörschner, gives nice examples for each kernel sentence. D. L. Gorlee's article on *Wittgenstein and Translation* is interesting and learned. Finally, buried in an even more learned and rather too detailed piece, L. G. Kelly makes a fascinating case for the early 17th Century apothecary Nicholas Culpeper as an accurate and even literal translator. (Like any good translator, Culpeper occasionally offends against his own norms — I say this to shock any reader I may still have.) The journal looks nice and should interest anyone interested in literary translation. (Does the repetition jar? Then let it jar.)

Stylistic Markers

The more an author uses his/her stylistic markers, the less meaning and force they have. Georges Duby uses *jouer le rôle* or *avoir la fonction de* (play the part of, have the function of) so often, that I translate his: *les Alpes qui jouaient si longtemps le rôle de conservatoire* as 'the Alps that protected them so long'. 'To be sure . . .'

Communicative Dynamism or Jargon?

The translator frequently has to choose between empty verb plus nominalization or straight verbalization. Thus for *ils subirent une dégradation, un renouvellement*, the neat 'they deteriorated, they were renewed' or the more forceful but jargonized 'they underwent a deterioration, a renewal'.

The Unfindable Word

Franchisme appears to be in no reference book. But bear in mind that in some languages, k, c and ch are in some cases interchangeable. Jakob Frank appears in the *EB (Encyclopaedia Britannica)* and the invaluable *Petit Robert 2* as an 18th Century Polish Jewish heresiac. Translate as 'Frankism, an 18th Century Jewish and Christian heresy'. The French is normally *frankisme*. An alternative term is 'zoharism'.

The Russian 'of course'

Easy to detect a Soviet's English, but *konechno* usually translates as 'yes', or has a zero translation.

The Nonsense of German Romantic Poetry

Michael Hamburger in a fascinating lecture to the Translation Division confessed his inability to turn Eichendorff into English poetry; the sense was so trivial . . . I quote from the indispensable Fischer-Dieskau *Book of Lieder:*
Es rauschen die Wipfel und schauern,
Als machten zu dieser Stund
Um die halbversunkenen Mauern
Die alten Götter die Rund. (Liederkreis). A cruel translation would be: The tree-tops rustle and shudder, as though at this hour the ancient gods were making their round along the half-sunken walls. '. . . George Bird and Richard Stokes turn this into: 'The tree-tops murmur and shiver/as though at this hour/the half-sunken walls/were paced by gods of old.' To me this poem is arrant rubbish, like most German Romantic poetry (except the great Annette Droste-Hülshoff and the unromantic Heine), shorn as it is of its to some people bewitching vowel assonances, but revealing a blind sleepiness that intoxicated too many Germans, and others. The way Schumann turned these and so many other verses into intense, glowing sounds of feeling is another matter. The 'ultimate' translation of Eichendorff's line: *Zu mir, phantastische Nacht* is Fischer-Dieskau singing it, which is unforgettable.

Goethe (not Schiller) is a case apart; *Über allen Gipfeln* is still waiting for its English translator.

The Metalingual Trap

A close translation of *Ces mâles jeunes et fougueux, comme dit la chanson, 'veulent mais ne peuvent pas'* gives 'These fiery young dogs', as the song goes, 'want to but can't'. In English, this only makes sense if the song is specified as French, which makes the reference rather pointless. Therefore it seems sensible to get rid of it, and translate as 'These fiery young dogs want to mate but can't'.

Translating into L.2

So many translators in industry have colleagues who think they should be translating both ways, even that translating into one's own language is kids' stuff, that the true test of the translator is the 'prose', that to write in a foreign language all a translator needs is knowledge of the standard grammar and access to the relevant dictionaries. It is surely time that the public were educated to know that translators in this country are normally only expected to work into their own language, and that while they can make themselves understood, they get no practice in the written foreign language. Non-idiomatic language is as easy to detect as a foreign accent. Translators have to be 'ambassadors' for their companies, and they can't do this properly if they make mistakes, even trivial ones. Tourist material in the 'away' language may be a delight, but instruction manuals and warning notices are more likely to be disastrous.

Reflexive Verbs

English shies away from reflexive verbs, which usually represent processes, where 'to be' plus past participles represent states. But it has abundant resources to translate them: progressive tenses, 'go', 'get', 'grow', 'turn', 'become' plus verb; passives; transitive verbs that lose their objects to adverbs of manner ('it reads well').

Permettre De (or *Permettere Di*) once more

Two more deletion procedures for translating this verb:

1. *Ici aussi, la prise de sang permet de réduire très sensiblement ce risque.* 'Here again, a blood sample considerably reduces the risk'.

2. *Ici encore, le frottis associé au dosage hormonal permet d'augmenter la certitude.* 'Once more, if one takes a smear to determine the hormone level, one can be more confident (that this is the right moment)'.

'One-to-two' Verbs

Not uncommonly, verbs in political or administrative language will not translate neatly one to one, but require a TL verb plus verbal noun. Thus, *infléchir une politique*, 'to (reorientate) change/modify the direction of a policy! Compare the notorious (in translation) *sich auseinandersetzen mit* . . . 'come to terms with', 'have a look at' etc.

IX
SEPTEMBER 1990

The Translation of Janáček's Opera Titles

Katya Kabanova, From the House of the Dead, The Excursions of Mr Brouček, The Makropoulos Case (sometimes *'Affair'*; Michael Ewans, a brilliant critic, even invests the Czech *věc = Sache* or 'thing' with mystery and terror), there is no problem in these translated titles. *Osud* ('fate' or 'destiny') has become *Osud*, wrongly suggesting that this is a Czech person or town. Remains the delightful *Prihody Lisky bystrousky*, literally, *'Events of the Fox Sharpears'*. Max Brod, the Austrian-Czech-Jewish, later Israeli, writer who also befriended Kafka and Hašek (*The Good Soldier Svejk*), translated this as *Das schlaue Fuchslein*, hence *The Cunning Little Vixen*, perhaps the only non-faithful translation of the title of a great and serious opera which can be justified, although it sentimentalizes the original in typical Austrian fashion. As the music is so much more important than the words, it doesn't matter. The finest of Janáček's works, *Jenůfa*, has rightly had its title changed from *Její Pastorkyňa* (*Her Foster Daughter* or *Her Step-daughter*) by its translator, Max Brod.

Janáček's Town

The main street of the city of Brno (till 1919, Brünn), die Zeile till 1919, Masarykova (1919 to 1939), Hermann-Goering Strasse (1939–1945), Gottwaldova (1945 to 1990), is Masarykova again. The Masaryk University, founded in 1919, renamed Purkyn University from 1945 to 1990, is the Masaryk University again. Janáček's Piano Sonata, written to commemorate the death of a worker demonstrating in favour of the establishment of a Czech university in Brno, is variously called *1.X.1905*, *Street Scene 1.X.1905*, *From the Street ('Z ulice)* or *Presentiment and Death*, the titles of its two movements.

The Cyclist's Paradise

In the wonderful park that surrounds the Kroller-Müller Museum outside Arnhem, with its two hundred white bicycles as well as Van Gogh and Co., there are numerous notices:
Fietsen die U elders aantreft laten staan.
Leave the bicycles you find elsewhere, on the spot.
Im Park abgestellte Räder bitte stehenlassen.
Les bicyclettes se trouvant ailleurs doivent rester où elles se trouvent à ce moment.
Of the three translations, only the German is both competent and polite. (*Bitte*, like 'please', is a beautiful word for toning down formality.) The English could be suitably 'modulated' to: 'Please do

not move (remove?) the bicycles you find lying around in the park'.
French regrettably has no 'please', and can only be peremptory: *Les bicyclettes abandonnées doivent être laissées sur place* or, less ambiguously, *Ne touchez pas aux bicyclettes abandonnées que vous trouverez dans le parc.*

The Eternal Problem

An article in the Council of Europe's *Forum*, entitled *Evoluzione e rivoluzione delle campagne italiane* by Corrado Barberis, *Presidente dell' Istituto nazionale di sociologia rurale*, begins: *Da una ruralità di esodo a una ruralità di immigrazione. Da una ruralità di inerzia a una ruralità di iniziativa. Da una ruralità contrassegnata da uno spirito di sconfitta a una ruralità improntata a volontà di conquista: ecco, in estrema sintesi, l'evoluzione vissuta dalle campagne italiane a partire dal 1970. I risultati statistici di questa inversione sono del tutto apprezzabili.*

Literal translation: Evolution and revolution in the Italian countryside by C. B., President (Chairman?) of the National Institute of Rural Sociology.

From a rural life of exodus (population flight) to a rural life of immigration. From a rural life of inertia to a rural life of initiative. From a rural life marked by a spirit of defeat to a rural life imprinted with a will to conquest; that is, in an extreme synthesis, the development lived by the Italian countryside(s) from 1970. The statistical results of this reversal are entirely appreciable.

The English edition has the same title and superscript as this literal translation. The first paragraph reads: 'From an unsociable, inert, defeatist countryside to a welcoming one which takes the initiative and is determined to conquer: these are some of the salient features of the development of Italian country life since 1970. Statistics reflect these changes.'

My comments are based on the following assumptions:

1. The translation must reproduce the facts. 'Unsociable' for *di esodo* and 'changes' for *inversione* imply them too faintly.

2. The language of the SL text is not 'sacred', but the main emphases should be reproduced. They are.

3. The translation should conform to normal social usage.

The translator rightly cuts out padding such as *contrassegnato, spirito, improntato, risultati.*

A possible close ('communicative') translation would be: 'From an inert defeatist countryside, from which the population has been drifting, to a countryside marked by immigration, initiative and the will to succeed (conquer?): these are the basic features in the trend of Italian rural life since 1970.

The statistics clearly demonstrate this reversal.'

Art Galleries

It is time all reputable art galleries and museums added at least one translation to the titles of their exhibits. The Kroller Müller has English translations (the Van Goghs not always consistent), but the Prado is as monolingual as the National Gallery and the Musée d'Orsay. The Prado should finally determine the correct title of the only painting which (in the Prado, not in repro), in my experience, has the power, the impact and the humanity of the greatest music and literature, — the confrontation of the terrified animal humans with the faceless mass machine — Goya's *El Tres de Mayo de 1808, en Madrid: los fusilamientos en la Montaña del Principe Pio*. ('The executions — shootings? — of the Third of May'.) Again, the Prado should issue a standard translation of the title. The painting is popularly referred to as *Los Fusilamientos.*

Translation, History and Culture

This is the title of a new collection of essays edited by Susan Bassnett and André Lefevere, published (at £27 for 130 pages!) by Pinter. The essays are well varied, literary and interesting, descriptive rather than evaluative, and influenced by reception theory. Like David Lodge, Elzbieta Tabakowska finds Bakhtin's theories useful, in attempting to ensure that a translation should be 'polyphonic' rather than a work on two instruments. There is a brilliant piece by Mahasweta Sengupta, who quotes Susan Bassnett's unhappily put: 'The translator cannot be the author of the SL text, but as the author of the TL text has a clear moral responsibility to the TL readers.' Taking Tagore as an example, Sengupta shows the consequences of a translator being faithful to the TL audience in a way which undermines the quality of the translated material. She then contrasts Tagore's poeticized version of his poem *Gitanjali 4-5* with her own close translation of the original, claiming that Tagore became corrupted and colonized by Edwardian English, from which he later freed himself. I suspect she overstates her case (she only gives one example), but this is how 'literal' translation ought to be used — as a moral and literary weapon.

The Fifth Purpose of Translation?

I take it that the five main purposes and uses of translation are:

1. To contribute to understanding and peace between language communities and groups.

2. To promote information and technology transfer, particularly to third and fourth world countries.

3. To explain and clarify ethnic cultures and their differences.

4. To make works of high moral religious and aesthetic importance in the arts and the humanities, as well as scientific works, available throughout the world. (Its original purpose.)

5. To facilitate foreign language learning.

This fifth purpose has always been controversial. Informal and *ad hoc* interpreting and translating (the social component in language learning) are additional to the four basic skills, which are individual: listening, speaking, reading and writing, but translation also has a place in developing these skills, ancillary to and as a component of a language learning course.

Translation as an Ancillary to a Language Learning Course

It always strikes me as strange if language learners do not at an early stage familiarize themselves with the cognate relations, if these exist, between their language and the language they are learning. Recently I was surprised that few of my Spanish students of English were aware that initial Spanish 'h' was often equivalent to English initial 'f' (e.g. *hambre*, 'famished'; *hembra*, female; *hijo*, 'filial'). No Italian student realized that Italian 'consonant plus 'i' plus vowel plus consonant' is normally English 'consonant plus 'l' plus vowel plus consonant' (*chiaro*, 'clear'). W. E. Weber's *The Intelligent Student's Guide to German* (Pitman, first published 1938, regrettably out of print) makes superb use of Grimm's and Verner's Laws to teach German vocabulary and grammar. Frederick Bodmer's great *Loom of Language*, revised by Lancelot Hogben, first published in 1943, recently reprinted as a paperback, discusses lexical and grammatical relationships within Germanic and Romance languages in detail, and includes some invaluable lists of common words for these languages (but not Romanian); unfortunately he ignores the Slavonic languages, which only have the indigestible G. Z. Patrick's *The Roots of Russian*. I still want a manual which tells me in handy form why say *potolok* means 'ceiling' and *otrava* means 'poison'. What is required are learner's books showing, with numerous examples plus both idiomatic and literal translations, (a) the relationship between:

1. p, b, v, f, ph, pf, w, etc.
2. t, d, th, s, ss, z, cz, ts, etc.
3. g, k, ch, gh, h, y, i, zero, etc.
4. all other intervocalic, as well as the interconsonantal relationships (b) the meanings of all prefixes, suffixes and common roots in an Indo-European branch, or in two or three cognate languages. Normally, such information should be acquired outside a language learning course. It has several uses: (1) it helps the learners to guess or discover the meanings of words, (2) most importantly it helps them to memorize the words and their meanings, (3) where appropriate, it illustrates and explains culture, etymology and diachronic linguistics, (4) it exercises the imagination.

Aids to language learning which may or may not be incorporated in a course are 'fundamental' (or basic) word lists with translations, based on word frequency, separating grammatical (function) and lexical words; topic words, including say twenty basic topics (kinship, jobs, food, accommodation, etc.) with the items in order of frequency; the most common word families — it always seems strange to me to teach say 'vulgar' without 'vulgarity'. All these words must be translated by their typical, most common meanings. As regards lists of idioms, they should be current and common, marked 'spoken' and/or 'written' where appropriate ('last but not least' and 'be that as it may' are written), and should be translated both idiomatically and literally. Idioms, whose meanings are barely deducible from their component words (e.g. 'in all conscience', 'prisoner of conscience'), can be distinguished from phrases. Phrases, which are transparent ('a nice turn of phrase') should be listed separately. A start should also be made with lists of verb plus object and adjective plus noun collocations and their translations under particular topics. The *BBI Combinatory Dictionary of English* (M. & E. Benson and R. Ilson; Benjamins; 1986) has carried on a long time after the great Albrecht Reum left off, but the collocations still have to be grouped in topics for language learning, and translated both idiomatically and literally.

Lastly, there is a place for lists of *faux-amis* (in order of frequency); key words both in general and in particular areas of intellectual life; lists of the commonest transferred (loan) words, classified according to topics; and lexical sets in specialized vocabularies.

The use of the literal translations, always contrasted with idiomatic translations, is (a) to assist comprehension, (b) to help memorization, (c) to increase vocabulary (e.g. 'bucket' in 'kick the bucket' or 'sod' in 'under the sod' if the idiom or the phrase is ever used).

Translation as a Component of a Basic Language Learning Course

A good language teacher discovers and works out her own teaching method; translation has no place in many language teaching courses, because the teacher uses the direct method, sometimes brilliantly. (However, the two radical variants on the direct method, one dispensing with writing for the first weeks of a course (*Credif*), the other restricted to listening and repitition without comprehension, (the Rand Morton method), are distortions that sacrifice valuable aids).

The four basic skills in language learning, whether productive (speaking and writing) or receptive (listening and reading) are all practised in the foreign language, and therefore translation (and here I include all the background resources I have outlined above), has an essentially supportive role only. It must be remembered that most of the distinguished work in EFL and ESL that has been done in the British Council and elsewhere since the War makes the assumption that the teacher does not even know the students' language (sometimes languages), that she practices the direct method of necessity. Even C. J. Dodson's translation method, which starts with translation, uses it as a crutch to be cast away as the course proceeds, and is realistic as it assumes that the student begins by thinking in her own language.

However, I propose to outline the use of translation in courses conducted mainly in the foreign language which call on a plurality of eclectic teaching methods. In the initial stage, assuming an ostensive method exploiting first the classroom situations and episodes, then pictures, diagrams, videos, etc, objects, when clearly depicted (often they are not) can be pointed out and some actions mimed or implied in the foreign language; other actions, qualities and grammatical words can where necessary be translated and then repeated in the FL to secure retention ('overlearning'). Grammar, when introduced, should be explained in the foreign language, but the terms translated at first mention. There is no harm in mixing languages orally, provided the students recognize it as part of the method.

L.1 to L.2 translation can be used regularly but sparingly as a form of control, that is to verify, by way of translating words, idioms, sentences or a connected passage, knowledge that the student is expected to have acquired. This is the quickest, most efficient and objective method of testing knowledge. As basic skills are being learned, any kind of 'unseen' or 'prose' that skips a stage in a planned course is out of place. 'Controlled' readers can be introduced fairly early, mainly for enjoyment; a few words can be translated or looked up, but this is not a basic part of the course. Realia are indispensable, but here translation is usually superfluous. In all or any cases, there is no harm in translating a few odd words, when plainly the students are thinking in their own language (the effort helps the memorizing process) to guess the meaning of the word — it's a pity if direct method becomes dogmatic.

At an advanced stage, if translation (out of or into the FL) becomes one of the aims of the course, it must be made clear whether it is being introduced for language enrichment (where paraphrase, literal translation, free translation, synonymous versions all have their place) or for communication (normal social usage) which should be accurate as well as idiomatic.

Autonomy

'Autonomy' is not always 'autonomy' in other languages. In Italian, it may be 'fuel distance', 'range', 'self-government' in *autonomia di governo*, 'more latitude' in *autonomia in campo agricolo*. In Spanish, it may also be (military or air) 'range'. In French, it may also be 'fuel distance'. Which suggests the term is most frequently used in Italian, least frequently in English?

Default Translation?

Elément essential de la société limouxine comme dans les collectivités rurales traditionnelles. Now decide whether *limouxine* is a misprint for *limousine* ('Limousin society'), or means 'Limoux society', Limoux being a small town in Aude? The context is impenetrable.

Translating Havel

A recent number of the UNESCO Courier, which is translated into about a dozen languages (a record for a periodical?) and is a resource for any translation critic, publishes an interview by a Spanish journalist with the Czechoslovak president. The translation into English of the 'sacred' (i.e. authoritative, as Havel is a great person), 'Spanish' (invisible Czech) text is close:
El hombre ha perdido el sentimiento de responsabilidad que teniá con respecto a algo trascendente, que lo sobresaba. In the English issue, this becomes: 'Man has lost the sense of responsibility he had previously felt towards something higher than him, something which transcended him'. The problem is, as often 'man', Czech has *člověk*, Russian has *čelověk*, German has *Mensch*, Greek has *anthropos*, English and the Romance languages have 'humanity', 'mankind', 'humans', 'people'. Because of the prominence of the three succeeding masculine pronouns, I think 'Humans' would be preferable here.

To Render Ageism

Lear is the most forceful and tremendous attack on ageism and the psychological and social difficulties of old age in my experience; it is also a sensitive study of the difficulties of being old. For Goneril's 'dotage' (1.IV.280), with its dramatic irony, French has *gâtisme*, German *Senilität*, Italian *rimbambimento* (are they good enough?), but there is no difficulty with the frequent collocations with 'old' and 'age'.

Acknowledgements

To Matthew Newmark for help with the Maupassant in the last number; to Tonni Cooper with the Dutch in this one.

X
NOVEMBER 1990

Untranslatability

Martin Weston, who after Anthony Crane knows more about translation than anyone I know (his book on legal translation is due out in November), has suggested to me that the phrase *On est bien chez toi* is quite untranslatable, in spite of its simplicity and its perfect familiarity as a concept. He suggests: 'It's nice, your flat'. 'It's nice, being in your flat.' 'It's cosy here.' Intuitively, I propose: 'I always feel (quite) at home here/at your place/in your flat.' (*Bei Dir, fühle ich mich immer so wohl.*) Undoubtedly the concept (or the feeling) is universal, not even culturally tinged. I think the French expresses it best, and there is a slight semantic and linguistic gap in the English and the German.

Political Mistranslation?

Saddam Hussein has claimed that owing to the resemblance between the Arabic words for 'shield' and 'prevent' (danger), Western journalists had wrongly claimed he was using his prisoners as a shield. His statement is unconvincing, as no one would have attributed such a claim to him.

Double Purpose Book

Alan Duff's new book, *Translation*, (OUP), is admirably suited for teachers and students of EFL at undergraduate level as a course in language enrichment. It could also be profitably used in professional translation courses where English is the target language. Duff provides an abundant variety of short extracts from well-written contemporary English texts, and draws attention to the richness of English styles and vocabulary, as well as its peculiar grammatical features which force choices on the translator. He asserts that translation develops three qualities essential to all language learning: accuracy, clarity, and flexibility. 'It trains the reader to search (flexibility) for the most appropriate words (accuracy) to convey what is meant (clarity)'. At an advanced stage of language learning, this is indisputable. The book is splendidly structured and written with compulsive enthusiasm.

Synonymy

The English language, according to R. Clabourne's *Life and Times of the English Language* has more than three times as many words as any other language. Large English dictionaries have 400 to 600 thousand words, Russian 150,000, French 130,000. (English has 50,000 words in current use, French and German 20,000 each.) Therefore, in principle, it should be easier to produce an accurate translation into English than into any other language, as English should have fewer lexical gaps. Whether this is in fact true is not easy to establish, as other languages may have more words which each have a larger number of accepted senses.

In any event, this comparison illustrates the necessity and the importance of synonymy as a translation procedure at all and particularly the latter stages of translating. (Standard example: English has: quick, fast, rapid, speedy, swift, fleet (plus velocity and celerity, plus tempo, rate, pace); German has: *schnell* (plus *rapide, geschwind, Geschwindigkeit, Tempo);* French has *rapide, véloce, vite* (plus *célérité, tempo, pas*)). It is not surprising that *Roget's Thesaurus* is an indispensable aid for any translator into English. After language dictionaries and encyclopaedias, a dictionary of target language synonyms (two types: (a) lists under a head-word: (b) defining and contrasting the meanings of synonyms) becomes the translator's main resource, since finally, she is mainly wrestling with the target language. The main alternative to synonymy as a translation procedure is componential analysis, that is, a one-to- two or three or four translation, say *stürzen* = fall heavily (suddenly, etc); it is more accurate but less economical, and unlike synonymy, is not used extensively for one text. Normally, it is only used for lexical units of some importance.

A Note on Translation in Leningrad

Leningrad, a great international city where foreign voices are heard in museums, concert halls, art galleries, public buildings, hotels and the main streets, has been kept pathetically monolingual. Many visitors cannot penetrate the rebarbative Cyrillic capital letters (in many varieties of typeface), let alone the italics, faced with street signs and public notices. In the enormous Hermitage museum, the absurdly brief Mecca of all tourists, the only concession is that the picture titles are printed in Roman as well as Cyrillic script. The brochures describing the masterpieces in each room are also in Cyrillic. A big translation contract should be given to the University.

The Name of Leningrad

St. Petersburg was founded in 1703 by Peter the Great. The name appears to combine allegiance to the saint and the Czar (the Peter Paul Fortress and the Cathedral of St Peter and St Paul were built at the time) and acknowledgement of German culture. In 1914, as the Russians were at war with the Germans, the city's name was changed

to Petrograd, and in 1924, after Lenin's death, to Leningrad. A petition
is now circulating in the city to revert to the name St. Petersburg.

Sound and Sense
'The linguistic sign is arbitrary', Saussure wrote, and the statement
has become a canon of modern linguistics. I would prefer to modify it
to: 'Linguistic signs have become mainly arbitrary'. I think there is a
circumstance of sounds behind all speech. These sounds reflect the
expression of spontaneous feelings, in particular pleasure and pain,
animal cries (including bird song), and the impact of rain, wind, storm,
water and fire on the environment. These sounds are universal, but
they are culturally modified in this or that community. Saussure rashly
identified arbitrariness with absence of motivation; human behaviour
is normally motivated. The signifier (phonic substance) 'sister'
(Saussure's example) appears to be arbitrary, but it cannot be known
whether its etymological archetype is motivated.

I speculate that in prehistoric times, humans anthropomorphized
their environment, and perceived all elements and objects as female or
male. The words that represented them reflected their sounds to some
degree. When humans began to identify and name objects (the neuter
gender), they also began to dissociate them from sounds. (Note that
adjectives of quality (which are all human but can be transferred to
animals and objects) and their adverbs and nouns ('soft', 'clear', *dolce,
doux, fein*, etc.) are pre-eminently associated with sounds.) The
Leningrad linguist Stanislaw Voronin refers to the study of the link
between sound and sense as 'phonosemantics' (which has the merit of
being a transparent term), and rightly points out that it has important
implications for translation. Sound has meaning, not only in poetry
and rhetoric, but in all emotional expression. There have been many
studies of onomatopoea, alliteration, assonance, metre, sound sym-
bolism, synaesthesia, linguistic iconi(ci)sm, etc, but no classical or
standard work on phonosemantics. In fact, since Saussure, the subject
has rather fallen into disrepute. The childish argument is often pressed
that if 'sh' has a caressing or a friendly sound, what about 'shirk',
'shock', 'shoddy', 'shout', 'shudder', 'shrew', 'shyster', etc? The fact is,
there is no focus on 'sh' in these words. Marouzeau (*Petit Traité de
Versification française*) has demonstrated that all human sounds or
phonemes, when foregrounded, have meaning (compare Rimbaud's
famous sonnet *Voyelles*), usually affective meaning, and sometimes
multiple meanings; but as in music, such meanings can often be
disputed and misinterpreted. However, perhaps a majority might
agree that 'k' is hard and forceful, 'm' is soft and dreamy, German
'ch' is snarling? I recommend Stephen Ullmann's *Semantics* on this
subject.

The Subject of Translation

The subject of translation is first and often last the source language text. The translator may have to decide whether it is worth rendering faithfully, if it is morally or/and factually true, or adapting or modifying it for target language readerships, or exposing it to implicit linguistic or moral criticism with a sharp translation. The source language text is always there. It only disappears in oral translation (interpreting). It is the translator's continual resource and recourse for fresh insights. In many jobs, after the detailed comparative check of the original with the translation, and then the essential independent check of the translation (how does it read?), the final check is for loss (leakage) of source language meaning.

In some writing on translation, target-language orientation is stressed by introducing the role of the employer, patron, client, etc. This role may or may not be important, but it is usually concerned with generalities rather than the details of a translation.

Limits of Literal Translation

This on the back of a postcard from Chiavari on the Italian riviera:
Lungomare e porto
Promenade along the sea and harbour
Promenade le long de la mer et port
Promenade den (sic) Meer entlang und Hafen.
'Along the sea' appears unnecessary in the English, and *le long de la mer* possibly in the French, as the *Promenade des Anglais* is not far away in Nice. In German, *Promenade* is perhaps not so common in this sense, so *dem Meer entlang* (alt. *Strandpromenade*) is justified. 'Esplanade' is available in English, but has a different meaning in French and German.

Neologisms

Why do I jib at 'translatology' but not at 'phonosemantics', a rarer word? Because phonosemantics is a readily defined scientific subject, whilst translatology is large and shapeless.

The Responsibilities of the Translator

The translator is responsible for the moral and (to the best of his ability and competence) the factual truth of the translation, but not dogmatically, since dogma in this sense is always counter-productive. Factual mistakes have to be corrected, either within or outside the text, depending on its degree of authority. Moral errors, that is, textual deviations from animal, human or ecological rights, have to be corrected inside or outside the translation, unless the translator is confident that the readership is aware of them. Thus Ralph Manheim can produce a 'straight' translation of *Mein Kampf* for a scholarly readership, but a 'popular' translation should be at least twice as long as the original, the corrections being made in extensive notes. (There is one in San Diego University library, on the Calexico campus.)

The Riddle of Translation

Extract from *La Nouvelle République*, the newspaper of the Centre-Ouest region of France, Blois edition: *LA DYNAMIQUE BLÉSOISE, 'A pour affaires économiques' d'avril met les villes en équation et classe 212 villes de France selon leur capacité à créer des enterprises et des emplois.* Translation comments:

1. *Blésois.* Most Romance languages form adjectives even from the names of the smallest villages, often reverting to an older form of the name. This may be due to the Romance language preference for adjectives of substance, while Germanic languages have premodifying nouns. 'Classical' examples:

Charleville; *carlopolitain.*
Charleville-Mézières; *carolomacérien.*
St. Etienne; *stéphanois.*
Biarritz; *biarrot.*

2. 'Dynamic' is a European vogue-word, so perhaps 'The Dynamic of Blois'.

3. The reference to the month (*d'avril*) indicates that a monthly publication is being quoted, and fortunately spares one the task of translating its title, which has to be reproduced and glossed as a monthly economic survey of French towns.

4. *Met en équation* indicates a further semantic extension of the 'fast growing' *équation:* 'relates towns to each other'.

(The occasion for such a translation would only be a personal commission or an academic exercise.)

Grammatical Terms

I have often looked for a serviceable grammar with reasonably transparent terminology to describe texts and translations. Quirk et al (*A Grammar of Contemporary English*) is encyclopaedic and perceptive, but some of its terms are opaque (e.g. 'style disjuncts'). I recommend the Collins *Cobuild English Grammar* (1990) (a spin-off from the *Cobuild Dictionary*) which has a clearly written glossary. It is based on Halliday's systemic grammar. However, it has irritating gaps.

Here is a list of grammatical concepts, and my suggested terms, which I miss in most grammars:

Example	Term
I do play . . .	Emphatic present
I did play . . .	Emphatic past
A smiling face	Dynamic verbal adjective
A charming person	Stative verbal adjective

Example	Term
Swimming is good for you ⎱ I like swimming ⎰	Verbal noun
Writing a letter/working with you is a pleasure	Gerund
An establishment	Stative deverbal noun
The establishment of this system	Dynamic deverbal noun
The writing of this book	Continuous verbal noun
I think that . . .	Comment clause
In my opinion	Comment phrase
Hopefully, personally, probably	Comment adverb
Kindness	Adjectival noun
Nervous	Adjective of quality
Nerveux (as in *centre nerveux*)	Adjective of substance
Of course, *eben, ja, vous savez*	Phatic or modal particle

The older I get, the sillier I
  become
	Correlative comparative
	  sentence.

English-French Translation

Henri Van Hoof's new book, *Traduire l'Anglais*, (Duculot, Paris 1989) is the best and most comprehensive introduction to English-French translation that I know, and I also recommend it to French-English translators. Much of it is based squarely on Vinay and Darbelnet (*Stylistique comparée du français et de l'anglais*) and it also has useful sections on collocations (pp. 92–94), puns, titles and dialects. The word 'culture' doesn't appear once, which is rather remiss, but I found it a relief. Some of the 'idioms' are a little quaint ('a deuce of a liar', 'a terror of a child', 'to fetch a sigh'). The latest upmarket translatology is thankfully missing from the bibliography. The author argues convincingly in favour of accurate translation.

Foreign Language Examining Now

The Aims and Assessment Objectives of the Associated Examination Board's 1991 Advanced Level 'Modern' Languages Examinations make no mention of translation. Yet under 'Reading Comprehension', a passage of about 300 words is to be translated into English, and 'the candidate will be required to render the passage with due attention to precise detail and shades of meaning', which sounds finicky enough. In another paper, 'Use of Written Language', 'some questions will involve translation of limited (*sic*) sections'. So translation gets in by the back door again. As before, there is more stress on knowing about literature than reading it.

At a time when a paper such as the *Guardian* acknowledges the importance of translation by publishing translations from ten

European newspapers, including *Lidové Noviny*, every week, the A.E.B's attitude to translation remains as antiquated as that of the 'progressive' foreign language teachers of the 60s.

Literary Translation and the Essence of Literature

Fritz Senn, an immensely stimulating and erudite writer who has contributed to two collections edited by Mary Snell-Hornby, *Ubersetzungswissenschaft — eine Neuorientierung* (UTB Francke 1986), and, with Esther Pohl, *Translation and Lexicography* (Benjamins 1989), claims that 'literature is what cannot be paraphrased': 'Being or not being, this ain't the problem' (Hamlet) won't quite do. The 'message' is inseparable from its wording. Sound, word order, repetition, grammatical structure — they all contribute to the sense'.

This is a bold statement. I would modify it by suggesting that it applies primarily to lyrical, then to dramatic, then to epical poetry; then to short stories; then to novels; then to plays (tragedy, comedy, farce, in descending order). And in general, to all good and serious writing.

'Translation, however', Senn goes on, 'is paraphrase; the words in which the supposedly same thing is being said are others, foreign ones. Priorities must be set. Correctness (of sense?) normally dominates against, say, sound or the length of the word.' (Is this true of poetry?) Thus far, I think Senn is right, but when he says that 'Translation is more "para" (i.e. paraphrastic) than anything else within the same culture' (same language?), I think he is profoundly wrong; translation, strictly speaking, is more or less paraphrase (but normally, not much so) but it is always more accurate than any paraphrase in the same language. Usually, 'a table' is *ein Tisch, une table, una tavola* rather than a 'flat horizontal slab or board supported by one or more legs, on which objects can be placed'. Note also that translation, being more concise, has greater impact than monolingual paraphrase.

Senn often takes his examples from Joyce, where frequent word play, complicating the conflicting claims of sound with two or more senses, greatly adds to the difficulties of translation. His discussion of some English, French and Italian translations of a sentence from Kafka's *The Trial: Störend schwebte das ewige licht davor* is illuminating (excuse my word play) and concentrates on sense, brevity and emphasis, but it is a pity that he does not, as any translation theorist should, offer his own version, presumably English, as he writes in the language. So I suggest: '(He illuminated the altarpiece with a torch.) Disturbingly, the eternal light from the altar hovered in front of him.' But I can only describe this effort as *pis-aller*. Compare with:

'The light from a permanent oil lamp hovered over it like an intruder. (Muir)

'The perpetual light of the sanctuary lamp hanging in front got in the way.' (Scott/Waller)

La lumière du tabernacle contrariait celle de la lampe électrique
(Vialette)
La lampada perpetua appesa davanti gli era di ostacolo. (Claudio
Magris, surely the best.) These four versions miss the word-order
emphasis. By the way, Senn constantly complains that the dear translatologists
aren't helping him. Not surprisingly, as I can't imagine X or Y *reading*,
let alone loving poetry. But there is still Jiři Levy's outstanding book,
translated as *Die literarische Übersetzung*, and still waiting for its
English translator.

Finally, Senn says, literary texts are overdetermined, carry no
wastage, no noise (in the communication theory sense), their
fittingness is all-round. (In contrast one may say that translation is
underdetermined, but not to the extent that Quine claimed.) When,
however, in his last boutade, Senn claims that 'translatology will have
to devote itself to the problem of translating movement, change,
distortion, deviation — in other words, how to translate translation
itself', perhaps he forgets that the translator can only do this by doing
another translation, now or a generation hence.

Plenitude or Fullness?
Plénitude has 14 lines in the Petit Robert; 'plenitude' has only three
in the Collins. Therefore 'fullness' is the more likely translation.

Jollity in Jesolo
'We asked: ''Why Jesolo for your holidays?'' ' says a brochure for
the Venetian resort. 'Because', the well-rounded beauty in the
illustration replies, 'Jesolo can be reached so easily that my husband is
able to come and see me every week-end, and each time he finds me
more and more sun-tanned'. I assume this is a close translation of the
Italian original, and, as it is sexist, the translator should have left out
the reference to the husband, and confined him/herself to Jesolo's
accessibility and its warm weather. Another illustration of a topless
girl lying on the beach is accompanied by the caption: 'The services on
the beach are easy and free'.

XI
JANUARY 1991

Possibilities of Translating

Most of the elegantly written articles in *Hermeneutics and the Poetic Motion (Translation Perspectives V*, edited by Dennis J. Schmidt 1990; managing editor: Marilyn Gaddis Rose, CRIT, SUNY, Binghamton, NY 13901 USA) argue the question of the possibility of translation. This may seem strange at a time when the necessity, importance and increasingly widespread practice of translation is virtually universally recognised. However, the authors appear to assume, though they do not say so, that they are only discussing texts where the manner is as important as the matter.

Before commenting on a few of these essays, I propose to make a few generalisations. Exact translation is usually impossible, if only because all languages have different grammars and unequal numbers of words, and, where relevant, reflect different cultures. Mathematical truths such as 'One plus one equals two' can, however, be perfectly and exactly translated into any language. Texts that transmit a message without emphasis on emotional tone or sound of words can always be satisfactorily translated, even if they show up lexical gaps or cultural differences in the target language: 'the bottom line' (a variation of the originally Marxist 'in the last analysis'), the real translating difficulty, is not cultural, but personal language, when it expresses some valuable and original thought of the SL author.

Here then is John P. Leavey, Jr., a philosopher, wrestling with Gadamer on translation (the translations in the first sentence are mine): 'In the understanding of texts, translation is *Rückverwandlung in Sprache* ("re-transformation in language") and *Nachbildung* ("re-shaping", "reformation", "reconstruction"), a cause for resignation for the loss; rarely, translation is *Nachschöpfung* ("re-creation") or *Nachdichtung* ("re-composing", "re-rendering"), a series of terms difficult to translate in English. But in all cases, translation is always *after*, supplementary, with a gap, an unbridgeable gulf, *nach* or *zurück*, whether *Verwandlung* ("transformation"), *Bildung* ("presentation" or "formation", *Schöpfung* ("genesis" or "creation") or *Dichtung* ("saying" or "poem").' Now this is a good exercise in translating and distinguishing certain German concepts (some of Leavey's noticeably aberrant), but is it any more than a statement of the obvious, viz., that the original precedes the translation, and that the latter is some kind of explanation or interpretation of the former?

Marilyn Gaddis Rose is trying to derive a new translation 'meta-theory' from post-modernism in translating Sainte-Beuve's *Volupté*, and she uses the all too familiar terms as well as a few new ones (regimes, transversal pertinencies, moves (*coups*), *différend* (from Derrida to Lyotard)); translation is a language game, which it certainly is, but the implication that it is a game rather than life or reality or truth is dangerous.

The Unfindable Again

La démocratie montante ne sera point — tout le présage — la salvatrice des rares cerveaux qui conservent en serre, par cette hyémale époque, les fleurs d'un printemps possible.

The meaning of the 'unfindable' *hyémale* is clear by its contrast with *printemps*: in a Grecolatinism, confusion of *u*, *y* and *i* is sometimes possible, and in fact the *O.E.D.* and the *Petit Robert* add *hyemal* as an alternative to *hiémal*. So I suggest: 'Everything indicates that the rise of democracy will not be the saving of the few intelligent minds which, in this wintry time, preserve the flowers of an eventual spring.' Note that the shift from French 'adj. plus noun' to English 'verbal noun plus' of 'plus noun' is rather more common for German than for French; also note that 'eventual' can mean 'possible' as well as 'final'.

Grecolatinisms

In principle, current Grecolatinisms are likely to have acquired a larger number of senses in Romance than in other languages, as they have existed for a longer period. Thus, say, the semantic range of *honorable* (F) is larger than 'honourable' (E). (*La progression est honorable*. 'This improvement is creditable (praiseworthy)'.)

The Bilingual Trap

Personal as well as geographical names from bilingual countries may have to be checked. Thus a French writer showing off refers to *La Dentellière de Van der Meer*; this is simply Vermeer's *Lacemaker*. Note also: Pieter de Hooch (F) or Hoogh or Hooghe (Du.); Quintin (F) or Quinten (Du); Massys (F) or Metsys or Matsys (Du); Antoine (F) or Antoon (Du) Van Dyke (F) or Van Dijck (Du); Pieter Van Laer (F) or Van Laar (Du); Rogier (F) or Roger (Du) Van der Weyden (Du) or de La Pasture (F).

Rembrandt, thank goodness, remains Rembrandt, or Rembrandt Harmenszoon van Rijn or Ryn. Note that these name-changes apply only to some Dutch (cf. Italian) Renaissance painters.

The Translation of Metaphor 'Revisited'

I warmly commend Alicya Pisarska's *Creativity of Translators — The Translation of Metaphorical Expressions in Non-literary Texts* (which is probably only obtainable from the Institute of English, Adam Mickiewicz University, ul. Niepodleglosca 14,61–874 Poznan,

Poland), in spite of her complimentary references to me. ('When people agree with me, I feel I must be wrong.' Oscar Wilde). To begin with, she gives an informative and stimulating review of some of the literature on translation theory, metaphor and text-types. She then examines the translation into Polish of 120 metaphors taken from six 20th Century British non-literary works, plus Frazer's *Golden Bough*; she finds that 60% were translated by the same image; 18% by a different image; 16% were reduced to sense. The remaining 6% were distributed amongst four other described procedures. This suggests to me (but I am described as a 'universalist') that in these kinds of texts, Polish and English are less culturally divided than culture-sharing or universally bound. Finally, Pisarska discusses the creativity of translating and makes an interesting distinction between 'conceptual' (original) and 'ornamental' (standard) metaphors. I think she is mistaken in thinking that 'ornamental' metaphors (take 'wooden face') merely serve to enliven a dull text; all metaphors, even cliché metaphors, attempt to 'mean' real or imagined actions, processes, objects, qualities, etc., more comprehensively, succinctly, arrestingly, even decoratively or ornamentally than is possible in literal language.

The Mood Factor

Apart from legal and administrative texts, which require exact translation from start to finish, all translations to some extent betray the translators' moods, which may vary or alternate between severity and indulgence towards the readership or towards themselves. So where does that leave the 'science of translation' or 'translatology', if you translate *faire ses preuves* as 'prove oneself' or 'show one's ability', according to your mood?

The Craft of Translation

The Craft of Translation, edited by John Biguenet and Rainer Schulte (University of Chicago Press, 1989) is a superb book of essays on literary translation. The Introduction states that 'the activity of the translator starts with the reality of the word on the page' and discusses six English translations of the first line of Rilke's great *The Panther*. Raffel Burton at least adduces examples to support his view that the literary translator 'is engaged with far more than words, far more than techniques, far more than stories or characters or scenes. He is engaged with world views.' (I agree, but not with the priorities implied.) Margaret Sayers Peden, who writes beautifully, and adds at least three to the all too numerous metaphors for translation, reproduces nine translations of Sor Juana's *A su retrato*, including one by Samuel Beckett; her own is breath-takingly close:

Este, que ves, engano colorido . . .
This that you gaze on, colourful deceit . . .

es cadaver, es polvo, es sombra, es nada.
Is but cadaver, ashes, shadow, void.
The analysis, which emphasises structure, is fascinating. Edmund Keeley, bravely contradicting Robert Frost, suggests that some would say in many cases, what constitutes poetry is exactly what survives in a good translation. Donald Frame thinks that a prospective translator can look at a text and make an estimate of its maximum yield in his language: say 20% or 50% or even 80%. 20% seems unduly pessimistic, but if you take say Joanna Richardson's version of Verlaine's *Chanson d'automne* with all its sounds and rhythms, I doubt if it is worth more, and it's so difficult that I suspect it's not worth making more than an interlinear translation as an introduction to the original; the content is so slight that a 'plain prose' translation is hardly helpful. (I hasten to add that I disagree with John Weightman, who has said that the translation of French poetry is impossible; he is merely right for this instance.) Frame closes with sensitive and practical discussions of translating Molière, Voltaire, Rabelais and Montaigne. His term 'translation yield' is an acquisition. William Weaver's 'The Process of Translation' is an object-lesson in thinking aloud (*Lautdenken*) and it is likely to be far more useful to a student than any survey of translators' habits. Weaver takes one paragraph by the Italian novelist Gadda and shows how and why he gradually transforms his first draft into his final (and beyond) version. He illustrates several accepted translation procedures: the switch from one hold-all word to another, *congegni* switching from 'machinery' to 'devices' to 'apparatuses' to 'instruments'; the distinction between ordinary (social?) words (*sudore, lavoro*) and exotic (personal?) words (*zaffiro, detersi*) to cleanse onself.

John Felstiner discusses in fascinating detail the translation of some poems by the great Jewish-Romanian-German poet Paul Celan, who wrote the wonderful poem of the holocaust, *Todesfuge (Fugue of Death*, translated by Christopher Middleton).

Detective Work
Puzzling titles, sub-titles, headings, acronyms (e.g. the elusive LBOs, leveraged buy-outs) should routinely be looked for in the body of the text for clarification.

Normal Social Usage
As an introduction to normal social usage, or social (as opposed to personal) language, I recommend *Language in use: a grammar of communication in English and French* by Beryl Atkins and Helene Lewis, which is the last section of the *Robert-Collins* (in m⟨ ⟩experience the most useful general bilingual dictionary). This i⟨ ⟩ application of notional-functional grammar, and in⟨ ⟩ range of standard formulae/collocations and thei⟨ ⟩

Fortunately, there is now a parallel version in the *Collins German* (1991 edition).

A Common Transposition

Verbal adjectives ending in -able, -ible, -bar, -abile, etc., are often more common or non-existent in one language as opposed to another, and are conveniently translated by a relative clause with the verb in the passive, e.g. *un barème fiscal tolérable*, 'a tax scale which can be met without difficulty'.

Not Found (Revisited)

When a translator fails to understand a passage or a sentence or a word in the source language text, after exhausting all the usual and the lateral resources (informants, reference books, connotation, figurative sense of passage, misprints, etymologies, mistakes, misspellings, idiolect, bizarreries, neologisms, etc), she has (a) to fill the gap with her best guestimate for the context, (b) state: 'Not found'; (c) desirably, in a footnote, reproduce the relevant SL passage and its literal translation, and then succinctly state how she has arrived at her solution. Thus, in a piece of political journalism: '*tour de table fermé*' (representation excluded), 'exclusion from participation'. (Literally, 'closed turn at table'.) But *tour de table* may be becoming a vogue word.

Slang and Idioms

In principle, the translator uses the modern language in the appropriate register, whatever the period when the original was written. However, slang in general, and some idioms are so closely related to the present, linguistically rather than culturally, that they sound bizarre when used in translations of texts of a previous period. Thus in 1894 Monet wrote to a friend: *C'est entendu pour mercredi*. To translate this as 'Wednesday is alright', is, I think, acceptable; 'It's on for Wednesday' is not. *Il doit être remonté* is better as 'We must cheer him up' than 'We must buck him up'. Certainly this illogically goes against the principle that translation should be into the modern language, possibly because modern slang including its 'taboo' component is exclusively associated with modern characters.

Analytic and Synthetic Language

It may be useful for a translator to bear in mind that of European languages, English is the most analytical; since the Middle English clash between Anglo-Saxon and Norman French (1100 to 1450), when English was shorn of many of its suffixes, it has been a basically monosyllabic language; unlike other languages, it tends to eschew compounding and hyphening when it forms words. The logical consequence of this is the tendency to translate a foreign tri (plus) syllabic word by three plus shorter English words. (Scrap example: *Il est excessif de dire que* . . . 'It may be going too far to say that.') Note that Russian's disconcerting polysyllabic words often require monosyllabic English equivalents (*ostanovka*; 'halt'); many monosyllabic English adjectives (e.g. colours such as 'green' and 'blue' almost routinely translate into Russian trisyllables ('*żeleniy*'; '*goluboy*'): moreover, the many conversions on the model of *gorod* (R) to '*grad*' (Cz) ('city') and *moloko* (R) to *mleko* (Cz) ('milk') suggest that Russian may be the most polysyllabic of all Slavic languages. Further, there is no end to the monosyllabicism of British and particularly American English forms and multiple meanings of phrasal verbs, nouns and adjectives ('no show'; invisible). As English increases its stock of phrasal words ('upturn' for 'recovery', 'downturn' for 'decline', both of them 'neutral' rather than 'informal' words) it turns away from Romance and returns to its physical and transparent Anglo-Saxon roots.

Translation Equivalence
The cerebration and the brain racking about translation equivalence goes on for ever. Equally futile are the attempts to define it narrowly (in a sentence) or to compartmentalise it into 'adequacy', 'equivalence', 'correspondence', 'approximation', 'identity', 'interchangeability' (Catford) etc. (See for instance, Hannu Tommola's 'From ReReRe (Recker's Regular Relationships) to "complex" translating', in *Fachsprachen und Übersetzungstheorie* (University of Vaasa, Finland, 1990), a piece partially redeemed by its translation examples, and then shamed by its attempt to replace translation by a multi-stage translation method (acquaintance (does she mean 'comprehension?'), note-taking, writing, post-editing), which invites inaccuracy. ('I have nothing against* inaccuracy (tee hee), when it is needed, when it is motivated'.)
Translation equivalence cannot be defined. Normally, there are only degrees of translation equivalence. In context, equivalence may merely be based on an alliteration ('An Austrian army'; *ein einfaches Ei*). Nevertheless, translation equivalence, which is semantic, and correspondence, which relates to places (*Stellen*) in the SL and the TL text, are indispensable operational terms in translation. ('Adequacy' is a genuine dead duck, as it means different things in different languages.)

Two Extremes
If the notion that the words of a (religious) text should only be translated, if at all, literally, originated with theologians jealous of the word of God, the idea that SL words should not be translated by TL

---

*People who use this expression, mean its opposite.

words spelt identically or similarly originated with language teachers. Both notions are misguided, but the latter, which appears particularly deep rooted in the French and English educational systems, does rather more to distort the concept of translation and is pernicious. No student I suppose would go so far as to translate such a concrete thing as a *table* (F) as a 'stool', or a 'table' (E) as a *tabouret*, but say they get *objection* (F), they assail you with 'criticism', 'blame', 'protest', or faced with 'objection' (E), they produce *critique, protestation, contestation,* etc.

Why? Fear of being imitative, uncreative, parasitical, mechanical? Is it just tradition, a take over from Latin 'prose' and 'unseen', where 'good style' always counted for more than accuracy? Because close translation is so boring, so unenterprising? Whatever the reasons, they're silly.

Closely and oddly related to the second extreme is the reluctance to translate a common SL word denoting a quality used in its primary meaning by its usual TL equivalent. Thus why translate *une bonne année agricole* as 'a bumper year in agriculture', when 'a good year in agriculture' is accurate? (Incidentally, this illustrates that a French adjective of substance (*agricole*) is sometimes conveniently translated by a preposition plus noun ('in agriculture').

A Moral Tale

Erst kommt das Fressen, dann die Moral, wrote the misguided Brecht. Not much problem in translating that: 'First comes grub, then morality'? But when you come to the essence of morality, say 'kindness' and 'truthfulness', German can't get nearer than the rarer *Gütigkeit* and *Wahrhaftigkeit*, and French has *gentillesse* and perhaps *fidélité*. So we're back to the abstractions, 'goodness' and 'truth', where there are no translation problems.

Personal and Social

Some words are too personal for 'social' texts. Thus 'need' (personal) and 'requirement' (social) both translate *besoin*. Compare 'eat' and 'consume' and probably many more.

The Quality of a Condition

Wolf Friedrich in the excellent *Die Technik des Übersetzens* notes many cases where an abstract noun plus object noun translates into 'adjective of quality plus noun' for German. (*Die Dynamik des Markts*, 'the dynamic' (or 'buoyant') market). To a lesser extent, this also applies to French. (*Le dynamisme du marché*.)

From Concrete to Abstract

SL concrete nouns, whether used literally or figuratively, that show up lexical gaps in the TL normally have to be raised to a more general level in translation. Thus, in an economic text: *des ressorts et des freins sont en oeuvre, qu'on ne peut déceler en une si courte période* could become 'expansive and restrictive factors are at work, which can scarcely be detected in such a short period'. Admittedly, ten translators would probably translate *ressorts et freins* (lit. 'springs and brakes') in ten different ways, but they would all have this generalising character.

Schnäppchen

The GDR, wrote Günter Grass, will become a *Schnäppchen* for the Federal Republic. How to translate this dialect word? 'Snip'? 'Quick bite'?

Metalingual Trap

An article in *Problèmes Économiques* begins:
L'ANNÉE 1984 À TRAVERS LES COMPTES NATIONAUX
Sous ce titre, Les Notes bleues, publication hebdomadaire du Service de l'information du ministère de l'Économie, des Finance et du Budget, a publié l'article suivant dans son numéro 236.

Close translation: THE YEAR 1984 SEEN THROUGH THE NATIONAL ACCOUNTS

Les Notes bleues, a weekly bulletin published by the Information Department of the Ministry of the Economy, Finance, and the Budget, has published the following article in its issue No. 236 with the above mentioned title.

However, this is metalingually misleading, as a French magazine does not publish an article with an English title. Therefore the last five words ('with the above mentioned title') have to be replaced by: 'under the title, *L'année 1984 à travers les Comptes nationaux*'.

Marked and Unmarked

Normally, *le marché à règlement mensuel* ('market with monthly settlements') could be translated simply as 'the market', but if, in later paragraphs, it is contrasted with *marché au comptant* ('spot market') and MATIF (*marché à terme d'instruments financiers*, 'forward exchange market'), it could be distinguished and translated simply as 'the stock market'.

Transference

From spaghetti to cappelletti, objects seem to remain diachronically safe after transference. Not so abstract ideas. Consider 'verve', transferred (from French) in 1697 as 'special talent in writing' (*O.E.D.*), now 'enthusiasm, vigour, spirit', esp. in literary or artistic work' (*C.O.D.*) in English, but 'wit and eloquence' in French.

The Translator's Two Perspectives

Translators have to consider their texts from two points of view: referentially and linguistically.

First, they have to understand what the words are referring to: what has happened, what is happening, and possibly what will happen, and what are the agents or instruments implicated. To do this, they may have to infer or intuit (the translator's tried and sorely tried hunch) a few linguistic gaps in the text. All words, even function-words like 'as' and 'towards' and 'the', refer to some kind of extra-linguistic reality, and this has to be visualised by the translator, even if it is only fiction or fantasy. Secondly, they have to visualise their translations in their appropriate target language settings, to ask themselves: Can you actually, can you really see these words on the page? This goes particularly for certain typical and regular settings, say the financial columns of a newspaper. Thus, in *Le Monde* (27.2.90): *'Purge', 'pause', 'consolidation', les qualificatifs abondent au terme de cette semaine où la place parisienne . . . a été secouée par la crainte de l'inflation et de la hausse des taux d'intérêt.*

Close translation; ' "Purge", "pause", "consolidation", there is an abundance of qualifying terms to describe the Paris Bourse shaken by fear of inflation and a rise in interest rates at the end of the week.' This translation recasts the syntax and keeps the lexis, but I still can't see it on an English page. Maybe, 'At the end of the week, when the Paris Bourse has been shaken by fears of inflation and higher interest rates, there is a need, amongst other things, for a return to stability (I assume Dominique Gallois meant *assainissement* by *purge*?), a pause, and then consolidation'. Of course, I'd prefer to translate what Dominique actually wrote. But I can't, I can't see it, I can't visualise it. Besides, Dominique is not de Gaulle, my eternal model of authority and good writing. If s/he were, my version would be different. Note also that there are even some internationalisms like *a contrario* or *a priori* which would be perfectly 'convincing' in a French but not in an English economic text.

Secousse Sans Panique = Shock Without Panic

The satisfying thing about this literal translation of the title of an economic text is that it reproduces the assonance. A large number of good titles are rich in sound effect, and translators too readily assume it is impossible to reproduce or compensate it.

The Invisibility of the Translator

In principle, the translator should be invisible, and a translation should not read like a translation, but should read as an independent text about to start its own life. In fact, things are not so simple. To begin with, translations should be published as such, with the translator's name and details of the source language text. Secondly there may be features of the source language, idioms like the German *grüne Lungen der Grossstadt*, 'breathing spaces', 'green lungs of the city', grammatical structures like 'the to him dear memory', extended use of words ('you can do that smoothly'), where 'imitative' translationese (*ruhig*) may turn into creative translation. Thirdly, translated idiolect as well as source language cultural features may 'betray' the translator; to some people, *Finnegan's Wake* would sound like a translation in the original as well as any other language. Fourthly, translators may have to declare themselves with their *sic* or their square brackets. Fifthly, the translator should always be invisible when following normal social usage.

The Non-neutrality of the Translator
Like art and sport, translation is potentially or implicitly political, if politics is regarded as a concern of national and international, or public morality. Translators cannot be neutral, where matters of fact or morality are concerned. They have to intervene, inside or outside their texts.

Informative Texts
Translators are always entitled to rewrite informative texts, if they are confident that their versions are going to be better than their originals. Thus they may impose their own style on them.

The Monet Exhibition
The important Royal Academy exhibition, *Monet in the '90s*, which was organised by the Boston Museum of Fine Arts, was entirely monolingual. It was a pity that the original titles of the paintings were not reproduced. *Les Meules*, for instance, was translated as 'Cornstacks', instead of the generally accepted 'Haystacks'. The paintings are beautiful and endlessly fascinating, but there is no 'pity and terror' in them, they are not on the level of Goya or Van Gogh.

Guardian Europe
The weekly *Guardian Europe* (Fridays), which includes translations from fourteen European newspapers by Pholiota Translations, London N1 9AA, marks a significant advance in the extension of translations in this country. It would be useful, not only to translators and teachers, if the original titles and the numbers and dates of the respective issues were appended to each translation.

The Despair and Relief of Translating
Sometimes when I translate, I am hoping to release better words

from my unconscious, my memory hold, I go on repeating the start of a sentence and stop, expecting something fresh to emerge, to pop out. Sometimes it does: it's a relief, and I start my smirk. More often it doesn't, and I despair.

XII
MARCH 1991

Word Order

Since so many translators appear to ignore source language word order and its meaning, it might be useful to recapitulate its main functions:

1. It distinguishes statements from questions and commands. Statements indicating a sequence of events are, in natural word order (i.e. following the normal train of thought) shown as agent-action-affected object, or SVP, e.g. 'Man kills dog'. Descriptive statements follow the sequence: topic-predicate, e.g. 'Grass is green'. Questions in natural word order begin by inverting agent and action (or the auxiliary that indicates time and number) e.g. 'Has he?' Commands begin with action and omit the agent, e.g. 'Run away'. Within a sentence, natural word order, which is always more apparent in analytical languages like English rather than in synthetic languages like Russian, suggests that an unmarked noun group follows the sequence: 'determiner-descriptor-headword' (e.g. 'a good lad') and that an adverbial group, indicating place, time or manner (in that order) follows the main sequence of events, e.g. 'He arrived in Brno on Friday without mishap'.

2. It follows the rules of language imposed by the prevailing clerks or clerics (that is, the political hegemony) which may run counter to natural word order and the popular spoken language. (Natural word order follows the spoken rather than the written language; many contorted but concise German or Latin participial clauses have to be unravelled in English.)

3. It distinguishes old from new information, normally putting old information first, e.g. 'He arrived'.

4. It indicates emphasis: natural word order puts the emphasis on the last 'content word', e.g. 'He gave a laugh'. (In natural word-order, function words like 'it' or 'then' are not stressed.) When particular stress is put on something, natural word order is altered or italics are used. Each language has its own lexical or grammatical emphasizers which normally have correspondences in other languages, and which set off (*déclencher*) a change in word order. English, in the lexis, has 'notably', 'precisely', 'obviously', 'for sure', 'really', 'of course', 'for certain' — they are often used phatically rather than emphatically, thereby flattering the reader; in the grammar, it can make use of existential sentences (e.g. 'There are . . .', 'There lived . . .'), cleft sentences (e.g. 'It was last night John appeared') or pseudo-cleft sentences (e.g. 'What you need is a rest').

French and German have corresponding emphasis devices, but Italian's facility for giving the subject 'end-weight' (e.g. *'Sono io'*; *È stata uccisa la sua moglie* ('It's me'; 'It's his wife who's been killed') is particularly useful for any translator.

These paragraphs owe much to Firbas (functional sentence perspective is always concerned with word order), Quirk and Greenberg, but unfortunately I know of no book principally about word order.

Micmac

The French word, meaning anything from 'funny game' through 'funny business', 'fuss', 'carry-on' to 'mix-up', or, more soberly, 'petty intrigues', 'suspect dealings' (*intrigues mesquines, agissements suspects*) illustrates the continuous influence of alliteration, rhyme, assonance, monosyllabism, repetition, abbreviation, on language, to reduce the gap between words and objects (onomatopoeia), and to make the word's sound attractive . . . Saussure, when he insisted on the arbitrariness of language, was depriving it of its roots: in the case of *micmac*, Middle Dutch *muytmaker* ('mischief making') to *meutemacre* ('rebellious') to *miquemaque* (1640), reaching perfection, i.e. *micmac*, in 1691.

Understandably, it has not changed since. (I note also as a newspaper heading, FROCK SHOCK, illustrating the irresistible attraction of monosyllabic C+V+K (consonant + vowel + final letter K) in English.).

Swearing at the Dictionary

Swearing at the dictionary must be any translator's favourite pastime. No longer out of date, prudish or anti-technical or anti-literary or anti-linguistics — the *Concise Oxford Dictionary* is quite reformed — the worst difficulty is trying to find a word when it forms part of an idiom, compound, collocation or proverb. You look for *coup de tête* in two columns devoted to *tête*, you find 'V. *coup*', and then you have over two columns of *coup* to search through. The second headache is trying to find out the currency of an item. Dictionaries are notorious repositories of mothy idioms. Other register categories are now handled better. It's a problem for Eurolex. (Why not Cosmolex?)

Hatim and Mason Again

Basil Hatim and Ian Mason's article, 'Genre, Discourse and Text in the Critique of Translation', published in *Bradford University Occasional Papers No. 10, Translation in Performance* edited by Peter Fawcett and Owen Heathcote, is again a pleasure to disagree fundamentally with. The article is steeped in post-structuralism (i.e. Barthes, Foucault and Co.), which ignores any moral values in literature, say Matthew Arnold's statement that 'Poetry is a criticism of life, by the laws of poetic truth and poetic beauty', and stresses that literature feeds on itself (intertextuality), and changes with each reading by a single or a different reader; both propositions have indeed a limited truth. Therefore Hatim and Mason are not concerned with the assessment or the standards of translation, nor their relation to extra-linguistic reality (e.g. facts), but rather with the 'cultural semiotics of language'. After an excursus on Freud, where they fail to point out how seriously Strachey's translation has distorted Freud (see Bruno Bettelheim's *Freud and Man's Soul*), they take Richard Howard's Proust as their 'issue'. Using two rather banal quotes from Reiss and House in support.

'It seems to be unlikely that translation quality assessment can ever be completely objectified in the manner of the results of natural science subjects' (Reiss) (who ever thought they could be?), they appear to assume that any assessment, because it cannot be 100% objective, must be 100% subjective, and therefore should be avoided. And having justifiably identified the genre of the business letter and its standard translation, they then put Proust into the genre of 'reflective semi-fictionalised biography' and distinguish its 'discoursal values' as though they were typical of the genre, giving a few one-word (*sic*, though these are committed text-linguists) examples of each value, and signally failing to point out any originality in Proust's text. They then indicate that the first Scott Moncrieff translation is 'monitored' whilst Howard's version is 'managed', that is, an evaluative version of Proust. The idea that a translator should not be trying to 'evaluate' or 'manage' Proust, but should be trying to render him as closely as possible, should in fact be emphasising with him (as Scott Moncrieff did, and Terence Kilmartin perhaps better, but neither as finely and poetically as Andreas Mayor) never seems to occur to them. They are heavily influenced by relativism, which is defined in the *Fontana Dictionary of Modern Thought* as the view that beliefs and principles, particularly evaluative ones, have no universal or timeless validity, but are valid only for the age in which, or the social group or individual person by which, they are held. This is the view I oppose.

A Translator's Mark

Vorsätze dieser Art schleppt man durch die Zeit, Einmal hat man es eilig, bei nächster Gelegenheit, fehlt die Lust.

Literal translation: 'Intentions of this kind one drags through time. Sometimes one is in a hurry, at the next opportunity, the inclination is lacking.

Close translation: 'You keep putting off resolutions like these. Either you're in too much of a hurry, or, next time, you can't be bothered.' A translator's mark, in non-authoritative informal passages, is to bring out the contrasts more clearly.

On est bien chez toi

Anthony Crane points out ('personal communication', as they say), that this is one of the rare occasions when *on* translates as 'one'. So, 'One always feels at home here'. This nicely forestalls Martin Weston's objection to my 'I always feel at home here' as too subjective. So O.K., unless you never use 'one', out of inverted snobbery. Certainly *on* is more wide-spread than 'one'. 'One' meaning 'I' in spoken language is reserved for the aristocracy.

A Sexist Metaphor

Les 'pros' de l'immobilier ont des sensibilités de jouvencelles. Literal translation: 'The professionals of property have a damsel's sensitivity'.

Close translation: 'Property developers are as sensitive as adolescent girls'.

However, I would translate this as 'Property developers are oversensitive'. As this is a non-authoritative text (from *L'Évènment du Jeudi*), I would think no more of it. If it were an authoritative text, it would depend on the occasion. I might add a *sic* to the close translation or delete the metaphor and tell the client.

I am aware that many intelligent readers will disagree with me. The objection has been made that the Jesolo brochure I quoted in *Paras* No. 10 was sexy rather than sexist (the illustration certainly was). If it was (I don't think so), then I withdraw because I have no objection to sexy language — the distinction between sexy and sexist is sometimes fuzzy. (Compare eroticism and pornography.) However, the Jesolo advertisement did suggest that the husband worked throughout the week, whilst the wife spent her time lazing on the beach.

But I have to clarify my position. Normally I favour the accurate reproduction of the meaning of a text, provided it does not infringe factual or moral truth. (Moral truth, based on the various human rights documents, is still evolving, and will be complemented by universal animal and ecological conventions.) If a text evidently infringes factual or moral truth in a way that may deceive the readership, I have to react in some way. I would normally alert the author and client, the commissioner of the translation. I would correct any factual mistakes, outside the text (notes, square brackets, preface, etc) if the text were authoritative; if the text were non-authoritative, I would correct them within the text. Moral infringement in a text is not so simply handled. I would normally correct (often inadvertent) sexist language. I would refuse to translate a non-authoritative 'immoral' text, say of racist or anti-homosexual propaganda, unless it included some kind of disclaimer. If such a text were authoritative, say written by an important writer or statesman or philosopher, I would indicate the instances of prejudice in notes or a preface, unless I were confident that the readership could do this for themselves, say in a scholarly edition of the translation.

I claim I am neither censoring nor bowdlerising any text, nor suppressing what I don't like — there is nothing subjective about human rights, which I subscribe to as an individual and as a translator. But I do not agree that the only good reason for changing an image or an idiom is that it is so culture-bound that a literal translation would make no sense or the wrong sense. Some images (catty, fishy, wolfish) are dead and do no harm, but one day they may be regarded as obsolete clichés. Others (bent, queer) have to be driven out and translators have to contribute.

More on French Economic Translation

1. Top heavy sentences. Sentences that begin with long noun-groups, premodified and post-modified by groups or clauses, appear to be typical of some French academic styles:

Institué par un décret du 9 janvier 1967, ce système de réserves obligatoires, déjà utilisé dans de nombreux pays étrangers, visait à . . .

(Literal translation: 'instituted by a decree of January 9 1967, this system of obligatory reserves, already used in numerous foreign countries, aimed to . . .')

(Close translation: 'This system of obligatory reserves, which was already widely used abroad, was introduced by a decree of January 9 1967. Its purpose was to . . .')

I suggest that translators should consider recasting top-heavy sentences.

2. Long sentences. Instinctive 'sourcerers' and 'immediate' translators like myself always have to reconsider and be prepared to recast long sentences in non-authoritative texts.

3. Key-words. The repetition of key-words within a TL sentence can sometimes help to 'ease' and clarify the translation:

À l'origine, le montant de ces dépôts non-remunérés était calculé en appliquant au volume des seules exigibilités de chaque banque un pourcentage fixé par la Banque de France à l'intérieur de limites définies par le Conseil National du Credit.

Literal translation: 'Originally, the amount of these non-remunerated deposits was calculated by applying to each bank's liabilities alone a percentage fixed by the Bank of France within limits defined by the National Credit Council.'

Close translation: 'Originally the amount of these non-interest bearing deposits was calculated by applying a percentage of the volume of each bank's liabilities, *a percentage* which was fixed by the *Banque de France* within limits defined by the *Conseil National du Credit*'.

(Acknowledgements to Jenny Marty, one of the awfully increasing

15%, i.e. the students who are brighter than the teacher.)

By analogy, a key word can conveniently be referred to (in the same sentence) by a hold-all word:

Le chômage engendré par la substitution du capital au travail accélérée par la hausse des coûts salariaux.

Literal translation: 'Unemployment engendered by the substitution of capital for work accelerated by the rise in wage costs.'

Close translation: 'Unemployment created by the substitution of capital for labour, a process which is accelerated by the rise in the cost of labour (or 'wage costs').'

4. Words ending in -ble. Generally, adjectives ending in -ble, -bar, -bile, -bil, etc., are intertranslatable, though Slavonic languages only appear to have a dual purpose past participle plus -yi suffix. If the TL equivalent is not as common as its SL correspondent, it can be replaced by '*which can be* plus past participle'. (*Ressources mobilisables*, 'resources that can be called on'.) When -ble words are used in one of the two possible senses, they may have to be clarified in the translation. ('Unreadable' as 'illegible' as *illisible*, or as *pénible à lire.*)

Compare also: *l'alibi d'une zone de libre-échange soluble dans le marché mondial.* Close translation: 'the excuse for a free exchange zone which can merge with the world market'.

5. The force of abbreviation. Who would think that an 'inaugural' meant 'inaugural lecture' (*leçon inaugurale* or *d'ouverture*)? Similarly, *effets* are *effets de commerce*, 'bills' or 'bills of exchange', and *un commerce* is *un fonds de commerce*, a 'business' unless it is 'goodwill'.

Translators sometimes have to look out for compounds with missing components.

6. Selecting the basic component of meaning. Faced with *la date-fétiche assignée au commencement du grand marché*, I think the best one can do is to review the components of *fétiche*, viz. religious, symbolical, magical, beneficial, charismatic, obsessional. Here perhaps 'the charismatic date assigned to the opening of the single market'.

7. Vogue words. I don't think translators should encourage the diffusion of vogue-words like *espace*. Thus for *ce que l'on est convenu d'appeler l'espace social européen*, which is slanted — who has agreed? and in which languages? — I would translate as 'what we may refer to as the social aspect of the European Community'. Note also that *libéral* has become a vogue-word in the sense of 'free-market' rather than 'conservative' or 'right wing' (compare Thody and Evans's invaluable *Faux-Amis and Keywords*):

L'emprise de l'idéologie dite libérale sur l'esprit public ira s'affaiblissant: 'the hold of free-market ideology on main stream opinion is about to weaken gradually'. (N.B., to my critics, this text is far from authoritative; if de Gaulle had written it, my translation would have been different.)

Notes on the Translation of Quotations

1. Typically, any sourced quotation in any type of text should be translated closely at the author's level ('Semantic' translation!). The translator, being at second remove, has no responsibility to the third readership for any pragmatic effect. Any 'corrective' factual or moral comment has to be made outside the translation. If the author of the quotation is likely to be unknown to the third readership, a gloss can be added inside or outside the text, e.g. 'Diderot, the 18th Century French philosopher'. (Preferably outside the text if it is authoritative or the gloss is long.) Typically, the style of the translated quotation should not be adapted to the style of the rest of the text.

2. If the quotation is translated from the target language, the original should be reproduced. If a source language quotation has already been translated and published in the target language, the published version should be reproduced, unless there are serious grounds for a fresh translation, which should normally be stated in a footnote. If the author is still in copyright, permission to reproduce the translation should be sought. If the Bible is quoted, the version (and its date) used should be stated.

3. If the quotation is unattributed and/or the translator decides that its language is not important, she can render it in indirect speech, provided the text is not authoritative.

4. Quoted publicity, notices and propaganda, which are normally anonymous texts, may be translated at the level of the source of the target language and its culture, depending on whether the readers are to be respectively informed or persuaded. So you can translate *Cointreau kann man mit und ohne Prinz trinken* as 'You can drink Cointreau with or without your Prince' (alt., 'lord and master') or 'You can drink Cointreau with or without your heart-throb', depending on the purpose of your translation. (N.B. *Prinz* is not sexist, it's light and ironical.)

5. If a quotation is given from the target language, it should be reproduced in the translation; if it is from a third language, it should normally be reproduced and then translated in brackets.

6. A quotation in indirect speech should normally be translated into indirect speech. However, if the quotation originated in the target language and is well-known and/or important, it can be rendered in its original version.

7. If the source of a quotation is unattributed or is of little importance, it can be deculturalised if appropriate and translated communicatively. *Nur mit entsprechendem 'Geläut der Totenglocken', ahnt Fischer, 'wäre das zu schaffen'* (literally, 'Only with a corresponding sound of the death-knell, Fischer had a foreboding(!), could we get that') could be translated as 'Fischer suspected that if that was done, it would be doomed to failure'.

8. Quoted proverbs should be translated by their standard equivalents, if these exist, *Morgenstunde hat Gold im Munde* (lit. 'The morning hour has gold in its mouth'), ('The early bird catches the worm'). (Both proverbs are equally shudder-making.) Quoted proverbs without standard equivalents should be rendered 'communicatively'.

9. If a quotation is obscurely or carelessly given in the SL text, it should normally be closely translated without inverted commas, but the quotations are sometimes italicised, whilst the words in inverted commas used ironically, figuratively or apologetically are left in normal type.

10. Single word or single collocation quotations, for which French economic journalists have a penchant, are hardly worth keeping in quotation marks, unless they have their own importance, are quoted from an important text, and 'shine through' from the source language text. Thus: *les quelques cas particuliers, qui échappent au dispositif d'ensemble seront 'étudiés':* 'the few special cases not mentioned in the body of the text will be investigated (studied)'. Or again: *Le gouvernement conserve la possibilité d'arrêter les 'mesures d'urgence' qu'une situation de crise ou une 'calamité nationale' exigeraient:* 'The government reserves the right to adopt any emergency measures required by a crisis situation or a national disaster'. None of the quotation marks seem worth retaining here, though the words come from an important government order (*ordonnance*). It would always be possible to add the French words in brackets after them. (Note that in considering words in inverted commas, it is not always easy to decide whether they are quotations or whether they are being used in a special sense.)

10. If, as often, the title of a source language text reappears in the body of the text, it should be readily identifiable in the translation, and in particular, content-words in the title should not be replaced by synonyms in the text. Thus a title such as *Urlaub an verdreckten Stränden*, 'Holidays on filthy beaches', if it comes up again in the text, should be reproduced in the translation, not glossed as 'vacationing on dirty sands'. Allusive titles can sometimes only be understood when they are repeated in the text. A translator should note the irritating habit of women's magazines such as *Cosmopolitan* of having two titles for one article, a sexy one for the cover and a more prosaic one on the front page. The *Spiegel* is equally misleading.

11. If a source language author uses a more or less well-known quotation, with or without quotation marks or attribution, say from a poem, the quotation can be incorporated 'communicatively' into the translation, if the readership is unlikely to have heard of it; 'What he wanted now was other people's wealth. O, for a beaker full of the warm south'. (The extract is from Howard Jacobson's *Coming from Behind*; the second sentence from Keats's *Ode to a Nightingale*). Amateur

translation: *Was er jetzt wollte, war der Luxus von anderen, Ein herrliches Glas Wein, in der Wärme, im Süden.*

(This important subject was too cursorily discussed in my *Approaches to Translation*; readers of German should get hold of Christiane Nord's *Neue Federn am fremden Hut*, pp. 36–42, in *Der Deutschunterricht*, Vol. 1/90).

Adapting Metaphors as a Translation Procedure

This procedure, also cursorily described in my *Textbook of Translation*, ignored by Alicja Pisarska (*Creativity of Translation*) because it was not mentioned in *Approaches*, is described in a brilliant as yet unpublished essay by Chris Everley, who is another of the 15 plus %, as a major translation procedure. She attempts to use it when literal translation doesn't work and there is no standard equivelent, and prefers it to switching images or reducing to sense.

When a metaphor is adapted in a translation, the main image remains or is slightly modified, whilst the collocation or the setting is changed. Thus, to take one of Ms Everley's examples, *les cousins de l'est retrouvés* ('the cousins from the East rediscovered') becomes 'the Eastern countries are once again part of the family', or, of a press report, *sans coups de ciseaux* ('without scissor cuts') becomes 'Without radical cuts'. Semi-similes like 'he seemed to be . . .', 'he appeared to be . . .' as translations could be described as adapted metaphors, as are standard translations of proverbs such as 'a rolling stone gathers no moss'. (*Pierre qui roule n'amasse pas mousse*.) Provided there is no cultural clash, it is often possible to adapt a metaphor (*Dieses Zimmer ist der reinste Eiskeller*, 'this room is like an icebox'), but the procedure is not usually available for the more colloquial and preposterous type of metaphor such as 'that cuts no ice with me' (*Das kommt bei mir nicht an; ça ne me fait aucum effet* (Collins) — how feeble.

Titles

The meanings of titles, as I have hinted, can often be discovered when they are repeated contextually, but what is one to do with a financial text called *L'Europe, un vol-au-vent à la sauce financière* which makes no further reference to any dish? A vol-au-vent is light and crisp, a *sauce financière* is rich and heavy.

Translating Poetic Discourse

Myriam Diaz-Diocaretz, the author of *Translating Poetic Discourse*, is obsessed by strategies and discourses, as well as omniscient readers, paradigms and translator-functions. Behind this there is some keen analysis and translation into Spanish of the feminist and sometimes lesbian poems of Adrienne Rich. She boldly clarifies the gender of genderless personal pronouns, for instance.

The Thin Line of Values
When Saddam Hussein was referred to as a 'despot' on Iran radio, the BBC at Caversham decided this was a mistranslation, as Iran is a neutral country. However, we were told that the Farsi word *'tohud'* was used to describe the Shah, which suggests that 'despot' may have been a Freudian slip. Note some other linguistic casualties: 'correlative damage' is 'civilian deaths and injuries'; 'take out' is 'destroy'; 'sortie' is 'bombing raid'. But the worst casualty, as always, is God or 'God', who, what with Hussein and Bush, is indeed having his or her work cut out.

The Eternal Unfindable
Acribie in a French text? (*Pourquoi le critiquer avec la même acribie?*) I knew the word, I had seen it before, I knew it meant 'meticulousness', 'finicky detail', 'overscrupulous accuracy'. I failed to find it in French, English, Italian, Spanish dictionaries, not even the Webster. I considered various spellings and misspellings. Then I found it, there it was in the German dictionaries, as *Akribie, akribisch*, even in the new good Penguin. What a relief.
The word derives from Greek *akribeia* — acro = tip, top, a point, cf. acronym, acropolis. (Etymology or other associations are the best way to remember (internalise) the form of meaning of any word.)
And it's a lovely expressive word: the *kr* is relentless (scrupulous, critical, cribbing), the repeated *i* is sharp, spitting (*sang craché* — 'spat out blood' — see Rimbaud's *Les Voyelles*), finicky, acrimonious.

Of Course
Never trust anyone (any man) saying or writing 'of course', they're probably lying, I've said it for years. 'Of course' is yet another phaticism (stereotype of phatic language) trying to lull your reader or interlocutor into passive assent. It's 'untranslatable'. *Bien sûr, bien entendu, selbstverständlich, natürlich* — none of the words shine through, the smooth 'course' is missing. And the Russian misuse of the word is notorious. And it's another war casualty: 'Of course one regrets, we all regret, the civilian casualties . . . but . . .'.

XIII
MAY 1991

Some Principles of Translation Restated
Within a general frame of reference, I think it is useful to categorise all texts as (a) expressive or authoritative, (b) informative, (c) persuasive or directive. In principle, (a) are translated at the author's level, and preserve the source language culture; (b) are translated at the readership's level, and make use of the overlapping cultures of the source and target languages, or, where this is not possible, of culture-free universal expression; (c) are also translated at the readership's level, and follow the target language culture. Thus the *Sejm* becomes the *Sejm* in (a); the Polish parliament in (b); the Polish House of Commons in (c). Needless to say this scrap illustration is subject to many subsequent contextual constraints.

The Occasion of a Translation
The occasion of a translation defines the particular circumstances and purpose of a single act of translation. Typically, it can be taken for granted, say it is for a corresponding readership or the translator is translating to please herself. In other cases, particularly when one is teaching translation, a realistic occasion must be posited. Thus, translating an article from the business section of a newspaper, it is normally unrealistic to suggest it should be translated for an 'equivalent' target language newspaper, as normally, nothing longer than a sentence or a paragraph is likely to be translated. Therefore a 'safe' realistic occasion for translating a technical or institutional text is normally a commission for a full translation from a professional in the same field. Cultural 'estrangement' may have to be accounted for. Professional economists, sociologists and philosophers, as well as lawyers may have widely different 'discourses'. (I use the term in a sense that includes values, reference points, attitudes and register.)

Reference Libraries
Reference libraries are the core and power house of any self-respecting library, and the stock in trade of any translator. Data banks and term banks complement them in specialised fields, and freelance translators have to be in a position to access them. However, many libraries are now concentrating on computerised information to the detriment of their reference sections. It is strange that some public, university and college libraries have not even got the full range of up-to-date English let alone bilingual dictionaries. And even now there are

people who regard the O.E.D. in the same light as others regard
Oxbridge, i.e. unique in excellence.

A Translator's Moods

A translator will rarely reread her translation, at any time after
translating, without making a few or many changes. That is the mood
factor in translation.

Lexical Gaps

Translating, one keeps wondering how one language manages
without the words in another. How do French and English make do
without *Nachwuchs, zimperlich* and *sauber*? New Blood? Fussy? Clean?
How inadequate.

The Oldest Translation Argument

The word means X but you wouldn't really call it X here.

Translation in Leningrad Again

Leningrad is still excessively monolingual, but most TV news
bulletins are accompanied by an announcer using sign language,
perhaps a faint reminder that the state was founded to produce a less
unfair society. The titles of the paintings in the Russian Museum,
unlike those in the Hermitage, are all translated into English, some of
them intelligently: thus *Edut*, which sounds enigmatic, is translated as
'They are coming; the entry of a foreign embassy in Moscow in the 17th
Century'. But descriptive leaflets in each room are in Russian only,
where even the Prado has them in several languages. All street and
shop signs are in Russian, except for one shop on the Nevsky
(Prospekt) which proclaims *Essen: Obst, Fleisch, Gemüse*, i.e. 'Food:
fruit, meat, vegetables', though whether these were obtainable there I
hadn't the heart to find out. At the University, English is avidly taught,
but Dickens and the Oscar Wilde of The Picture of Dorian Grey are
still used for language teaching purposes.

The Third Correlation

In a non-authoritative text, if the content is more important than the
style — the more badly written the text, the more it has to be rewritten
and restructured in the appropriate register, in normal social usage,
with a sensitive choice of language.

Weston on Legal Translation

Martin Weston's *An English Reader's Guide to the French Legal
System* (Berg, Oxford, pp. 155, 1991) is a splendid and absorbing book
which I enthusiastically recommend to all translators, terminologists
and students of French institutions. I regret that the title was not

expanded to *An English Reader's and Translator's Guide to* . . . , but this does not detract from the book's value. The book consists of two parts. Part I, theoretical and practical approaches to translation, discusses the linguistic issues, translation methodology (including functional equivalence, word-for-word translation, transcription, neologisms, choice of procedure and consistency) and the business of legal translation. Part II, the French legal system, putting translation principles into practice, has chapters on French and English law and their branches; legislation; the courts; the legal professions; the investigation, prosecution and punishment of crime; and a conclusion. There is a comprehensive bibliography and an excellent Index of French legal terms referring to the pages where the terms are explained, a variety of translations discussed, and a recommendation firmly made. The book is clearly and attractively written, free of linguistic-translatological jargon, and beautifully produced. I 'blush' to note that whilst Martin Weston has found numerous misprints and erros in my work, there appear to be none in his; he is a scholar. (Just once, Lyon is spelt as Lyons!) I also emphasise that whilst I have had to be 'tactful' in discussing the work of authors I know personally, I have experienced no such inhibitions in this case. I shall now comment on some issues raised in the book.

Recognised Translations

Weston makes a reasoned case for translating *juge d'instruction* as 'investigating judge', whilst he admits that 'examining magistrate' may by now be too entrenched as a translation to be displaced'. I fear it is, since 'examining judge' is established (*consacré*) by the EC Glossary and the Collins-Robert. I think the translator has to give in in such cases, though where appropriate he should gloss the recognised or official with his preferred version. In my case, this applies to *Verfremdungseffekt* ('distancing' rather than 'alienation' effect) and *Mitbestimmung* ('work force participation' rather than simply 'co-determination'). If the translator does not at least mention the standard translation, the readers may be seriously misled.

Functional Equivalence Against Neologisms

In informational texts (like Weston I prefer 'informational' to 'informative' here, but was reproached ten years ago for jargonising unnecessarily), I prefer functional and cultural equivalence to creating neologisms, which is a 'last resort'. However, I regard transference as the basic translation procedure for cultural words (literal translation for universal or non-cultural words), and both 'croissants' and 'university of the third age' are part of the English language, even though the words were imported some time before the referents, which are now both a part of British English culture. You have to be careful about culture! The Czech for the universal 'sea' is *moře*, as common a word in Czech as in English, but physically it is not a part of Czechoslovak culture.

Metropolitan Versus Common Market French?

A gap appears to be developing between French and English terms for French and non-French institutions. Thus the French *Conseil des Ministres* is normally the French 'cabinet', whilst both the EC and the ACAP (African, Caribbean and Pacific States) *Conseil des Ministres* are translated in the EC Glossary as 'Council of Ministers'. Again, *conseil des prud'hommes* is variously translated as 'industrial arbitration court', 'industrial tribunal', and 'industrial conciliation tribunal' (Weston), but in the EC Glossary it is 'conciliation board'.

The Law

Weston rightly points out that the Continental conception of law is much wider than the English one, 'and in France it encompasses matters dealt with in England under the heads of government, public administration or political science'. Outside the UK, the law is the point of entry for a vast number of public and business careers. Hence the narrowness of *le common law* compared with *le droit commun*, and the cultural focus on words like *droit, loi, arrêt, arrêté, décret, règlement, ordonnance.*

Relevance and Universals

E. A. Gutt has recently written a book, *Translation and Relevance* (Blackwell), which I look forward to reading. At present, I regard Wilson and Sperber's Relevance Theory, as well as Grice's co-operation principles as more or less useful maxims for efficient communication rather than as aspects or wholes of linguistic theory, but they have the merit of being culture-free, with the implication that close but not perfect translation is always possible when cultural terms and expressions are analysed on the basis of common human intelligence, emotions and sense. Good writing and bad writing remain so when translated closely into any language. It is strange that Vladimir Nabokov, who later became the protagonist of (absurdly) literal translation, 'couldn't resist the chance to improve on Gogol's famous jingle-bell peal in *Dead Souls* with "The middle bell trills out in a dream its liquid soliloquy", whilst Constance Garnett's 'The ringing of the bell melts into music" may not be so eye-catching, but it is exactly what Gogol wrote.' (Miranda Seymour, *From the Russian with love*, *Sunday Times*, 6-1, 7.4.91) Here Nabokov had not even the excuse of being faced with a culture-bound original sentence and good becomes bad writing.

Technical or Common Language
Partir avait la force d'un réflexe véritablement national. (Extract from a magazine article about a Portuguese explorer). (Literal translation: 'Parting had the strength of a genuinely national reflex.') It is sometimes difficult for a translator to decide when a technical term becomes sufficiently common to be classified as common language, particularly if the word exists in both languages. If the above mentioned sentence were in a psychological or physiological context, I would translate *réflexe* as 'reflex'. Otherwise, perhaps: 'Going abroad was a spontaneous reaction which was truly national'. (*Réflexe*, but not 'reflex' is currently used in this general sense.)

The Oldest False Friend
Gérard Depardieu is said to have missed an Oscar for *Green Card* because he told a film critic that he had assisted at a rape at the age of nine.

End Weight
'End Weight' can be used by a translator to strengthen the force or communicative dynamism (CD) of the end of a sentence, particularly by translating a verb by a phrasal verb or by an 'empty' verb plus a verb-noun (a deverbal).
Examples:
Finalement, il a été récompensé de sa patience.
'In the long run, his patience paid off.'
Pauvre de moi, soupira-t-il. Il le soupirera plus d'une fois.
'Poor me', he sighed – a sigh he was to breathe more than once.
Il se raconte.
'He wrote about his travels.'
Compare, as the conclusion of the feature: *Le lecteur aussi.* 'So does the reader.'

The Degree of Vividness of a Metaphor
It is sometimes difficult to judge how literally to interpret a metaphor. Thus the French *gâteau* and the English 'cake' (but not the English gâteau) enter into several idioms and collocations, but how to translate: *Pour le lecteur, son livre est un énorme gâteau succulent et parsemé d'horreurs, d'or et de saintes épices, dont l'Europe était folle.*
Succulent strengthens the case for 'a succulent cake'. But this is the magazine article again, and so the metaphor is hardly important. One could write: 'His book is an enormous treasure-trove (or "adventure-packed delight") strewn with horrors, gold and the sacred spices for which Europe was crazy'.
On the other hand, whilst *perle* and 'pearl' are standard and comparable metaphors, *sans une perle en poche* cannot mean 'without a

penny in his pocket', since neither the French nor the English words
are metaphors for 'money', and it can only mean 'without a pearl in his
pocket'.

The 'Mr' Dilemma

Whilst it seems perfectly natural to premodify (!) any kind of non-
British person with Mr or Ms in newspapers, I think in more formal
texts such as books and academic journals the appropriate foreign
titles should be retained. Alternatively, house-styles should replace
them with first names. Incidentally, German seems to be combining
first names with the 'Sie' form among men, which, forty years ago, was
only usage amongst women (ladies).

Students in Leningrad

The part-time students of translation I taught in Leningrad
University had no difficulty in identifying 'the longest serving prime
minister in the Western world' or in glossing Wat Tyler and the
Peasants' Revolt. They have to translate Somerset Maugham, Dickens
and Wilde's *The Picture of Dorian Grey*, and sought my views. I took a
random sample from Maugham's novel *Theatre* (1928), and found its
plain informal language, steering clear of slang, remarkably modern
and implicitly easily translatable. One sentence: 'She had a fine Jewish
nose and fine Jewish eyes' might have been glossed by the translator;
possibly 'Jewish eyes' are 'dark eyes', but it seems dubious to me. I was
asked if Dickens's famous quotations were worth memorising; I
considered they were worth memorising as illustrations of character,
but not for expanding one's knowledge of modern English. I found
Dorian Grey excruciating — jewelled and artificial — and suggested
that only anyone capable of empathising with it should attempt to
translate it. This applies to the translation of any literary work, but I
would be more encouraging to a prospective translator of the four
great comedies, *The Ballad of Reading Gaol* or *De Profundis*.

Notes on Drama Translation

1. It is a serviceable principle to classify drama according to three
genres: tragedy, comedy, and farce, allowing for the fact that the
genres may be mixed within a single play, particularly in modern drama.
Typically, tragedy is serious and sad, and is translated closely,
preserving every component of the source language culture. Comedy is
humorous and may or may not be serious; the closeness of its
translation depends on the degree of its seriousness; and the source
language culture is normally retained. Farce is light and funny, is
adapted rather than translated, and is transferred to the target
language culture; fun is its essential element, and has to be preserved in
the form of language and stage business.

2. It is a common practice in the theatre today to have a foreign play closely translated by a fluent linguist and then modified or adapted by an experienced dramatist. It is a sensible idea, if the principle described above is borne in mind, and always assuming that no professional translator in the relevant language is available, and the dramatist is not simply being commissioned for his name. Sometimes it becomes an ego-trip for the dramatist, or a disaster.

3. Adaptations of serious or light plays should be judged on their own merits, and not be critically compared with their originals. Sometimes, like plain prose translations of poems, but from an opposite angle, they can be seen as useful introductions to their originals.

4. The translator is concerned with translating drama, which since the beginning of the 19th Century has included stage directions. She is not concerned with the acting or stage version, which is the responsibility of the producer except at a producer's or actor's specific request for a modification, addition or deletion of a line (*Stelle*). The distinction between a reader's and a spectator's version is artificial, implying that the first is literary and the second dramatic, and misleading.

5. Sirkku Aaltonen of Vaasa (Joensuu) University has recently published a paper on *Problems in Drama Translation with special reference to the Irish drama of Synge and O'Casey*, which raises interesting questions. She follows K. Bednarz (*Theatralische Aspekte der Dramenübersetzung*, Vienna, 1969) in first discussing a general linguistic problem, the translation of the Hiberno-English dialect into Finnish. Quoting Jiři Levy (the most sensitive of all writers on translation), she states that it is mandatory to render intact those linguistic forms that have a significant semantic function. In the case of dialect, this could be social class, level of education, contrasting humour, richness and vividness of language, and the 'lilt' or rhythm, and I think it has to be reduced to a few indicative items. Aaltonen notes that the slightly contemptuous Gaelic diminutive '-een' (as in 'priesteen' can be rendered into Finnish (*kirkonmies* or *herran palvelija*), and this is not difficult for Italian (*-ino*) or German (*-chen*) or French (*-et*).

6. Discussing the dramatic framework, Aaltonen notes that something is usually lost in translating allusive titles; invented personal and place names should be recreated rather than transcribed to retain their connotations as far as possible; sometimes Finnish can introduce a dialectal feature absent in the original, as compensation. *Realia*, or culture specific common nouns are usually replaced by common TL cultural terms (like 'county' or 'parish' — 'ward' or 'borough' would be too specific), or generic terms ('district'). Where language is used for dramatic purposes, alliteration should not be missed. (In fact, O'Casey

notoriously overdoes alliteration, but in German his puns can usually
be recaptured.) Aaltonen criticises the two Finnish translators for
'losing' the malapropisms (which ought to be easy to translate into any
language?) and the famous key-word 'chassis' (in French, *chaos* could
be mispronounced; in German it could become *Chaosismus*?) in the
characterisation of the Paycock.

7. 'Theatricality in the dialogue', which is presumably Bednarz's
term, though I'd hardly dare to re-translate it (can it be *Theatralität*?)
refers to elements in the language that invite or imply action or
behaviour on the part of the characters, therefore pragmatic language
or paralanguage, like mumbling or stuttering. They can be used for
widely different purposes (to indicate confusion, drunkenness, embar-
rassment, hesitation, physical handicap) but they are probably
universals, so can be translated neat. Aaltonen is doing useful work,
not only in analysing drama translation, but also in calling attention to
the two great and unduly neglected dramatists (neglected partly
because of the H.-E. dialect.)

Terminology

'This book', Juan Sager states in his introduction to his *A Practical
Course in Terminology Processing* (Benjamins, Amsterdam 1990)
'denies the independent status of terminology as a discipline but
affirms its value as a subject in almost every contemporary teaching
programme.'

It is a clearly written, well structured book, containing much
fascinating detail. There are chapters on Definition of Terminology,
the Cognitive Dimension, the Linguistic Dimension, and the Compilation, Retrieval and Usage of Terminology. It is I think a pity that
Sager does not discuss the translation of technical terms, and in fact
restricts his examples and his bibliography largely to English. The
book lacks a sense of controversy; there is no reference to the views of
Picht, Arntz or Maillot. It deserves an expanded second edition,
including an alphabetical bibliography (by authors), a subject-index,
and possibly a revised title.

The Use and Abuse of Repetition in Translation

'The French', that is, the tinpot 'immortals' (members of the
Académie française, almost all of them male) and the *inspecteurs
d'Académie* who guard the French language, abominate repetition.
Even personal names are not usually repeated; they are replaced by a
referential synonym, which in translation is sometimes better premodified
by a repetition of the personal name; thus (invented example): *M.
Giscard d'Estaing . . . Le député d'Agde . . .* ; 'Giscard D'Estaing . . .
Giscard, the deputy for Agde in the National Assembly'.
English inevitably has to make more use of repetition than most

other languages, since it has only one gender for objects, whilst the others have two *or* three. French tends to make use of pronouns such as *ceci, cela, celui-ci, celui-la, c'est* which are better translated by 'this plus the noun referred to.' Example: *C'est essentiellement des pays industrialisés que peut provenir un mouvement de reprise. Celui-ci a commencé a se manifester en 1983.* 'A trend towards recovery will come mainly from the industrialised countries. Such a trend began to appear in 1983.' Further, English can make an elegant use of repetition in translating complex sentences, particularly to precede adjectival clauses:

(Adapted example): *Très tôt, le législateur est intervenu pour assurer et organiser la protection des intérêts des tiers d'une entreprise défaillante, et c'est dans cette perspective qu'ont été définies en 1967 les procédures de règlement judiciaire et de liquidation des biens.*

'The law intervened at an early date to provide for and organise the protection of third parties in a troubled company; to protect these interests, the procedures for judicial composition proceedings and for selling off the assets were defined in 1967.' (See *Paras* (12) for another example.)

The use of repetition often helps to clarify or emphasize or concentrate a statement; it avoids the use (again!) of fillers and circumlocutions like *dans cette perspective*. Repetition of the same or similar words can jar, and repetition can be the symptom of a meagre or poorly deployed vocabulary, or it can be unnecessary, as in this sentence, but listen to the great Fowler: 'The first thing to be said is that a dozen sentences are spoilt by ill-advised avoidance of repetition for every one that is spoilt by ill-advised repetition', which he contrasts with 'elegant variation', where the rule of thumb against repetition is shown to have the most disastrous consequences'. (*Fowler's Modern English Usage.* H. W. Fowler. Revised by E. Gowers, OUP 1965.) Tell that to the immortals! (Recently, a translator-colleague of mine was reprimanded by an American publisher for not paying proper respect to the mothy style of her author [G. Duby]. 'Didn't she realise he was a member of the *Académie francaise!*')

The Name Leningrad
The question of renaming Shostakovich's city has been deferred, as there are more urgent social problems and renaming would be excessively expensive.*

Officialese
I define 'officialese' as a smooth bureaucratic wrap-up of real facts.

---

* The referendum (on renaming) is being held on June 12 and a lot of statues may come tumbling down afterwards. P.N.

Normally, it is the translator's job to penetrate the verbal fog and clarify the meaning. Thus I think it is unfair to keep *La nation reste toutefois une instance de régulation spécifique et un lieu d'identification privilégié* as 'The nation remains, however, an authority of specific regulation and a place of privileged identification', even though it sounds rhythmical (three *-tions*) and the word 'privileged' is becoming as 'with it' in English as it is in French. So I suggest: 'The nation, however, still has the authority to make specific regulations and to offer an individual identity to its citizens', filling a yawning case-gap ('citizens'). And again, is *exclusion sociale* anything more than 'marginalisation'?

Enlightenment at Last
It has recently been announced that the Turkish government has lifted its ban on the speaking of Kurdish by Kurds in their own homes (cf. Catalan under Franco).

Removing Class Barriers
A book review refers to *cet essai de sociologie comparative, volontairement accessible a l' 'honnête homme' européen* (this essay in comparative sociology, which is readily accessible to European 'gentlemen'). The 17th Century *honnête homme* often rendered as 'gentleman, man of breeding', surely has to be de-sexed and de-classed simply as ' "cultured" or "educated" Europeans'.

An Impossible Language
How long can French go on with its frequently ambiguous use of *politique* and *expérience*?

Zionism
The term 'Zionism' is current in too many senses and causes much misunderstanding. When it is used to embrace Israel's promise to offer a national home to any Jew in the world who honestly seeks it, then that is a noble sense. When it is used for purposes of national self-aggrandisement, in defiance of United Nations resolutions, to absorb Biblical Palestine, to annex 'Judaea' and 'Samaria', that is, to swallow up the Occupied Territories, then that is an ignoble sense. (See the Fontana *Dictionary of Modern Thought* for other senses.)

XIV
AUGUST 1991

An Aphorism
Translate the words if you can; if you can't, translate the sense.

On the Use of Philology in Translation
1. Up to thirty five years ago, it was the prevailing culture to identify the original with the true sense of a word. One was told to avoid the word 'nice' except in the sense of 'accurate, neat, delicate' ('a nice stroke'), which was its 'true' meaning. (In fact, its original meaning is 'ignorant'.) Then American (structuralist) linguistics swept philology away. For a few years, meaning itself, and with it semantics, was in some disrepute, provoking pain and protest from the leading British semantician, Stephen Ullmann, a refugee from Hungary. On the European continent, meaning was still studied, but the influence of Saussure and Bally tended to discourage any historical approach to language. Linguistics was to be essentially synchronic; and diachronic or historical linguistics was to be hived off.

2. The Chomsky revolution changed most of that, and linguistics has become more humane and perhaps systematic rather than scientific. Semantics is reinstated. Nevertheless, even the respectable sounding 'diachronic linguistics' isn't much studied. 'Diachronic linguistics, whose goal is the study of language change, development and history, is at best marginally and occasionally relevant to translation', writes Joseph L. Malone. (See below.) A tell-tale use of the phrase 'at best'. The statement is nonsense.

3. It is an illusion to think of an *état de langue*, a language at one period, as a static homogeneous ensemble. At any given time there are obsolescent, clichéd, current and in-coming words, collocations and idioms, as well as, but to a lesser degree, grammatical units. A translator has to be aware of the effect of time on the meanings of lexical units, particularly if translating a text composed a generation or more ago, or even a modern text written in old-fashioned language. (Paul Valéry, a great poet, attempted to reinvigorate the Latin and Greek meanings in French words.) Generally, the more a word is used, the wider the meaning it covers and the weaker its force becomes; when it nears cliché-point in the source language, the translator of a non-authoritative text may decide to replace it with a more vivid target language word.

4. Knowledge of philology and etymology in translating is more useful for literary than for newspaper texts; for the greco-latinisms in scientific texts it is valuable, though not indispensable. Translators can

profit from partly historical word studies as diverse as those of C. S. Lewis (*Studies in Words*), R. E. Waldron (*Sense and Sense Development*), Owen Barfield (*History in English Words*), Ernest Weekley (*The Romance of Words!*), Albert Marckwardt (*Introduction to the English Language*) and, the best, Raymond Williams (*Key Words*). History pervades language, and it is arrogant to cut oneself off from it. I memorise words best by finding out their derivations, which provides me with a 'bridge-word', even if I invent it with my own folk-etymology. (Thus, *niais*-ninny-simple/silly). And I regret any mono-lingual dictionary that has no etymologies, even the *Cobuild*, because it deprives the reader of a valuable practical aid.

Surtitling
Surtitles (*Übertitel, surtitres, sopratitoli?*), that is, sequences of captions projected above or to the side of the stage, translating the opera text that is being sung, have in the last five years enhanced the appreciation of opera in many opera houses. Tentatively introduced with questionnaires for each member of the audience at Covent Garden, the director says he now relies on them when presenting any new foreign work. No one has yet suggested screening them in the original for English operas (choruses, heavily orchestrated works), but I suppose that even that may come. In many respects up to now, music lovers have been deprived of an entry to opera and foreign songs (including Britten's in four languages) owing to a lack of translations.

German Compounds
German dictionaries don't seem able to keep up with the vast number of their compounds. Thus *Steppenreiter*, a not uncommon word for 'nomads', already appears in Hitler's *Monologue im Führer-Hauptquartier 1941-44*, but not in the reference-books.

Structure and Structuralism in Language
I think that in any challenging text, a translator has to look for taxonomies, hierarchies, oppositions, contrasts, complementarities, clines, gradations and sudden gaps. Take the following extract from G. Caire's *Les Syndicats Ouvriers* ('The Trade Unions', since *syndicats* is a wider term than 'union' in an economic context), P.U.F. 1971: *Les partenaires susceptibles de s'affronter pendant les négociations sont les suivants sans qu'il y ait nécessairement correspondance d'un groupe à l'autre:*

Groupe ouvrier	Groupe patronal
Section locale d'établissement	Directeur d'établissement
Syndicat d'entreprise	Directeur d'entreprise
Fédération d'industrie ou union départementale	Fédération professionnelle ou chambre patronale

Confédération ouvrière   *C.N.P.F. (Conseil National de*
Patronat Français)
Proposed translation for a textbook for specialists, which should
reproduce the French terms in the table in brackets after each English
version: 'The parties representing the two sides of industry who may
face each other during the negotiations are the following, although
each group may not precisely correspond to the other:

Workers group	Employers group
Union branch at site or company establishment	Head of company establishment or place of business
Company's union branch	Head of company
Unions amalgamated at *département* level	Local employers or trade organisations
Unions at national level (CGT, FO, CFDT)	National employers organisation (C.N.P.F.)

Notes:
1. *Partenaires:* Soon after the establishment of the Federal Republic
of Germany in 1949, the two sides of industry were designated as
Sozialpartner to indicate the collaborative and thereby to rule out the
idea of the confrontational nature of the economy. The concept is
widely accepted in French and EC thinking (*partenaires sociaux*), but
the EC Glossary austerely notes that the UK Civil Service only uses
'social partners' to mean 'husbands and wives'.
    2. The table is a double inverted hierarchy: from bottom to top, (a) in
order of importance (b) in order of size and geographical area.
    3. 'Establishment' for *établissement* is used in the sense of 'an
operating unit of a business' to distinguish it from 'a firm or enterprise
which is the controlling unit'. An explanatory synonym ('place of
business') is added to clarify the sense. An *établissement* could be a
factory, plant, works, workshop or branch.
    4. Terms such as *chambre patronale* are reproduced and glossed
rather than translated, since a translation might be construed as a
standard translation, which would not be necessary for a 'local' term
such as this one.
    5. The table 'balances', but on the employer side there is no strict
correspondence to the *département* dimension.

Translation's Concern
    Translation is potentially always concerned with the factual, moral
and aesthetic truth, in the sense that when these truths are infringed and
the readership is likely to be deceived, some kind of intervention is
probably required. By 'aesthetic truth' I mean the principles of good
writing, which would only be implicated in translating non-authoritative
texts.

The Metalingual Quicksand

It is all too easy to start translating a passage and to miss the fact that it has become metalingual, i.e. relates only to the source language. Take the following:

Quel patrimoine?

Parmi les diverses définitions concevables du patrimoine, cette étude en retient une relativement étroite, celle qui correspond en principe à l'assiette de l'impôt sur les successions et qui serait probablement aussi celle d'un éventuel impôt sur la fortune: en ce sens, le patrimoine d'une personne est constitué par l'ensemble des éléments aliénables et transmissibles qui sont sa propriété à un instant donné. Here the red-light word is *définitions*, and a close translation would be: 'the definition of *patrimoine.*'

'Amongst the various possible definitions of the term *patrimoine*, we shall choose a relatively narrow one, approximating to 'wealth', which in principle covers the assessment of inheritance tax and which would also probably cover the assessment of wealth tax where relevant (*éventuel*); in this sense, a person's *patrimoine* or wealth consists of all the disposable and transferable components (*éléments*) of his or her property at a given time'. An alternative, less accurate translation, would be entitled 'The definition of wealth'; deletes the first two lines of the above translation; starts 'The term "wealth" in principle covers the assessment, etc,' and deletes the further reference to *patrimoine* (which has a wider range of senses than wealth, viz. 'inheritance', 'assets and liabilities', 'patrimony', 'fortune', 'net worth', 'funds', 'wealth'). Thus the metalingual element can always be removed in a translation, but this removes the source language culture as well as the language, and, in the case of the above passage, such a 'neutral' or 'universal' translation would distort the sense of any further sentence anchored in source culture (French) ordinances or laws.

The Metaphor Trap

Whilst metalanguage is normally signalled by the use of a pun or a linguistic term peculiar to the source language (gerundive, aorist, supine) or a metalingual signal such as 'literally', 'by definition' or 'word for word' or 'often called', metaphor can occur or start without warning, and the translator's only clue is that a non-metaphorical interpretation will not make sense. Thus in a newspaper article: *Wobei die Gerichte sich vorwiegend gärtnerisch betätigten, auf andere Weise als weiland Flick, aber in idealer Arbeitsteilung: Hatte der Grossindustrielle sich jahrzehntelang um die 'Pflege der Bonner Landschaft' bemüht, so sorgten nun die Gerichte dafür, dass auf unbedungten Flächen Gras wuchs.*

Here I think the metaphor has to be converted to simile, and the sense unobtrusively suggested:

'At the same time (*wobei*) the courts for the most part (*vorwiegend*) acted like skilled gardeners (*gärtnerisch*), demonstrating an exemplary division of labour (*in idealer Arbeitsteilung*, apportioning their work in exemplary fashion?) unlike the now defunct (*weiland*) firm of Flick; whilst Flick (der *Grossindustrielle*, an unnecessary referential synonym) had spent many years (*jahrzehntelang*, many decades) cultivating the Bonn politicians, (*die Plege der Bonner Landschaft*) the courts now made sure that grass would soon grow over the unfertilised surfaces again, and the affair would soon be forgotten (alt. 'and everything would run smoothly again.') The sense of the last 'addition' is derived fairly safely from the subsequent paragraph. For ease of reference, I have intercalated a few German words to show correspondence, adding a few alternative translations, since no two translators would translate this passage in the same way.

Note then that *gärtnerisch* starts derailing or 'metaphorizing' this passage, making a 'material' (concrete, substantial, real, hypostatic, literal, physical, objective — there's some lexical gap here) translation impossible. This is an instance of adapting metaphor as a translation procedure.

Gutt's *Relevance and Translation*
E.-A. Gutt's *Relevance and Translation* is an exceptionally challenging, luminously intelligent and always enjoyable work. Gutt's thesis is that the two main translation theories of today, the functionalist ('translation behaviour') theory of Vermeer, Reiss and Holz-Manttäri, which he calls 'action-theoretic' (not a good translation of *handlungs-theoretisch*) and the descriptive-classificatory theory are bankrupt and should be superseded by Sperber and Wilson's relevance theory, (*Relevance: Communication and Cognition*. Dan Sperber and Deirdre Wilson, 1986, Blackwell), which makes any kind of translation theory unnecessary.

Nevertheless, Gutt himself does set up a theory of 'direct translation' ('descriptive use') and 'indirect translation' ('interpretative use') which remarkably resembles those of other writers, and he makes frequent use of these terms, though he finally states, somewhat surprisingly, that the choice of the one or the other of these approaches is not 'theoretically significant; the distinction between them is purely theory-internal', whatever that is supposed to mean. It is a pity that Gutt never hints at a distinction between translating a lyric and a soap advertisement. Relevance, says Gutt, 'is a universal principle believed to represent a psychological characteristic of our human nature,' (p. 188). Precisely, and he never demonstrates that it is any kind of a theory. Is relevance any more than common sense, like Grice's co-operative principles? If it is a theory, then is it a theory of logic, language or psychology? Or is it just a minimax recipe for efficiency, where the 'contextual effects' are as large as possible and the effort to process them as small as possible? (p. 30, adapted). Relevant to what or to whom? Presumably to the 'receptor language audience being addressed by the translator as the great communicator?' (Gutt doesn't realise how overburdened the language is with excessive 'relevance and communication'.) But who is this 'receptor language audience'. What if it consists of the great unknown masses, or, as in John Cairncross's case (Penguin *Racine*), just the one, lonely translator?

Gutt seems to imply that one doesn't translate what the readers already know and one has to add, by interpretation, what one assumes they don't know. Nothing could be more relevant as a principle, but it is only occasionally true, since most messages, like lessons, start with the known before they go on to the unknown. Too often, what Gutt says is theoretically correct but typically incorrect: thus 'A man crossed the road' is not normally an 'abstract mental picture that has to be inferentially enriched' (p. 131), i.e. put into context! It stands up on its own. He is sometimes hard on writers who try to help with practical problems of translation. Thus quantities applied to distances, weights, currencies etc. may be intended literally or figuratively, and it doesn't need relevance theory to tell me that in a diary any sum should be accurately transferred to retain the local colour, whilst in a poem, 'Few pence in purse had I' can be rendered as *Ein paar Heller/Groschen hatte ich*, and this was what Levy intended (p. 120). There is no 'exception' here. Add a few complaints about some unlovely terms ('interlingual interpretive use') and the excruciatingly overused 'crucial' and that completes the debits.

The credit side begins with Gutt's sensitive attention to the more particular translation issues. He writes well on the powerful yet indeterminate force of metaphor, and the 'communicative clues' in sound-based poetic properties, including onomatopoeia, and the stylistic value of words. His choice of translation examples, both from poetry and the Bible, is always interesting and — wait for it — pertinent, apposite. He makes some telling contrasts between direct and indirect translation parallel examples, and between naturally colloquial and formal renderings. He is instructive on formulaic expressions, and, too briefly, discourse markers, (pp. 144–148): *so* (German) as 'so', 'in this way', 'as a consequence'). He makes some interesting remarks on stress relating to a Biblical quotation (p. 142), and it is a pity that his wide reading, though it includes Jiři Levy, rightly the most cited author in the book (apart from Sperber and Wilson 'of course'), ignores the literature on communicative dynamism and end-weight, i.e. Firbas and the main Prague linguists.

Gutt is a civilised, subtle (at times too subtle) writer, many removes from the translatologists. This is a book which it's not only a pleasure to disagree with, but which one should, I shall, frequently return to.

Linguistics and Translation
Joseph L. Malone's *The Science of Linguistics in the Art of Translation* (1988; State University of New York (SUNY) Press) is an exhaustive and an exhausting book. It not only makes use of many technical terms; it invents a dozen or so more: trajections (why not shifts or transpositions?), transduction, transjacence, parallax, antispanning, contentive — all used in a translational sense — are some of the more important. Malone uses over two hundred translation examples from twenty-two languages, including one each from Malay and Unondaga. However, he constructs such an enormous and idiosyncratic terminological apparatus that it is hard to imagine a reader who is going to take it seriously, and a sentence like: 'Rhoemetalces is a "semantically present" subject of *avenging* without coindexing by (11.5), but there is nothing for (11.5) to coindex until a construct (zero or other) is provided by (11.4)', which is typical of the book's make-up, is not exactly inviting. Hidden behind this is an occasional sense of humour, much learning, and the interesting information that from Homeric Greek onwards, several languages use the same words for 'right' and 'left' as for 'east' and 'west'.

Interpretation and Translation — Some Distinctions
Assuming that in general terms interpretation and translation have the same purpose, that is, to reproduce the meaning of a text accurately and economically in a second language, interpretation has the following distinctive features:
1. Tone of voice, indicating irony, sarcasm, strong feeling etc.
2. Paralanguage, included pauses, grunts, laughs, cries.
3. Gesture and body language.
4. Interpretation normally simulates speech and 'privileges' idiomatic, colloquial language.
5. Consecutive interpretation tends to be a summary, and if the original delivery is rapid, simultaneous tends to some reduction. The interpreter frequently has to précis; he has to be a natural 'précis-speaker'.
6. Interpretation should be immediately comprehensible, clear and unambiguous.
7. Allusions and cultural terms may have to be explained in 'neutral' terms or in terms of the target culture.
8. Interpretation is normally sentence by sentence.
9. Techniques of anticipation and stalling have to be developed to cope with non-SVP word order.
10. After delivery, the source language text disappears (is 'deverbalised'), and can never be recovered. This preeminently distinguishes interpretation from translation.
11. Metaphor is likely to be reduced to sense, or at best adapted,

since an equivalent image may not come readily to mind.
12. Sentences are likely to be co-ordinate rather than complex. Complex sentences are not usually used in speech, which in fact eschews punctuation.
13. Interpreters are even more time-bound that translators. The simpler the language, the better, since they cannot revise and the listeners cannot think again.
14. In moderation, interpreters should make more use of phatic language, if only to make the listeners comfortable, particularly at the beginning of a speech or a rejoinder.
15. Interpretation is mediation. The interpreter sometimes has to keep the dialogue going, to slightly modify and moderate feelings. Interpreting a sentence such as Norman Stone's 'Clearly there is a need for the civilised powers, perhaps even the Russians, to intervene to save Third World peoples from disasters of the Third World kind' at an international conference (an imaginary event), there would surely be a case for replacing 'civilised . . . even' with 'industrialised powers, including the Russians'.
16. Where appropriate, interpreters should keep grecolatinisms, loan-words, internationalisms. Inevitably they contribute to the convergence of political and public language.

Amnesty International

Amnesty International (AI) is an internationalism. A month after the Wall came down (*die Wende*), East German newspapers were referring to AI without further explanation.

Syntax versus Lexis

The semantics of syntax is general, indicating emphasis, mood, sequence, statement, etc. The semantics of lexis is particular. In translation, syntax is more pliant and resourceful than lexis, and has precedence over synonymy. Thus, *une année contrastée* is 'a year of contrasts' not 'a variable, changing (etc.) year'.

Aberystwyth Word Lists

AWL, a French-English Glossary containing new words found in the French press, including word-classes, translations and relevant citations, appears twice a year. Recently a summary edition of four years work, *New French Words*, has also been published. Acronyms are included. This is a worthy successor of the regretted *Petit Termophile*, and is a linguistic and cultural treasure-trove. All enquiries to the editor, Geoffrey Bremner, 12 College Road, Reading RG6 1QB.

Languages in South Africa

Anne-Marie Beukes has recently read a remarkable paper on

'Training Translators in post-Apartheid Democratic South Africa', in which she convincingly demonstrates that Afrikaans has an important part to play in the new South Africa. It seems to me to be essential that the Government and ANC now jointly set up a non-governmental body with a powerful research department, a National Language Council, to advise on all matters of language planning, language education, language services, and the foundation of translators' and interpreters' associations. The age of the hated 'bilingual (*sic*) republic' is finished.

International Finance

The *Penguin International Dictionary of Finance*, compiled by Graham Bannock and William Manser is innovative in including a large number of key foreign-language terms, including institutional terms from the most powerful financial countries, indicating national references, as well as acronyms, (*CAC, ADEF,* etc.). Further, it distinguishes American from British/English terminology. I couldn't find 'thrifts' (US) in any other reference book.

The Cultural Gulf

'The Cultural Gulf' is the title of a fascinating and wide-ranging article by Richard D. Lewis, who recently wrote on Strine in this journal, in the current issue of *Cross Culture*, a magazine about inter-cultural communication published three times a year by Riversdown Services Ltd, 107 High Street, Winchester, Hants SO23 9AH. Richard Lewis describes not only the cultural 'gulf' between Bush and Saddam, but also between Churchill and Hitler (and in turn between Hitler and Franco), contrasted with the mutual comprehension between Churchill and General Mannerheim, 'his theoretical foe', and potentially at least 'high ranking Germans of his own class'. He rightly stresses the primary role of religious differences, which dominate every aspect of the prevailing Arab and sometimes inversely, the prevailing American cultures, and is evident primarily in style of language, leading to palpable translation difficulties. ('Hostages' are 'guests', etc.) Whilst Marx overstressed the factor of social class, Richard Lewis perhaps understresses it, but his analysis of Arabic oratory (mercifully, he avoids the cliché term 'rhetoric' as a generic term), so close to naked emotions, is brilliant.

Much work is now being done, and notably at the Centre for International Briefing at Farnham Castle (Surrey) on the study of cultural differences, and it is important, but it is usually on the basis of 'In Rome, do as the Romans do', which is alright in the first instance, as an introduction. Not enough, perhaps, is being done on the *tertium comparationis*, which is not a compromise, not a middle way, but a universal, at root a non-cultural behaviour, nor on its language, which has its basis in universal rights and obligations, which can still leave the apparent sensuous and material cultural differences to flower. In spite of the culture, a 'hostage' is not a 'guest'.

XV
OCTOBER 1991

Layers of Translation

At the bottom layer of translation, the translator has no choice: in simple sentences like 'He came in', 'The sea is deep here', 'The picture is large', where the translation is one-to-one, at least typically. As soon as there is choice — and given the different grammars, the vast differences in lexical quantities, the quirky lexical gaps, the cultural disparities, choice comes soon, translation becomes approximation. Translation becomes an interpretation. Just as 'acting is a judgement of character' (David Hare), so too the translator judges the character of what s/he translates. At the top layer, the translator is concerned with language as sound, puns, and metalanguage, or constraints of metre and formal structure, and translation is at its most approximate, and choice is at its widest. Nevertheless, in total translation, the scientific factor, accuracy and economy, pertains at every layer.

Two Museums

In the Mauritshuis at the Hague (*den Haag* or *'s-Gravenhage* (Du); *la Haye* (F); *la Haya* (S); *l'Aia* (I); *der Haag* (G)), the paintings are marked only with the names of their painters and the dates on their frames. The more important ones in each room can be identified by reference to cardboard-backed printed sheets in Dutch, English, German and French, which give their titles, small photographed reproductions and brief useful analyses, which are pleasingly closely translated from the Dutch. (An interesting 'howler' was the translation of *deugdzamheid* (*Tugendhaftigkeit* (G); *Vertu* (F)) as 'virtuosity' (from 'virtuoso') instead of 'virtue' or 'virtuousness'.)

I think this is a good translation service, superior to the usual monolingual and bilingual systems, which should be a thing of the past, but it is a pity that the remaining paintings cannot at least have their titles translated at the bottom of the sheets. (Some of the finest Dutch paintings are hung in this museum, such as the Vermeer 'Head of a young girl'.)

At the Stedelijk Museum of 19th and 20th Century art in Amsterdam, all paintings have brief details in Dutch and English only, which is regrettable, particularly in the case of the 'third country' paintings, but which is the way things are going in a country where shop-window signs are in English as often as in Dutch.

Translation and Précis-writing

Looking at the Transavia flight magazine, where all articles are in

Dutch and summarised in English, I stress again the importance of SL
to TL précis writing in translation training and education, and
consequently the need to include it as an obligatory subject in all
professional translation examinations. (In educational courses, a
subject that is not examined is not taken seriously.) Professionally,
translators need this skill when they are working in news agencies,
when they are making abstracts of papers and articles for professional,
scientific and academic journals, when they are sub-titling for films
and TV, if they are engaged in consecutive and to some extent in
simultaneous interpretation, in many routine jobs in the translation
departments of companies and government offices, and in all the
aspects of journalism.

However, I am mainly concerned with précis-writing as translation
training, with the value of an exercise in continuous concentration on
what in a text is most important, either to its author, or to its readers,
or perhaps 'in fact'; as in translation, the triple distinction may not exist,
but if there are marked cultural differences within the topic in its
source and target setting, say in political science or *cuisine*, the précis
may have to be skewed or filtered, modifications may have to be made,
and if the original evidently infringes the truth, the précis-writer may
(or may not) intervene in some way.

The précis-writer, like the translator, has to distinguish the essential
thread of thought that runs through a text, to understand the language
and the reality that the language denotes: so, *in petto* (i.e. scrap
example), 'The Morning Star' becomes 'Venus' (if I may revive Frege),
'the Venice of the North' may become Annecy or Stockholm or
Bruges, 'the Swan of Avon' or 'the Bard' becomes Shakespeare, 'it was
a difficult act to follow' might become 'she could not emulate her
predecessor'(?!) . . . in fact all tropes, metaphor in particular, unless
they occupy a paragraph or longer, usually have to be reduced to sense.
Key words, key phrases and key sentences have to be reproduced as
strictly as the translator renders authoritative quotations; there should
be no concessions to synonym, paraphrase or fear of repetition. In an
'argumental' (Webster; how else distinguish from 'argumentative'?)
text, contrasts and continuations have to be sharpened, sentence-
connectives often inserted, and facts distinguished from illustrations.
Always the positive has to be accentuated, the negative as far as
possible eliminated, as in the Fred Astaire song. Except when
addressing a specialist, statistics should be rounded off and fractions
or ratios preferred to figures, since they are more easily grasped by a
reader. Letters or numbers, rather than dashes, should introduce the
items of a series. Whatever the register of the SL original, the TL précis
should normally be written in a matter-of-fact 'neutral' style; therefore
emotive language should be avoided. There should be practice in
reducing 1000 words to 50; 300 to 150; 100 to 10; 250 to 150 words

approximately, within 10%; the convention of reducing by a third or a quarter is arbitrary.

Précis writing is a continuous practice in generalising information (compare translation, continuously forced to move slightly from the particular to the general or vice-versa), in linguistic economy and in assessing the importance of words, facts or concepts.

Further it is a splendid educational and social instrument, discouraging verbosity and tautology (the interminable bores and 'monologgers', the people who love the sound of their own voices, particularly in committee and in professional transactions), since all intelligent conversation (read discourse, if preferred) is a continuous exercise in précise-production, thoughtfully and sensitively adapted to a particular audience. In English teaching, the virtues of brevity, clarity and simplicity tend to get unduly canonised in relation to personal expression, but in précise-writing, as in all kinds of translation, the ability to abbreviate, to clarify and to simplify within a structured text is essential.

I must confess that of the many subjects I have taught, I enjoy précis-writing most, and am fortunate to be teaching it now. The only 'proper' way to 'teach' précis is for teacher and students to write their précis as homework, and then to read it out sentence by sentence and debate it in class, criticising each other's versions. Finally the students should be given an, in my case, rather radically revised teacher's version. (There is a good book on teaching précis to translators by Pamela Russell of Ottawa.)

John Dodds on Translation

I have greatly enjoyed reading *The Theory and Practice of Text Analysis and Translation Criticism (Vol. 1 Literary Prose)* by John M. Dodds (Campanotto, Udine, 1985). He writes convincingly and naturally, and manages to discuss say Barthes and Derrida without reproducing the jargon. The book is in two parts, and deals with analysis and criticism under similar heads. Each part is followed by about a dozen literary texts, the first set being English texts for analysis, with six undogmatic 'models', the second, Italian texts followed by one or sometimes two English translations, with four commentaries. There are excellent glossaries for both parts. The book is for Italian students of English and English students of Italian at university level, but anyone with an interest in translation should be interested in John Dodds' lively discussions, and he gives much practical advice to translation teachers. I find his enumeration of three readings prior to translation: initial, analytical and interpretative, helpful as one form of approach. The sections on phonological, syntactic and semantic equivalence are stimulating, and there are always pertinent examples, in some cases unfortunately without his own translations. There are some funny remarks on the limits of 'communicative' translation, e.g. why Dante's *Nel mezzo del cammin di nostra vita* is less suitably translated as 'When I was thirty-five years old' than as 'In the middle of the journey of our life'. There is a pointed discussion of dynamic equivalence, but the concept is too summarily rejected for great literature, since a similar (not identical) response by say Koreans and Slovenes to say Shakespeare's superb: 'Time hath, my Lord, a wallet at its back' (*Troilus and Cressida 3.3.145*, the greatest of his less known plays) would at least confirm the speech's universal validity, the culture-bound element in 'wallet' being a triviality.

I quarrel with one statement: 'Translation criticism is descriptive and not prescriptive, it analyses what a translator has or has not done and not what he might or should have done' (p.v.), which is fortunately in contradiction with pp. 259 and 260, which state that a translation criticism should conclude with 'a quality control assessment of translation equivalence, including a clear classification rating'. Like the 'translatologists' on the Israeli-Belgian axis, John Dodds seems fleetingly under the illusion that anything that is not descriptive must be prescriptive, that one cannot separate analytical facts from a critical personal opinion which adduces them, and which is therefore not subjective. On the contrary, it is the critic's business to evaluate, and if he (in this case!) is also a teacher, to suggest better solutions, often alternatives, for some difficulties.

A Question of Translation Yield

'That poetry is untranslatable is a basic tenet of modern criticism', wrote David Lodge in at least the second edition of his fascinating *The Language of Fiction* (1984). He produces no evidence for this surprising statement (surprising, because 'modern criticism' is not concerned or interested in translation), except to add 'and appears to follow logically from any critical theory which holds that form and content are inseparable, and which accounts for the literary effects of a given work principally or exclusively in terms of its verbal organisation (p. 18). Admittedly, he quotes from Shelley's '*A Defence of Poetry*', ('It were as wise to cast a violet into a crucible that you might discover the formal principle of its colour and odour, as seek to transfuse from one language into another the creations of a poet') which is hardly 'modern criticism', and he forgets that Shelley produced about seventy pages of poetry translation, including Dante, Homer and Goethe's *Faust*. David Lodge also confesses his unease when reading translations of novels, understandably admitting that he cannot pretend to 'possess them as he does an English original', and rather inadequately adducing a single example, a sentence of Proust translated by Scott Moncrieff, which he analyses in interesting detail, stating that a good deal of the meaning is conveyed and a good deal is lost. However, he never thinks of asking himself whether the translation could have been improved: for instance, the treble rhyme that so irritates him: 'straw . . . double-doored corridor' (*paille . . . dans le couloir à double porte*) could have been replaced by 'passage with double doors' and put in its right place in the sentence, which Lodge also criticises. To be fair to Lodge, always an engaging critic or novelist, he later quotes Auden in defence of poetry translation, and admits that 'in terms of literary' (what's 'literary'?) 'meaning and effect, *chat* is closer to "cat" than "female quadruped".' Translation, as I have stated before, is the most direct rendering of meaning, and is always superior to paraphrase.

On the general question, poetry and translation are indissolubly linked. Most English poets have translated poetry, even Robert Frost ('The poetry is what gets lost in the translation') must have translated Latin and Greek poetry, and David Lodge fails to make distinctions. It is all a question of 'translation yield', to use Donald Frame's term, which I have previously discussed (*TL* Vol. 30, No. 1, p. 29) that is, the proportion of the relevant meaning that can be transferred. The proportion is likely to be lowest in the case of lyrical poetry, but the translation will always be worth making. Plain prose translations are invaluable, if only as an entry into the original, and Verlaine's *Chanson d'automne* may still find its inspired translator-poet; in the meantime, a plain prose translation rather than Joanne Richardson (*Verlaine: Selected Poems*, Penguin Books 1974) will have to do.

The *Tertium Comparationis*

The *tertium comparationis*, or the *tertium quid*, the potential point of comparison between the translation and its original, is the factual, moral, linguistic and logical truth. These are universal, non-cultural truths. The *tertium quid* may be Chomsky's deep structure or Nida's kernels or normal social usage, or logic transmuted into language, or elegant, precise expression. I speculate it as a flexible concept. But it is the linguistic truth which must preclude the translator from reproducing poor writing in a non-authoritative text. No self-respecting translator would make a translation knowing it to be shoddy. After rewriting and/or recasting the original, s/he has to contact the employer or the author, explaining the reasons for the stylistic changes made, and persuade and 'educate' them tactfully. Typically, they should be grateful for the changes.

The Factual Truth

Similarly, the translator should not knowingly reproduce factual inaccuracies that occur in the source language text. In this point I disagree with Jean Herbert (quoted by Peter Wareham two issues ago) when he stated in *Le Manuel de l'Interprète* (Georg, Geneva, 1952) that 'The translator has no responsibility whatsoever for the content of the texts he translates'. However, Herbert was discussing interpretation, where conditions are different. I believe the translator should, where she thinks it necessary, check the facts of her original; however I am not maintaining that she has responsibility for the truth of all statements in her translation — that would be absurd. If I ever wrote that the translator is responsible for the factual truth of what she translates (I cannot find this statement, but I may have made it), then I must now modify it. The translator should, at the least, check all implausible-looking figures (Magnalium, an alloy with 10% to 40% magnesium), symbols and proper names (Roumania, Rumania) — they may be misprints or mistakes, and, being a temporary expert in the topic, do her best to check suspicious-looking statements. But the responsibility for the factual truth must be shared with the author and the 'agent' (i.e. the employer, the translation agency, the translation section of a firm or of an international organisation — there seems to be no satisfactory generic term), who desirably have their own checkers or revisers. The final responsibility must rest with one of these three (translator, author, or 'agent' if there is one), depending on the occasion of the translation, the contract, and the nature of any mistakes or defects. This is sometimes a complicated question, and this discussion is simply tentative, like so much in these *Paras* . . .

Translation at Maastricht
     There are several stimulating pieces in *Translation and Meaning Part 1*, the proceedings of a conference held at Maastricht (ed. M. Thelen and B. Lewandowska-Tomaszczyk; Euroterm, Maastricht 1990; ISBN-90-72614-03-8). Robert Wilkinson's *Translating into European English* is worth reading whether one agrees with his thesis or not, as he gives many examples of change or degeneration in British (European? influenced by non-British) English, such as: decline in use of 'fewer'; replacement of '-er' and '-est' by 'more' and 'most'; increased use of existential 'there is', 'there are'; French sense of words like 'interesting', 'eventual', 'realise', 'control', etc. I think the piece should be seen as a warning rather than an encouragement, but it is important.
     Eva Koberski and Sally Petrequin Jessen ask some amazingly naïve questions about why a number of English and non-English students translated the following poem, by Jacques Prévert (*Paroles*):

ALICANTE
Une orange sur la table
Ta robe sur le tapis
Et toi dans mon lit.

Doux présent du présent

Fraîcheur de la nuit
Chaleur de ma vie

identically as:

ALICANTE

An orange on the table
Your dress on the carpet
And you in my bed.
Sweet present of the present.

Freshness of the night
Warmth of my life.

Could it be because no more accurate translation is possible? Because there is complete cultural overlap, and therefore culture and romanticism are irrelevant? Because this is an 'explicit' text, where one-to-one translations of all words are available throughout, and nothing else is appropriate? (The distinction between explicit, mixed and implicit texts, though perhaps rather too obvious, is well made by Hanne Martinet here.) An explicit text requires almost no linguistic and/or referential interpretation, whilst an implicit text is at the other end of the scale.

Mohammed H. Heliel's discussion of 'Lexical Collocations and Translation' is comprehensive and thorough, and pertinent comparisons are made with Arabic. Kitty van Leuwen-Zwart usefully refers to John McFarlane's paper 'Modes of Translation' (*Durham University Journal 147*, pp. 77–93, 1953), in which he insists on the need to analyse translation procedures before one makes value-judgements. She rejects the concept of translation equivalence; I think it is an essential and essentially operational term which implicates so many variables that it is as fruitless to pursue it as to abandon it. Peter van Nunen contributes some fascinating examples and comments on cultural difficulties and word-order in literary translation (Russian to Dutch, English and German).

Finally, Mona Baker ('My own feeling is that Translation and Interpreting are going to be the disciplines of the near future') (*sic.*) describes a course book of translation she is about to publish (with Routledge) which has some original features:

1. English is assumed to be the source language, from which students will translate into a variety of languages. (Therefore I assume the book is addressed to non-British readers, but she does not admit this.)

2. Her approach is non-Eurocentric, and she gives many examples from Arabic, Japanese and Chinese. (She rightly states that some European languages have a smaller share of the market than these, but

disconcertingly quotes M. Croft to show that the most important languages for non-literary purposes remain, in order: French, German, Spanish, Italian, Arabic, Japanese, which goes against her argument.)
3. In the body of her book, all examples are back-translated, presumably closely but not literally. 'Original' target texts in the foreign languages will be appended.
4. All target texts are previously published, and not her own, for the purpose of introducing the readers to 'the world of translation'. As an example of translation by cultural substitution, she first quotes from Stephen Hawking's *Brief History of Time*:
'A well-known scientist (some say it was Bertrand Russell) once gave a public lecture on astronomy . . . At the end of the lecture, a little old lady at the back of the room said: 'What you have told us is rubbish. The world is really a flat plate supported on the back of a giant tortoise.'
and then quotes the target text, which is back-translated from Greek:
'Alice in Wonderland was once giving a lecture about astronomy . . . At the end of the lecture, the Queen looked at her angrily and disapprovingly. What you say is nonsense. The earth is just a giant playing card, so it's flat like all playing cards.'
Ms Baker comments on this strange translation by explaining that Alice and the Queen are well known in Greece, but she does not try to justify the new metaphor for the 'world', describing it simply as 'interesting'. I wonder if Hawking would see it that way. But Ms Baker 'feels it is important to give trainee translators a realistic account of the strategies actually used by practising translators, not of the strategies linguists (*sic*) think they should use'. Presumably in her fear of being prescriptive, normative, judgmental, pedagogical, etc., she refuses to criticise any of her target texts. I would have thought that as she is writing a course textbook, she must be a teacher, and therefore concerned with standards of translation, and particularly of professional translators. However, I share Ms Baker's interest in back-translation (i.e. translation of translation), both to explain an example from a language the reader may not know, but also as a yardstick for the truth, i.e. a quite different reason, and am curious to read her quite original book.

Incidentally, Ms Baker criticises me for providing no back-translations at all (not true), which means that my readership is restricted to speakers of European languages only. In fact I am mainly writing for English-speaking readers, but *Approaches* has appeared in Arabic and Italian, and some of my papers in Chinese, so she may be wrong.

This well-produced compilation, which includes eleven papers on computerised translation, concludes with rather a futile discussion about meaning.

Subsidiarity and Confederation

Anthony Crane has pointed out to me that all kinds of historical connotative meanings probably lie behind the terms now being adopted by the European Communities. If the EC is to become a confederation, one must bear in mind that in English a 'confederation' is a looser association than a 'federation', whilst in French it is a transitory state between federation or dissolution. 'Subsidiarity' in its new sense preserves the right of decision making at the lowest reasonable point of authority or instance, and therefore the health of the confederation (acknowledgements to Richard Nice), but Clifford Longley in *The Times* of 6.7.91 has described the large body of Catholic teaching implied in the term.

Martyrs for Translation and the Truth

Tyndale (d. 1535) was amongst the earliest translator-martyrs. Etienne Dolet (1509–1546), who, Eugene Nida has stated, formulated the first theory of translation in his *Manière de traduire d'une langue à l'autre*, the first book on translation, was tortured, strangled and had his body burned for the heresy of 'translating' one of Plato's dialogues.

On July 12, 1991, Hitoshi Igarashi, the Japanese translator of Salman Rushdie's *The Satanic Verses*, was found stabbed to death.

Christopher Taylor on Language and Translation

I unreservedly commend *Aspects of Language and Translation: Contrastive Approaches for Italian/English Translators* by Christopher Taylor (Campanotte Udine, 1990). It covers an exceptionally wide range of translation topics: historical background; functional grammar (including useful contrastive discussions of Italian and English word-order, pp. 20, 58, 61, 134, 155, discourse analysis and functional sentence perspective); lexis (particularly good on acronyms and etymology), which Taylor actually enjoys and which is 'centrally' important (from Latin to Vulgar Latin to the Italic dialects to standard Italian) in Italian semantics; text analysis (valuable remarks on irony and metaphor); phonological equivalence and onomatopoeia; text-types (literary, journalistic, technical and legal), summarily discussed and then exemplified by specimens with annotated translations. There is a combined name and subject index. The book abounds in examples with translations. Reading it one is always conscious that the author is a translator and evidently a splendid teacher — he advises and recommends, but his 'should' is not absolute — which does rather differentiate it from the translatological studies.

Taylor's distinction between linguistic, situational and background or 'world' knowledge (or meaning) for a translator may have been made before, but I have never seen it more usefully discussed. Of the three types, background knowledge is the most likely to escape the translator, since it may include an unattributed reference to a literary quotation, or an event temporarily in the news, or a feature (say 'yellow jersey' or *maillot jaune*) transferring from the referential (*Tour de France*) to a metaphorical ('taking the lead') sense.

Taylor's concept of grammatical metaphor appears to be wider than Halliday's, and may therefore be confusing; for Taylor, grammatical metaphors are alternative constructions to the most likely lexicogrammatical construction; e.g. 'My suggestion is that you go home now' rather than 'I suggest you go home now'. In Halliday (*Introduction to Functional Grammar*), I think grammatical metaphor denotes the metaphorical use of verbs (therefore linguistic, rather than rhetorical personification, which is a trope), e.g. 'The year saw many changes', 'Supper was followed by games'. Note that for German at least, a grammatical shift (the generic term that covers both types of metaphor) is preferable: *Ich schlage vor . . . In diesem Jahr veränderte sich vieles.*

Christopher Taylor is perceptive on institutional terms which are normally literally translated, but which differ in their functions, so that the literal translation is only valid where the target language readers are aware of the difference, e.g. between a 'chamber of commerce' and a *camera di commercio*. He is acute on what he refers to as the 'different frequency patterns of the two languages' illustrating from proverbs which can either be translated literally ('don't cry over spilt milk/*non piangere sul latte versato*), adapted ('to kill two birds with one stone'/*prendere due piccioni con una fava*), or be expressed differently ('the straw that breaks the camel's back'/*la goccia che fa traboccare il vaso*).

In short, this is a rich book, not merely for translators from or into Italian.

Religious Translation

Tension between original and translation is at its highest in the case of a sacred text whose intent is to prosetylise.

Don Giovanni Plain

In Music Theatre Works's modern (dress, amongst other things) production of Mozart's *Don Giovanni*, the Don's memorable *Mi pare sentire odore di femina* (lit. 'It appears to me I can smell a woman's scent/odour) becomes 'I can smell a woman', which typifies the difference between the sensuality of the original and the animality of this version, which makes no acknowledgements to Da Ponte and appears to be freely translated by Nick Broadhurst and Tony Britten.

Batti is variously translated as 'beat', 'spank' and 'slap'; Zerlina is a bimbo and Masetto a lout. (The vicious irony of his *Sì, signore, sì* aria (the detestable 'sir') gets lost.) With all that, it's a refreshing, exciting production which does not diminish the greatness of the opera, and it gets audiences which, I imagine wouldn't normally dream of going to an opera and which are enthusiastic.

Key-words Again
Normally, one expects key-words to be translated straight and repeated at each mention. However, in the absorbing introduction to his translation of Corneille's *Le Cid* (performed by 'Cheek by Jowl'), David Bryer (in *Landmarks in French Classical Drama*, ed. David Bradby, Methuen 1991) points out that it is impossible to capture Chimène's *gloire* by a single word, and he translates it variously as 'honour', 'glory', 'reputation', 'renown', 'name', 'good name'. His case is strengthened by the fact that Corneille could only dispose of about 1800 *mots nobles*, and English would probably use more.

The Monolingual National Gallery
The titles and details of the fascinating paintings in the Sainsbury Wing of the National Gallery are all in English. I think these should additionally be given in the language of the painter, throughout the Gallery, out of respect, to facilitate identification of titles in some cases, and to avoid the invidious dilemma of selecting a second world language. The (few) English paintings should have translations in French. This would require a rolling financial plan. I do not know how long the Gallery can continue to be free to visitors, but if a charge is made, I hope all who are in full-time education will be exempt.

Etymology Again
'Any historical knowledge we may have about the development and meaning of words is in principle irrelevant to their synchronic use and interpretation'. (*Introduction to Theoretical Linguistics*, John Lyons, 1969, p. 407). I think 'irrelevant' is mistaken; it is simply an important factor.

Basic English and Translation
C. K. Ogden (1889–1957), who devised Basic English, the simplified 850 word variety of English supported by Churchill and Roosevelt and entrusted to and abandoned by the British Council in the '50s, planned a large programme of translation of foreign works into Basic English. In *Basic English International Second Language* (Harcourt Brace and World N.Y.), Roosevelt is quoted as stating that a Basic English version of Churchill's 'I can offer you nothing but blood, toil, tears and sweat' would be 'blood, work, eye-water and face-water'. It is pointed

out that Roosevelt had the naïve idea that translation was simply a matter of word for word substitution, and that the actual Basic English version would be something like: 'All I am offering you is death and pain, bitter trouble and hard unending work'. In fact, Roosevelt's error was merely to ignore the figurative sense of Churchill's language. Incidentally, Basic English anticipated the later 'explosive' expansion of phrasal verbs with its 'operators' and directional prepositions (perceptively analysed), and it is ironical that while it was criticised for linguistic imperialism, English has reached precisely this predominant and dangerous position entirely without its assistance.

The Art of Translation

The Art of Translation: voices from the field, edited by Rosanna Warren (Northeastern University Press, Boston 1989; ISBN 1-55553-048-6), a civilised, intelligent and literary work, covers a wide area overlapping adaptation and translation relating to some well-known poetry, drama and fiction of the past. Thus Tony Harrison eruditely and often brilliantly discusses his *Phaedra Britannica*, but barely quotes *Phèdre*. Michael Ewans, the author of an outstanding work on Janáček's tragic operas, compares and evaluates some passages from Aeschylus. Seamus Heaney compares his two versions of *Buile Suibhne*, a Middle Irish text, with some others. Charles Tomlinson, the editor of the *Oxford Book of Verse in English Translation*, emphasises the importance of translation, retranslation, reworking etc. throughout the course of English poetry. Richard Sieburth sensitively describes his thoughts and second thoughts on translating Hölderlin. Some essays are perhaps poised at too great a distance from the works and their translations under discussion. Benjamin and Derrida are widely quoted, and so is Paul de Man's questionable essay on Benjamin (in *The Resistance to Theory*, 1986). I at least would dispute his challenging statement: 'The poet has some relationship to meaning, to a statement that is not purely within the realm of language . . . The relationship of the translator to the original is the relationship between language and language, where . . . the desire to say something is entirely absent. Translation is a relation from language to language, not a relation to an extralinguistic meaning.' As I see it, this is an unrealisable and not particularly admirable purpose, since there must always be some relation between words and reality. *The Art of Translation* will interest anyone conversant with its topics, and should stimulate literary translators.

Ibsen's *Lady from the Sea*

I warmly applaud the Women's Playhouse Trust production of Ibsen's realistic and imaginative 'feminist' masterpiece, *The Lady from the Sea*, 'in a new version by Heidi Thomas, from an original translation by Kari Dickson'. (I have not read either.) Kathryn Pogson (the superb Ellida) told me that the translation was 'too literary' (the play was written in 1888), and had too much repetition. Perhaps it's a pity that in the adaptation, the repetition was reduced, and a few lines like 'Be my guest' seemed to jar.

But the performance was for me a fine dramatic experience.

Back Translation

Back translation, the retranslation of the translation into the original, must be distinguished from Nida's back-transformation, which is the analysis of the surface structure of a discourse into its underlying kernels in the same language, typically prior to translation. (Thus, 'the beauty of her singing' or 'her beautiful singing' become 'she sings beautifully'.)

Back translation is the scientific element in translation, since it can measure approximately the deviation between the original and the translation. It can also be used to explain translation examples to readers unacquainted with the target language. It is usually a valuable test, but it is not always decisive in distinguishing a valid from an invalid translation. (The test question is: 'If the author had meant to write this, why didn't he do so?') Back translation may range from word-for-word translation to close translation which respects target language syntactic structures and collocations. There are perhaps six types of back translation:

1. Lexical, where the word is used in its primary sense and the target language has a clear one-to-one equivalent. Thus, *das schwarze Haus* is 'the black house', and if translated as 'pitch black', 'dark', or 'sombre', the critic would ask why the author hadn't written *pechschwarz, dunkel, finster, düster* etc. Note that if there is no clear one-to-one equivalent, the test is illuminating but less decisive: 'the dark house' would normally be *das dunkle Haus*, but *finster* (edging to *düster*, gloomy) is also possible, and exposes an English lexical gap.

2. Collocational. Since the typical characteristic of a collocation is that its 'secondary' collocate is not used in its primary sense, a back translation will often expose translationese. The most common type of collocation has a noun as its primary collocate. (What do you do with a 'shoulder' (shrug), 'nemesis' (meet), a 'prejudice' (hold)?) Thus, 'hold a prejudice'; *tenir (entretenir) un préjugé; ein Vorurteil halten (hegen)*. Collocations with adjectives ('dusty answer'; *en être pour ses frais*; mistranslated in Collins as *eine unklare Antwort bekommen; scharf abweisen*) or verbs ('hinges creak'; *grincer; quietschen, knarren*) are narrower, and idioms, being singular, are always shown up.

3. Syntactic. A literal or a close syntactic back translation may show up the non-existence (phrasal verbs, gerunds, verb nouns), or the infrequency of a structure in the source language, and may be instructively performed at the level of groups, clauses or sentences.

4. Word order. A change in source language word-order in the target language may be anomalous or may alter the emphasis of the original, making a lexical or a grammatical change preferable. (*Ihm wurde die Erlaubnis erteilt, . . .*; 'To him permission was granted'; 'Permission was granted to him'; 'he was granted permission'.)

5. Text length. A comparison between source and target text length

is not often discussed, although Nida and Taber (*The Theory and Practice of Translation* (E. J. Brill, Leiden, 1974), a seminal work, devote six pages to the topic (pp. 163–168). One would expect:

(a) A translation from a synthetic language such as Latin or German into an analytical language such as Vietnamese or Chinese to be longer than its original, since the synthetic language may have no definite or indefinite articles, and is likely to make more sparing use of pronouns, prepositions and auxiliary verbs.

(b) A 'communicative' to be longer than a 'semantic' translation, and *a fortiori* the source language text, since it is *per se* more explicit, and includes cultural and other background information which is not required in the original. Subject to (a) above, a 'semantic' translation should be of approximately the same length as its original; this is usually achieved in the translation of classical plays and has to be so in poems with prescribed forms, e.g. sonnets, haikus etc. In fact, all translations should be economical, strictly 'relevant', and should eschew paraphrase. Only general indications about relative text length can be given.

6. Metaphor. Back translations of metaphors (here I include all figurative language) may be useful in determining cultural differences as well as a translator's incompetence or 'metaphorobia' (i.e. metaphorphobia, not my coinage, the unnecessary weakening of a metaphor).

Translation Theory in Scandinavia

The above is the title of a volume (ISBN-82-992162-0-6) published by the University of Oslo in 1991, edited by Patrick Chaffey, A. F. Rydning and S. S. Ulriksen, which includes some remarkable papers.

Werner Koller, whose excellent *Einführung in die Übersetzungswissenschaft* (UTB, Quelle & Meyer) should go into a third edition and be translated, writes on 'A Linguistic Approach to Translation', claiming that most problems in literary texts at least are 'not in the domain of denotative meaning, but in the aesthetic and formal qualities'. He offers some fascinating multilingual translations of metaphors in Ibsen and Max Frisch. He insists that his sensible comments are 'descriptive, not judgemental', but a statement such as 'Maybe we could even state that they have different concepts of translation faithfulness' suggests irony rather than neutrality.

Koller takes me to task for writing that 'A translation theorist has to be a practising translator or a teacher of translation or preferably both'. Mine was a reaction to many students complaining that their T.T. lecturers couldn't teach and probabaly couldn't translate; besides, I was writing in the context of a post-graduate translation programme, where I would hope that most teachers would also be at least freelance translators, and the T.T. teacher should be no exception. Suggesting that, according to me, a literary scholar would have to be a poet is as irrelevant as suggesting that a food critic should have to have a *cordon bleu*. However, I think translation theorists have to produce their own examples and often their own translations, not as know-alls, *Besserwisser*, but because I assume they are teachers who have to be concrete and illustrate the points they are making. Every time I translate in these *Paragraphs* I stick my neck out, and invite criticism. There are now several writers on translation who prefer to produce as their examples published translations and analyse them linguistically, rather than evaluating them or contrasting them with their own versions. If one object of practising translation theory is to improve translation standards (which I assume must be the object of any teacher), I don't think it will do to passively 'accept' a translation simply because it has been published and has been produced by a professional translator 'in the market place', as it may be of poor quality.

I would add that translation theorists, like translators, have to know how to write: a passage such as 'There is no doubt a lot more has to be done to close in on the process of translation. Until this is done, hypotheses will no doubt go on being formulated as conjectures, among other things . . .' (not by Werner Koller of course, but in this collection) will not do.

Hanne Martinet contributes a discussion on the different uses of graphical devices (typographical conventions) and graphical marks such as italics, inverted commas and capital letters indicating stress and emotions in a French novel and its translation into Danish and English. It is strange that text-linguists usually ignore punctuation and prosody.

Gunilla Anderman and Margaret Rodgers briefly review the course of foreign language teaching in the UK, and warn of the danger of 'the translator being superseded by the star dramatist, often more interested in leaving his own signature all over the original work than in doing justice to it' in the English theatre.

Paul St-Pierre, in a stimulating essay on 'The Historical Nature of Translation', denies that it has any 'transhistorical' element, and regards any statement that 'this translation is better than that' as 'merely subjective'. Goodbye to standards again.

Judith Woodsworth demonstrates that the metaphors used by writers to describe translation indicate the essence of their concept of translation. From 'dress', 'garment', 'humble labour' to 'critical weapons'? Lars Wollin and Patrick Chaffey are always improving reading.

The Three Dots . . .

The punctuation mark . . . (*trois points de suspension, drei Punkte,*

sometimes enclosed within brackets), which normally appears at the end of a sentence, or a list of nouns, apparently has the following meanings:
1. And so on; etc.
2. Passage omitted. (The dots are sometimes within brackets.)
3. A brief silence, or a pause in a dialogue. (Particularly in French fiction.)
4. Suspense, followed by an unexpected outcome. Thus: *Krouchtchev décide de donner une autonomie aux Républiques. Il leur transfère de nouveaux pouvoirs du Gosplan, le centre assurant une coordination d'ensemble au travers . . . d'un nouveau bureau contrôlé par le PC.* (Khruschev decided to give the Republics a certain autonomy; he transferred to them a few new powers belonging to the Gosplan, creating a centre with general powers of coordination through . . . (believe it or not) a new committee controlled by the CP).
5. As a conclusion, suggesting perhaps that this is not the end. (See *Strange Meeting*, below.)
6. To indicate an interruption in dialogue, made by another speaker.
7. To imply a contrast. ('I work, whilst you . . .')
The three dots appear to be more common in French than in German or English; note the two series of three dots in *Étrange Rencontre* below; Note that the mad exclamation mark (repeated four or five times in expressionist plays!) is most favoured by German.

Shakespeare's Universal Humour: Dogberry
It is sometimes thought that puns being peculiar to one language are as impossible to translate as any cultural linguistic feature. Not true. Shakespeare's bumbling bureaucratic busybody, the fortunately inept petty official Dogberry (*Much Ado About Nothing*), is a wonderfully humorous creation. Admittedly he is mainly comic because of his blundering actions, but his misuse of 'learned' words, anticipating Mrs Malaprop, also makes one smile. For Romance languages, there are no translation difficulties, since most of the word play is from the Romance word stock. Thus 'comprehend' (apprehend) becomes *comprendre (appréhender)*; 'tolerable' (intolerable) repeats itself; 'decerns' (concerns) is *décerne (concerne)* and 'dissembly' (assembly) *dissemblée (assemblée)*. The German translation is trickier, but here too Tieck made use of Latinate words: *irritieren (arrestieren)* for 'comprehend'; *dispektieren* for 'suspect' (respect). In fact, by inventing lovely pompous 'German' words like *Injurie, aufs komplottste, odorös* (odorous, odious), *perspektivistisch* (could this be Kristeva?), he showed, rather better than François-Victor Hugo (no doubt a relative) that the important thing in this type of translation is ludicrous absurdity rather than pedantic accuracy, and Shakespeare would be only too pleased.

'Dogberry' is translated by Tieck as *Holzapfel* ('crab apple'), but F.-V. Hugo transfers the name, which is surely a cop-out, as the English suggests some kind of a dogsbody to me. Why not *Cournouille* (or Cornwall or better Cornwheel? — the French should shine through —) which means 'dogberry' and sounds rather pathetic. According to Webster, a dogberry is any of certain small fruits considered unfit for human consumption and therefore a word with connotations is required in any translation.

Errors in Translation

An error in translation could be narrowly defined as a case where a back translation or a segment of the translator's version would indisputably produce a segment of text differing from the original segment. If this were due to the translator's ignorance or incompetence, the result would be a poor translation. However, it might be due to the translator's concept of translation, placing more emphasis on say readability or raciness or imaginative flights than on accuracy; on the need to produce an equivalent pragmatic effect (say laughter or tears) on the reader (or spectator) rather than a denotatively equivalent version; or on the prevailing fashion (ideology) of translation, favouring the free rather than the literal, which is the concern of the reception theory school. All these factors have to be taken into account in reviewing the translations of the past; they should not deter one from proposing standards of translation fidelity to the facts, ideas and style of some texts, and the facts and ideas neatly and elegantly presented of other texts in the future.

Great Poetry

The greatest 20th century poem in the English language is not *The Waste Land* or *Byzantium* or *An Ancient to Ancients* but Wilfred Owen's *Strange Meeting* (as was recently stated by 'Centipede' in *The Guardian*). It is a universal poem, and its translation presents no cultural difficulties, but many linguistic choices. I quote the last five lines, and their translations, in *Ohne Hass und Fahne. . . No Hatred and no Flag . . . Sans Haine et sans Drapeau* (ed. E. Grassi; Rohwolt, Hamburg 1959), (a superb and unique anthology) as *Seltsame Begegnung* by the distinguished Austrian-English-Jewish (incidentally anti-Zionist) poet Erich Fried and as *Étrange Rencontre* by Jacques E. David:

'I am the enemy you killed, my friend.
I knew you in this dark: for so you frowned
Yesterday through me as you jabbed and killed.
I parried; but my hands were loath and cold.
Let us sleep now . . .'

Ich bin der Feind, den du erschlugst, mein Freund.
Wie hier im Dunkel sahst du gestern fremd
Durch mich hindurch, und stachst mich durch die Kehle.
Ich wehrte mich, doch ich war klamm vor Kälte.
Lass uns nun schlafen . . .

Je suis cet ennemi que tu as tué. Dans l'ombre,
Ami, j'ai reconnu ce regard dur et sombre
Qui me perça, hier, quand pour tuer tu frappas.
Je parai. Mais ma main, glacée, ne voulait pas . . .
Dormons donc maintenant . . .

Inevitably, the German translation (cognate language, monosyllables) is the more successful. Fried's first line is magnificent, but he has had to pay a semantic price for retaining the Wilfred Owen (assonant) rhymes. David's *Je parai . . .* line is good. Both translations are written with love, which gives a positive translation yield. Note that 'Let us sleep now . . .' is unforgettably 'translated' in Britten's *War Requiem* for German, French, English and all listeners. Which leads to *Ewig . . . ewig . . .* (the scrap of paper floating on the heaving ocean) at the close of Mahler's *Das Lied von der Erde.*
(The best 19th century English poem is *The Wreck of the Deutschland.* It has no rivals.)

Theory of Translation
I call attention to 'A False Opposition in Translation Studies: Theoretical Versus/and Historical Approaches' by Dirk Delabastita in *Target* 3:2 (1991). Delabastita, like Snell-Hornby, commendably argues for an integrative approach to a discipline that is inherently fragmented. He rejects four 'discursive strategies' (*sic*) to translation. He condemns 'normativeness' and ignores all questions of translation quality. He gives no translation examples, which could have been introduced, not to prove this or that point, but to clarify his often cloudy language. His sceptical discussion of word-play translation is not relieved by a single pun.

Paras
Much in these *Paragraphs* would probably be assented to by many people; much is controversial and tentative (a favourite word). Much looks to translation standards of the future. Nothing is prescriptive or normative. I prefer the 'should' to the 'absolute shall' (Shakespeare, *Coriolanus*, III.I.88) or the 'must', and my 'should' is a shorthand for 'typically' or 'in most circumstances'.
I write as a teacher and occasional translator, trying to assist and give advice to translators and therefore to contribute to improving

translation standards. I write as an author, and never as President of the Institute of Linguists, which unfortunately at present has no national language policy, let alone views about translation.* I also write as a human being committed to some universal rights, and as a person attempting to convey his love of particular artistic works. I make this statement in reply to the charge that what I write is 'what the President has laid down as his creed for student, client and general reader', which is pure and perfect poppycock.

The *Translator's Turn*

The *Translator's Turn* by Douglas Robinson (Johns Hopkins University Press, Baltimore and London 1991) is a strange, civilised and enjoyable book. It informs its statements with its Laurentian philosophy of the primacy of feeling and the body, hence the triumph of 'idiosomatics' (personal feeling) over 'ideosomatics' (conventional or ideological feeling). It is obsessed with 'mainstream translation theory' (including me, though I don't recognise myself and the mainstream theorists don't recognise me), to the virtual exclusion of translations and translators.

According to Robinson, mainstream translation theory is wrong because it is characterised by sense-for-sense equivalence and normative rules as well as (a) dualism — medieval mind versus body; source text versus target text; formal versus dynamic equivalence (Nida is misquoted as well as misunderstood), 'free' versus 'literal' translation etc; (but I now tend to replace 'semantic-communicative' with my three correlations (see *Paras* VI, p.36) and to stress the medial factors of the truth (factual, logical, aesthetic) and the translator); (b) instrumentalism (functionalism?); (c) perfectionism — the goal of perfect translation. (But the only translation theorist I know who wrote of ideal translation is Kade, not mentioned by Robinson; improving (*perfectionner*) translation skills is another matter.)

Robinson remains 'firmly' (cf. his pervasive use of the suspect 'of course') believing that the 'competent' translator does not need 'any kind of theory at all'. What about the student, who is now being 'drilled' (*sic*) with translation rules? What happens when she asks the teacher 'How (closely) do I translate this word/sentence?' and has no intuitive 'feeling' about it? Here I assume Robinson would turn to 'embodied dialogical turning' (p. 295) which is his conception of translation; this is the vague dual dialogue between the translator and the author and the translator and the reader which he derives from Bakhtin, a difficult and rather abstract writer who is best approached, I think, through David Lodge's brilliant *After Bakhtin*. (Try this book

---

* I have many times urged the Institute to agree and publish a national policy for languages; a policy for translation would not be in its remit.

too for the overblown Barthes and Paul de Man, both obsessed by language and reader to the exclusion of reality.) Robinson too often constructs Aunt Sallies of translation theory which he triumphantly demolishes, but he is usually above the *mêlée* of the translating activity. So what are the plusses? The book is well written. The book is (rather breezy) fun (outrageous sex). It is fine on turning bad writing into good translation (p. 116), and this is one of its few references to non-literary translation. And it is instructive on metaphor, and, so help me, metalepsis. I can't see this new theory of translation sticking (and even less the 'neuroscience of translation' which is abandoned after a pathetic paragraph or so in the Introduction), but it should invigorate thinking about the subject.

The Translator's Dilemma
'What is this bloke on about? What on earth do all these pronouns refer to?' (Acknowledgement to Matthew Newmark.)

Berliner Spielkarten
A company called *Berliner Spielkarten* asks me how to translate the caption: *Berliner Spielkarten & mehr* of their logo, as they want to start a British advertising campaign. I suggest 'Berliner Spielkarten — more than just playing cards!' But in view of *Vorsprung durch Technik*, keep the German? Perhaps it depends on the size of the company.

Justice as Translation
Justice as Translation by James Boyd White (University of Chicago Press 1990) is one of those leisurely, educated, civilised, lettered, bland books that contain too many semi-platitudes for me to be comfortable with, but who am I? (For me, impatience is a virtue, and patience a vice, since patience is so often an excuse for inactivity.) The book is concerned with the relationship between justice and 'implicit' texts, where the sense is always more figurative than literal, and where translation can only be as accurate and economical as possible. For White, translation is 'the composition of one text in response to another', a conversation between the translator and the author where each maintains their separate and different integrity, which is followed by a similar conversation between the reader and the translator. There are no translation examples, but one or two telling reminders of Ortega y Gasset's fine essay 'Miseries and Splendours of Translation' (*Miseria y esplendor de la traduccion; Glanz und Elend der Übersetzung; Splendeurs et Misères de la Traduction* — the French and German titles are presumably reversed on the analogy of Balzac's great *Splendeurs et Misères des Courtisanes*), where he refers to 'deficiencies', i.e. aspects of the meaning of the original that cannot be reproduced in the translation, and 'exuberances', aspects of the meaning that necessarily

appear in the translation but are not part of the original. These parallel undertranslation (excessive generalisation) and overtranslation (excessive particularisation).

Style

French has for too long been the language of Style, of smoothing out, of the *discours* (see Walter Redfern's *Clichés and Coinages*), where words are composed but not felt, influencing too many translations out of and into French and other languages.

Somatic Language

I don't deny ('of course'!) that language is somatic. If my (English) wife calls me *Sie*, or my son calls me 'Peter', it's a body blow. But to ask, of a word in a translation, 'Does it feel right?' or 'What's your gut reaction to that?', as Douglas Robinson does, *teaches* nothing. One needs reasons, not abstract, not 'emotionally directed or guided', but informed by humane and artistic values.

Responsibilities of Translating

Surely no professional writer (i.e. and e.g. a translator) should turn out work knowing or suspecting that it is inaccurate, slipshod or biased (without taking some kind of counter-measure?), just because the original is all of that?

Hegemonies

Why do the prevailing national hegemonies prefer such pompous verbs for their collocations? Thus 'deliver a lecture', *proporcionarnos deleite* ('give delight')?

The Translation of Verbal Irony

Irony is the often (not always) humorous or sarcastic use of words to imply the opposite of, or some degree of difference from, what they normally mean. Irony may be broad ('Some genius!') or ambiguously concealed ('I've known better afternoons'.) Sometimes, however, the irony may only be in the eyes of the beholder. It is indicated by tone, and in texts can only be detected when it is in contradiction with its context or with common sense. It is the most serious and powerful weapon in satirical comedy or farce, particularly when it is used to expose pomposity and deceit or to deflate self-importance. When it is subtle, it can easily be overlooked.

Irony can be closely translated provided that the relevant words have straight one-to-one TL equivalents, and the SL and TL readerships have similar cultural and educational backgrounds — a formidable proviso! Thus, 'Diplomacy is the noble art of lying for one's country' could be translated straight into many languages.

Where there is a cultural gap, it may be advisable, in persuasive texts, to add a comment phrase such as 'ironically understood', 'figuratively speaking', 'so to say', 'if I may invent a word' (or 'a phrase'), 'I may be exaggerating', or to use inverted commas or an exclamation mark — in all cases to alert the readership.

However, in serious literary texts, ironised cultural expressions or words are difficult to translate, since, if they are transferred without a classifier, they are unlikely to make the readership smile let alone laugh. (I shall return to this difficulty.)

Understatement (litotes) is often an important form of irony. It typically consists of a negative plus a qualitative term (e.g. 'not bad'). Qualitative words are often not easy to translate, as they may have no one-to-one equivalent ('fair', 'passable', 'nice', 'middling', 'standard', 'respectable', 'up to the mark', 'jolly', 'rather jolly', 'decent', 'all right' — but 'okay' is 'OK' in many languages) or have peculiar cultural criteria; thus the eminent *cynophile* Amanda Maclaren has pointed out that in the dog world, *bon* as a grading may indicate poor physical condition, *assez bon* shows many faults (both terms are considered poor gradings), while even *très bon* is often disappointing to the exhibitor; any degree of real badness however is simply *insuffisant*. (Note my ever so gentle and easily translatable irony.)

Situational or dramatic irony normally presents no translation difficulties.

I must point out that most dictionaries (but not the *C.O.D.*, excellent) are 'totally' ('Usher, show me the washroom', as the great dramatic critic, George Jean Nathan used to write) misleading in defining 'irony' as merely the 'opposite' of a word's ordinary meaning. It is precisely the degree of difference in meaning which translators have to assess so nicely; hence the ironical meaning of expressions like 'of course' or Colette's *sans doute*.

Nida

Eugene Nida, the most influential of all contemporary writers on translation, is often thought to have written nothing since 1974. I draw attention to *Meaning across Cultures* by E. A. Nida and W. D. Reyburn (Orbis Books, Maryknoll, N.Y., 1981, ISBN 0-8834-326-0); *Translating Meaning* by E. A. Nida (English Language Institute, 448 E. Foothill Blvd, San Dimas, California 91773, 1984); *On Translation* (with special reference to Chinese and English) by Jin Di and E. A. Nida (1984; publisher not known). These are rewarding books.

French Adjectives

French adjectives of quality or of substance, when they have no evident one-to-one equivalent in English, are typically expanded in translation. Thus un *retrait massif d'épargne* may become 'a large-scale withdrawal of savings'. Adjectives of substance usually translate as premodified nouns (*obligations monétaires*, 'money liabilities'; *à vocation monétaire*, 'money orientated'), but may translate as prepositional groups (*les sicav monétaires*, 'unit trust holdings in the money markets'.)

Connectives

It would be useful to have some statistical evidence for the frequency of sentence connectives in various text-types for various languages. In 'good' Latin prose, where a sentence connective was missing in the English, one was meant to begin every sentence with a relative pronoun. I would guess that 'logical' connectives are evenly proportioned in many languages, but as regards modal connectives or particles ('of course', 'naturally', *eben, ja, en effet* etc.), for 'my' languages, they occur most often in German, followed in order by Italian, French and English. Connectives, which Helen Chau Hu in an outstanding forthcoming study refers to as 'the nucleus of translating', often merit separate post-translating revision.

Justification

The trendy computer/printing technology term dates from 1551.

XVII
FEBRUARY 1992

Lebensgefährlich

At last British Rail has, to coin a phrase, grasped the nettle and the rail, and created DANGER OF DEATH! which no one would as yet say or see, from *danger de mort* and *lebensgefährlich*. It was high time too. (Acknowledgement to Paul Dodd.) In this matter of life or death, literal translation triumphs over natural usage, and though 'danger of death!' still sounds odd, it won't do so for long. Note also the recent 'traffic calming' (*Verkehrsberuhigung*), related to 'speed ramps' (*ralentisseurs*), replacing 'sleeping policemen'.

The Dynamics of Translation

Translation is a dynamic process, within limits. A translation is never finished (normally, you go on changing it a little every time you reread it) and never perfect. The main dynamic agent is therefore the translator, who sometimes goes on mentally wrestling with her job long after she has sent it off. The second dynamic agent is the changing target language, which requires another translation of an enduring work every thirty years. The source language text may be an agent of change if fresh semantic features emerge.

As a teacher, I am not infrequently reproached for underlining or crossing something out (in a piece of homework) which I later reinstate when it is discussed in class. Maybe I'm wrong, maybe I've been careless, and maybe I've changed my mind since. It's part of the dynamism of translation. But this is *no* excuse for leaving alternatives on the job or in an exam paper.

Translating Long Sentences

If long sentences are clumsily written in a non-authoritative text, one can either read them say twice, get the sense, write the sense in the target language, and then draw it closer to the original; or one can think out or write a more or less literal translation, and recast it till it makes sense and conforms to normal social usage. I prefer the second method, which also ensures one accounts for (and does not forget) any of the words. Typically, the TL sentence starts with the last segment, which conveys the communicative dynamism (CD) of the SL sentence.

Example: *Une réflexion sur la différenciation croissante, en termes de caractéristiques de fonctionnement de leurs 'marchés' respectifs, entre médecine générale où la concurrence entre praticiens s'accentue sous la pression démographique et médecine spécialisée qui échappe partiellement à ce phénomene, avec de plus grandes possibilités d'induction de la demande par l'offre et de constitution d'ententes de type oligopolistique dans certaines zones, contribuerait sans doute à mieux fonder la recherche de nouveaux modes de régulation.*

Literal translation: 'Thinking about the growing differentation, in terms of functional characteristics of their respective "markets" between general medicine where rivalry between practitioners is stressed under demographic pressure and specialised medicine which partially escapes this phenomenon, with greater possibilities of supply inducing demand and constituting agreements of an oligopolistic nature in certain zones, would doubtless contribute to a better justification of the search for new modes of regulation.'

Suggested translation: 'Undoubtedly we would to some extent achieve an improved basis for finding new methods of regulating health economics if we considered the increasing differentiation (in respect of the operational features of their respective "markets") between general medicine, where competition between general practitioners grows under demographic pressure, and specialised medicine, which is to some extent free from such competition; we should also find greater possibilities of stimulating demand through supply and setting up group practices in some areas.' Note: (1) When splitting long sentences, I prefer semi-colons to full stops. (2) I jibbed at 'oligopolistic' as it is pejorative, and went for what I think is the underlying meaning. (3) 'To some extent' (repeated!) is meant to cover *partiellement* and *contribuerait à.*

Three More Correlative Comparative Statements (see *Paragraphs* 6)

(d) The worse written the language of a non-authoritative text, the better and the more the translator has has to rewrite it by rephrasing and restructuring.

(e) The more explicit the language of a text, the more the translator remains at its linguistic level and the less responsibility she has for its underlying meaning. ('That's what the bloke wrote, so I'll leave it like that.')

(f) The more culturally embedded a 'persuasive' text (instructions, publicity, propaganda), the more SL cultural expressions have to be replaced by TL cultural expressions.

(I am devising these 'correlative statements' tentatively to partly dissolve the dichotomy between 'free' and 'literal', 'communicative' and 'semantic' etc.).

Two Poles of Translation

There are two poles of translation, one intended to capture 'full meaning', the second to convey 'simple message', and as usual there is a large interlapping area between the two. At the first pole, translation is descriptive, at the second it is a speech-act, illocutionary or perlocutionary, designed to produce a result or to have a result produced. (See *How to do things with words* by J. L. Austin.) The first is typically only partially successful and can be rated in terms of 'yield' (Donald Frame); thus the translation of a lyric (Verlaine in English?) may only have a yield of 40%, whilst a book on mathematics (no cultural clash?) may yield 95%. But at the opposite pole, say the translation of an advertisement or a manual of instructions or sometimes propaganda has to be 'happy' (J. L. Austin's word), and therefore 100% successful; otherwise it fails.

News from British Airways
More than £50 million was spent on translations last year by British companies aiming at Europe and other world markets for their products and services. Demand for translation services, including marketing brochures, letters, technical manuals etc. has risen by more than 50% in the last five years. (Every month British Airways publishes a miscellany *Business in Europe* in English, French, German and Italian; the translations are remarkably close.)

Paraphrase
A paraphrase expresses the meaning of a segment of text in other words. Intralingually, paraphrase is normally used to clarify or simplify. In translation, paraphrases like synonyms are always to be avoided where they are unnecessary (they often are), for which back translation provides the 'scientific' evidence. When a text segment cannot be closely translated (say *il me fait venir*), paraphrase in varying degrees of closeness has to be used; it may be lexical ('he summons, fetches me'), lexicogrammatical ('he sends for me') or mainly grammatical. (*Je ne peux pas le supporter;* I can't put up with it.)
A. Grozdanova, a Bulgarian linguist, has produced the following paraphrases, in order of closeness for the (Bulgarian) sentence:
1.0 Lekarite ne i davat da puši.
Her doctors won't let her smoke.
1.1 Lekarite ne i razrešavat da puši.
1. Her doctors do not allow her to smoke.
1.2 Lekarite ne i pozvoljavat da puši.
2. Her doctors do not permit her to smoke.
1.3 Lekarite i zabranjavat da puši.
3. Her doctors forbid her to smoke.
1.4 Lekarite i kazvat, če ne trjabva da puši.
4. Her doctors tell her that she shouldn't smoke.
1.5 Lekarite i kazvat da ne puši.
5. Her doctors tell her not to smoke.
1.6 Pušeneto i e zabraneno ot lekarite.
6. Smoking is forbidden her by her doctors.

1.7 Ne puši, zaštoto lekarite ne i davat.
7. She doesn't smoke because her doctors won't let her.
1.8 Zabraneno i e da puši.
8. She is forbidden to smoke.
1.9 Spored lekarite pušeneto e vredno za neja.
9. According to the doctors smoking is harmful to her.
1.10 Lekarite kazvat, če cigarite sa vredni za neja.
10. Her doctors say that cigarettes are harmful for her.

Note that the change of emphasis (theme-rheme reversal) in 7, 8 and 9 is ignored, and that many more variations are possible.

Acronyms

The following is a (tentative) frame of reference for the translations of acronyms, which I define broadly as a sequence of initial letters or syllables of two or more words denoting a single entity:

TYPE OF ACRONYM
1. International organization
2. National organization
3. Name of company
4. Technical entity
5. Geographical feature
6. Latin
7. Made up *ad hoc*

CONTEXTUAL FACTORS
1. Text type
2. Readership
3. Recency
4. Importance
5. Duration
6. Well-known?

TRANSLATION PROCEDURES
1. Transference
2. Reconstitution of acronym
3. Definition
4. No. 1 + No. 3
5. Write out in SL
6. Translate in full

The main principle in translating acronyms is to bear in mind the educational level and the requirements of the readership. Typically, an international organization (A.I.) is transferred; if 'required', it is written out (Amnesty International) and defined (say, human rights organization); or it is reconstituted (WHO = *OMS*), and, if required, written out and explained (*Organisation Mondiale de la Santé*, World

Health Organization)). A national organization (BM) may or may not be transferred, depending on its importance within the TL culture; it would usually only be written out in the TL (*Musée britannique*). The name of a private company is transferred. (GEC) if it is well-known in the TL; otherwise written out (General Electric Company). A geographical feature (KL, TCR) or the title of a book (*EB*) is written out (Kuala Lumpur; Tottenham Court Road, *Encyclopaedia Britannica*), unless the acronym is common in the TL. A Latin acronym (*e.g.*) is 'appropriately' translated (*z.B., p.ex.*). An acronym made up for the SL text can normally be reconstituted for the TL text, and should be, provided it is frequently used again; but the translator should discourage the practice of using or creating acronyms as an 'in' code, since translation is to reveal, not to exclude.

Keywords
I use the term 'keyword' in Raymond Williams's sense (but he never defined it): an important concept (typically but not always a noun) with a long culture history in one or more languages, sometimes an internationlism ('capitalism'), often with a universal core sense ('liberal') but then continuously loaded with new, more or less contiguous sometimes apparently contradictory fresh senses, both 'depreciative' and 'appreciative', some of which die whilst others live on. Some of these words ('populism') are used in a partisan way which is not known to others. I consider it to be one of a translator's responsibilities to explain, inside or outside the text, any keyword which, when translated, may mislead the appropriate TL readership; translation is to clarify, not to mystify. A reader is usually entitled to have a translation that offers no cultural difficulties. I discussed such keywords at length in *About Translation*.
So I hit on the important keyword 'Zionism', which I found I was using in a different sense to that of many others. My intention was simply to define some of the word's current senses. My own political views, though irrelevant (they appear to be precisely the same as Rabbi Julia Neuberger's, not to mention the spirit of Heinrich Heine, but not of Robert Maxwell), inevitably became apparent. But all my correspondents misunderstood my purpose. As is known, the UN 'Zionism equals Racism' equation has been rescinded. It was high time.
The meanings of the keywords 'communism' and 'socialism' are now in disarray, and have to be reinterpreted according to context. Several European communist parties have changed their names, usually replacing them with 'socialist'. The main sense of communism, 'advocacy of a classless society in which private ownership has been abolished and the means of production and subsistence belong to the community' may remain. 'Socialism', however, will probably be radically redefined, if its present semantic components such as 'state or

government control of all economic activity' and 'absence of economic competition' are to be dropped. The emphasis may be on combinations of co-operation, competition and capitalism(!) for the common welfare.

Desacralizing Vogue Words

In the last ten years(?) the media and the PR agents appear to have secularized 'mission' and 'vision', making them both into routine business strategies. Is the same fate about to overtake 'vocation', which according to my *Petit Robert* was secularized in French in the 70s, veering toward 'function' or 'task' and now appears in various drafts of the Maastricht treaty, 'obviously translated from the French' (my thanks to Anthony Crane, who sent me this extract from the *Times* of 12 October):

'In order to conclude in Maastricht and thus come closer to attaining European union, with a European vocation . . . (The treaty) must include all the questions related to security and defence with the aim, in the future, of a common defence.' The text may have originated in Dutch, but is French the general language of diffusion within the EEC?

Deculturalising Metaphor

In translating satirical novels, it is sometimes possible to de-culturalize a local metaphor. Thus in Evelyn Waugh's *Brideshead Revisited* 'Lyonnesse' can become 'Atlantis'; in Malcolm Bradbury's *Eating People is Wrong*, 'a Rupert Brooke without a Gallipoli' (actually, it was Skiros) can become 'a Byron without a Missolonghi' The alternative is to transfer the metaphors, but dynamic equivalence would be lost, and I doubt whether notes on Lyonnesse and Rupert Brooke would interest the foreign readership?

Spanish Translation Schools

Spain now has translation degrees at three universities: Barcelona (the 'autonoma'), Las Palmas, and the balmy Granada (F: *Grenade*). The interest in professional translation is enormous, and it is likely that Malaga and Vitoria will soon follow. Core courses on translation theory form part of these degrees. Granada publishes a wide-ranging periodical, *Sendebar*, which includes articles on *traductologia*, technical and literary translation, teaching, and terminology (edited by Luis Marquez Villegas. EUTI, Puentezuelas 55, Granada).

Mein Kampf

I have long considered that extracts from *Mein Kampf* should be in the syllabus of any course in European or German political or philosophical thought. The translation by Ralph Manheim (Hutchinson, 1974), with an introduction by D. C. Watt, is first rate. (The book was first disastrously 'translated' by Captain E. S. Dugdale as *My Struggle* in 1933 in an edition expurgated by the author.) D. C. Watt contributes an extensive and scholarly essay on the history and 'philosophy' of the book. Manheim's Translator's Note, a stylistic analysis is perceptive, commenting particularly on the journalistic clichés, the long sentences, the nominalizations and the particles. He uses notes mainly to point out factual historical mistakes and to quote the German when the translated sentence is particularly weird and obscure. Puzzlingly, he states that 'Many German writers feel that the substantive is the strongest and most impressive part of speech". This is surely true for any language. He closely and vividly reproduces the intolerable heaviness, intensity and repetitiveness of Hitler's discourse. (In one paragraph: infinitely hated . . . the whole existence . . . completely indifferent . . . positively terrifying . . . ultimate final aims . . . continuous lie . . . shown incomparably.) All these are literal translations, but *geradezu grauenerregender* gives a shudder-making alliterative indication of German force.)

St Albans
St Albans is a 'model' town for multilingual development. It is exceptionally beautiful and attracts an increasing number of visitors. The Cathedral publishes excellent brochures in four languages (no Dutch or Spanish) closely translated without misprints. But the superb museum is still monolingual, and the town needs multilingual notices.

Standards of Translation
I believe that there are good and bad translations, and that the difference between the two can be assessed through evidence, and that mainly but not entirely objective evaluations of translations can be made. Further, I assume that John Keats is a better poet than Bob Dylan, and that a Michelangelo mural is better than a *graffito* on the wall of a public lavatory; however, the drift of movements such as reception theory, deconstruction, structuralism, pop art, post-structuralism (which have influenced the translatologists, if not the translators), since they disconnect language or sense from reality or reference, lead one to question the existence of any moral or aesthetic standards, in translation as in art; the exclusive concern with the process and not the product of translation is equally detrimental, if it is to consist of an uncritical record or diary of translators working. (And what ever happened to Even Zohar's Transfer theory, interference theory and functionalist theory none of which recognized values or standards, and which were meant to swallow up translation theory?) I regard accuracy as the main criterion of quality in a full translation. If the purpose of the text is to achieve an effect, the translation will be accurate if it achieves it. In all other cases, accuracy covers not only the

maximum reproduction of meaning, but discrimination in assessing the value and importance of the meaning of various segments of a text.

The Tate Gallery

For foreign (? non-British?) modern paintings, the Tate appears to be following the good practice of keeping the original titles and translating them into English; there remains the obligation of translating the English titles into at least French and German. The recent entrancing Morandi etchings were well translated, although *poggio* is surely 'hillock' rather than 'hillside'.

I have rightly been reminded that it is more urgent to have multilingual notices in all hospitals (add: clinics, police stations, town halls, municipal offices, police courts, public libraries, post offices, all phone booths) than in art galleries. I believe that all public buildings should have multilingual notices, and that this should be a part of the Institute's national language policy.

The Translation and Adaptation of Plays

The lighter the play, the more it can be 'adapted', the less closely it need be translated. As emerged from a recent discussion between translator Ranjit Bolt and the critic Michael Billington, one does not translate *Tartuffe* in the same way as *Les Femmes Savantes*. *Tartuffe* has much humour (which in translation has to make the spectator laugh), but it is a serious play, and the women are more sensible ('feminist') than the men. *Les Femmes Savantes* is about pretentious blue-stockings, and it seems to me quite legitimate (i.e. in the spirit of Molière) to make them into fanatical and absurd 'feminists', as Ranjit Bolt has done.

Zaïde

Ruhe sanft, mein holdes Leben ('Rest softly, my sweet life') outclasses and outshines everything else in *Zaïde*, the recently revived *singspiel* (type of early comic opera) that Mozart wrote in 1780; the wonderful aria is rarely sung, let alone noticed. The closest equivalent of *sanft* is 'soft' (both derive from OHG *semti*), but *sanft* unlike soft is only used to express tender emotion, which is prolonged by the additional (alveolar nasal) continuant. *Hold* is an old-fashioned literary word, whose central meaning is 'gracious' or 'favourable'. *Ruhe sanft*, which is startling and out of this world, leads to *Zeffiretti lusinghieri* ('Flattering little breezes') in *Idomeneo* and to *Soave sia il vento* ('May the wind be gentle') in *Così fan tutte*. (I have to remind such readers as I still have that in spite of the bicentenary (*Mozartkugeln* — Mozart balls, what balls), when I mention the word Mozart (Schubert, Janáček etc), anything else including translation immediately becomes irrelevant.)

Phrasal Words Again

Basically, phrasal words restore to English its physical, non-abstract, Anglo-Saxon monosyllabic strength. They are also a resource for translating foreign reflexive verbs. Thus: *s'effriter*, 'crumble away'; *se coucher*, lie down; *se coincer*, wedge in; *s'enfiler*, 'make off into'.

Quine and Translation

In my opinion, Michael Dummett successfully refuted Quine's influential and misleading behaviourist theory on the indeterminacy (plus erroneousness and impossibility) of translation many years ago, but Robert Kirk appears to have done it again in *Translation Determined* (Clarendon Press, Oxford, 1966. ISBN 0-19-824-921-7). The book is addressed to philosophers, linguists and psychologists, not to translators, and I am not competent to criticize it, but it demonstrates little interest in any foreign language, let alone in translation.

The Linguistic Truth

I have already discussed four factors that tend neither to the source nor the target language text, but are medial forces, potentially or actually, in the process of translating: these are the factual, the moral, the aesthetic and the logical truth. A fifth factor may be tentatively designated as the linguistic truth. The linguistic truth is 'pure language', Walter Benjamin's *reine Sprache*, the ideal comprehensive language of which all natural languages are components, the language of completion or of supplementation (*Ergänzungssprache*), which fills in the grammatical and lexical gaps in each natural language such as are stimulated by outside reality; it is therefore a dynamic concept. It has perhaps its surrogate centres in Brussels for Euro-English, as well as in America. It is leading to the convergence of European languages through contact and large-scale interference. Its analogue is the Sacred Text, the Bible for English, the Koran for Arabic. Translation is facilitated because natural languages complement rather than equal each other. The complementarity existed from the beginning in a rudimentary form, but it is being worked out all the time, most notably in English, said to be three times larger than any other language, through the continuous adoption of foreign cultural terms and transparent Grecolatinisms, which, to a limited degree, deculturalize and universalize English itself. The force of linguistic truth is to make translation gradually easier, but there are various countervailing forces too.

Questions of Meaning

Meaning is often categorized (Ogden and Richards in *The Meaning of Meaning* distinguished about thirty varieties), but it might be more useful to sensitize the translator by asking meaning-related questions when a sentence or a sentence-component is obscure:

1. Is the sentence or one of its components being used figuratively?
2. Is the sentence ironical, and should the irony be made more explicit in the translation, particularly for Arabic?
3. Is a noun being used without its headword? ('Post' as 'letters' or 'post office'?)
4. Is an idiom being adapted or truncated? ('This point must not be "overegged" . . . "overegging the cake" ').
5. Does this represent a state or a process or an act?
6. Is a general word being used instead of a specific term? ('The army (one soldier) is coming').
7. Is this humorous hyperbole?
8. What is the purpose of this sentence?
9. Is the sentence in the wrong place? Have the wrong words been used? (Lateral thinking).
10 Is this an abstract or a concrete noun? (*La rupture* . . . 'break' or 'setback'? For whom? By whom? For what? Abstractions are particularly common in economic texts).
11. General or cultural expression?

In Praise of Approximations
Au long de quinze kilomètres, aucune construction n'apparaît. In such a context, *au long de quinze kilomètres* might be 'for fifteen kilometres' or 'for ten miles'; it could not be 'for 9.4 miles'. For translation, one often has to decide whether a figure is exact or an approximation. An approximation normally has more impact and is useful in calculating ratios and fractions which are even more effective; a precise figure (*18 Jahre 2 Minuten* again (*Magic Flute*)) is often ridiculous. (Note that both *trente-six* and *sitt:iin (= 'sixty' in Arabic) mean 'umpteen').

De Gaulle
Villages tranquilles et peu fortunés dont rien, depuis des millénaires, n'a changé ni l'âme ni la place. Ainsi, du mien.
'Tranquil and penurious villages, whose soul and whose market square, nothing, for thousands of years, has ever changed. Thus, my own village.'
Place as 'place' or 'position' would not make sense here, as it offends the 'logical truth'; besides, the *place* is the heart of most French villages.) Translating this great writer and great man, whom I revere, my only criterion outside literal translation, which includes the retention of emphases, is to retain the dignity and the harmony of the original. Even the normal shift from relative clause to past principle (e.g. *les terres que cultivent les habitants*) is undignified, so it has to remain 'the lands which the inhabitants cultivate'. The English has to

be modern, uncontrived, subject to no literary or poetic fashion, simple, serious.
Many structures, however 'French', should be kept: *Leurs familles, je les connais, je les estime et je les aime.* 'Their families, I know them, I value (esteem?) them and I love them.' De Gaulle is lovely.

Translation Theory

Translation theory draws first on general and applied linguistics (sociolinguistics, psycholinguistics, phonosemantics), since translation is finally linguistic, not cultural; secondly on stylistics, linguistic and literary criticism, cultural sociology, logic, moral philosophy and the relevant topic.

Arabic

At an international conference on 'Teaching and Translating Arabic' held recently at the School of Oriental and African Studies, University of London, convened by M. Salih and M. A. S. Abdel Haleen (the proceedings will be published), Dr Haleen noted and regretted the fact that whilst since the Authorized Version the English Bible has normally been translated by translator-teams (but Ronald Knox's New Testament is an exception), the Koran has only been translated into English by individuals. Basil Hatim and Brian Harris read remarkable papers on 'The Translation of Irony' and 'Redundancies in translation from Arabic'. It was a rich and thought-provoking conference.

French Economic Terms: Some Suggested Translations

Plan de charge, 'business plan'; *grands travaux* 'major projects'; *structure commerciale*, 'market oriented structure'; *personnel d'exécution*, 'operational staff'; *un établissement public symbole*, 'a representative public corporation'; *la prospective et la transversalité*, 'forecasting (forward planning?) and inter-company communication'. (All from I.O.L. DipTrans Business Paper, 1991). Add *la rupture (retournement) de la conjoncture*, 'abrupt economic setback'.

XVIII
APRIL 1992

Hymn to a Multilingual Coffee Maker

The Rowenta coffee maker (*Kaffeemaschine, appareil électrique*) has a manual of instructions in eleven languages: German, English, French, Italian, Portuguese, Dutch, Spanish, Danish, Swedish, Norwegian, Finnish. This type of technical translation is typically the easiest and perhaps the most tedious of any type of translation. There are no cultural or connotational difficulties, no metaphors (except dead ones), few idioms, no colloquialisms. In this booklet there are no new technical terms. This text only resists literal translation in (a) forms of address, (b) technical terms which describe the object from various points of view, and which may be more generalised or particularised, (c) syntactic differences, (d) the translators' apparently arbitrary decisions. The text has to be uniformly explicit, without undertones, and clearly, concisely and elegantly written, rendering the complete denotative meaning of the original; it may be tedious, but it will still give an indication of each translator's competence.

Eight brief extracts may be of interest:

German: *Erste Inbetriebnahme:*
Zum Reinigen des Gerätes empfiehlt es sich, 1-2 Brühvorgänge nur mit Wasser (ohne Kaffeemehl) durchzuführen.

English: Using for the first time:
It is advisable to clean the coffee maker before use. We recommend allowing it to run through its operating cycle twice, filled with water only, i.e. no ground coffee.

French: *Première utilisation:*
Il est recommandé de faire un premier passage avec de l'eau seulement (sans mouture), afin de nettoyer la cafetière.

Dutch: *Voor het eerste gebruik:*
Voordat u het koffiezetapparaat in gebruik neemt, verdient het aanbeveling deze 1 a 2 keer alleen met water (zonder gemalen koffie) te gebruiken.

Italian: *Primo impiego:*
Per pulire internamente la caffettiera, prima di usarla per la prima volta, si consiglia di riempire il serbatoio d'acqua ed azionare la caffettiera facendo 1 o 2 passaggi completi di sola acqua (senza caffè) procedendo nel modo sequente.

Spanish: *Primera puesta en servicio:*
Para limpiar el aparato se recomienda que antes de su uso normal se hagan primero dos o tres (sic!) cafeteras con agua sola.

Portuguese: *Primeira utilizacao:*

E aconselhável fazer una primeira passagem de agua (sem mistura de café), sómente para limpar a cafeteira.

Danish: *Forste ibrugtagning:*
Til rengoring af kaffemaskinen anbefaler vi at foretage en brygning med vand alene (uden kaffe).

Swedish: *Forsta anvandningen:*
For att rengora kaffebryggaren rekommenderas att genomfora de forsta 1–2 bryggningarna med enbart vatten (utan kaffe).

Norwegian: *Forste gangs bruk:*
For at kaffetrakteren skal vaere helt ren, lonner det seg a gjennomfore 1–2 traktinger bare med vann (uten kaffepulver).

Finnish: *(Suomi): Ensimmainen kaytto:*
Puhdista keitin kuumentamalla siina pelkkaa vetta (ilman kahvijauhetta).

Instruction manuals differ from the mass of technical writing in being addressed to a general readership, and with a particular sense of urgency and explicitness. The English passive, so common in technical writing, frequently gives way to the imperative form of address, though not in this example. It is the only one that uses the personal 'we' form and is perhaps the most agreeable translation. The multi-word nominalisations of English and German technical writing are also missing. The translations differ in their degree of explicitness (the Dutch omits the purpose of the exercise); the Italian, followed by the English, is the most verbose, and the Finnish, being the most synthetic, the most concise, and the most opaque.

Translation and the Nature of Philosophy

Translation and the Nature of Philosophy by Andrew Benjamin (Routledge, 1989; ISBN 0 415 04485 5) is more concerned with philosophy than with translation, though it purports to formulate a 'new theory of words', which I find elusive. Here is a typical extract:

'Difference understood as original difference — differential plurality as an original — both emerges in, as well as provides the conditions of possibility for conflicts of interpretation. For philosophical studies this has the fundamental importance of reorientating interpretation, moving it away from concerns with finality and truth [why truth?] and towards the textuality of the object of interpretation ... The importance of textuality takes place within the impossibility of the presence of a unified original frame of meaning that excludes semantic differential plurality (p. 38).' 'Of course', to use one of the author's favourite expressions, and of course no example is offered. The chapter on Freud's use of the term *übersetzen* is unenlightening, and there is a good discussion of five translations of a sentence from Aristotle's *Metaphysics*. But the 'post-structuralist presence' (blurb) pervades the book.

Translation of Film Titles

In a recent *Guardian* article (21 December 1991) John Wyatt pointed out that the film title *Chariots of Fire* was translated as *Les Chariots de feu*, meaning 'Trolleys of Fire', which can be described as a straightforward howler, whilst *Rita, Sue and Bob too*, which is a neat almost monosyllabic rhyme, became *Rita, Sue et Bob aussi* and puns as *Rita Sue et Bob aussi*, i.e. 'Rita sweats and so does Bob'. Some translated film titles are created for their effectiveness rather than their closeness to the originals: hence *Liaison fatale* for *Fatal Attraction; Les dents de la mer* for *Jaws; Docteur Folamour* for *Doctor Strangelove*. Many translated film titles, however, bear no relation to their original titles, and select another feature of their films: thus *Porc royal* for *Private Function; Bons baisers de Liverpool* for *Letter to Brezhnev; Les enfants du silence* for *Shoestring*. There is also the increasing practice of transferring titles, if they are neat (*Au revoir, les enfants!; Belles de jour: Jour de fête: La cage aux folles)*, and, in France, *My Beautiful Laundrette; Full Metal Jacket; Torch Song Trilogy*. Sometimes English titles get snappier English titles in France: thus *Feathers à la française* becomes *Fatal Games, Coal Miner's Daughter* is *Nashville Lady*, and *Wish you were here!* is *Too much!!*, which apparently is French for *C'est trop*. Finally, *No sex please — we're British* is *No sex please — nous sommes anglais —* described by John Wyatt as 'truly Federalist franglais'.

There can be no principles about the translation of the titles of entertainment films — let them stay amusing and illogical — but one would hope that the titles of serious films would be transferred or closely translated, as they are for operas and plays. Further, it appears logical that the titles of sub-titled films should be transferred, unless they are impenetrable and consist of more than two words, whilst the titles of dubbed films, which are likely to be for mass entertainment, should be appealingly translated.

The Grain of English

I think that the grain of English follows monosyllabic phrasal words and goes against polysyllabic grecolatinisms like 'interculturality' and 'translatology'; this even holds good for computer science, but not for medicine.

The Göttingen Group

Interculturality and the Historical Study of Literary Translations, edited by Harald Kittel and Armin Paul Frank (Erich Schmidt, Berlin 1991 ISBN 3 503 03015 8) appears to be the first study in English published by the Göttingen Centre for the Study of Literary Translation, which has links with Theo Hermans, Susan Bassnett, José Lambert and Gideon Toury. The group produced a manifesto, which I have not yet seen, but whose flavour can be gathered from the comment 'For the historical — descriptive study of translations . . . a source-text based approach is inadequate . . . but the exclusively target-side based approach recently promoted [presumably by the Centre?] is not the answer.' (p. 61). In fact, the answer proposed, a study of the SLT and TLT differences, is a rather overblown platitude; the text, a study of French and German translations of *The Waste Land* contains some fascinating details, but, in spite of the diagrams, merely concludes that a 'comprehensive theory of translation must take discontinuities between Scripture, literature and technical writing into account'.

Another contributor, Erika Hulpke, however, is an even bolder dissident: 'By comparing a translation with its source text, we can assess the effect of censorship more precisely than by studying an original work written under censorship conditions'. This seems obvious, if one substitutes 'translation' for 'original work' in this context; for in fact Ms Hulpke has written a fascinating brief study of a German translation written after the censorship laws of 1819 of Washington Irving's short story, *Rip Van Winkle*; the time of the action is moved back from 1776, after the Declaration of American Independence, to 1770, the reign of George II; the main character Nicolas Vedder, is no longer an independent ruler, but a civil servant; everything that might remind the German reader of a successful revolution is eliminated. Ms Hulpke's essay exposes the political abuse of translation, and does not concern itself with its place in the German literary 'polysystem'.

Birgit Wetzel-Sahm shows how Mark Twain's dead-pan humour was jigged up by an emotional and immature Karl May type style, whilst Wilhelm Graeber shows how in the 18th Century, after Lessing's vigorous criticism, e.g. in the *Hamburgische Dramaturgie*, second-hand translation of English via French into German, introducing a refined, stiff and humourless type of language, was gradually replaced by direct translation from English into German. José Lambert is concerned with the classification of literature according to its genres rather than its geographical origins by 'literary scientists' (*sic*), and shows scant interest in its interpretation.

Literary Translation

An engrossing conference on literary translation, confronting authors with their translators (Claude Delarue and Vivienne Menkes; A. S. Byatt and Jean-Louis Chevalier) was held at the London French Institute in January. The following conclusions possibly emerged:

1. Ambiguities are more common in fiction than in other texts, since the language is connotative.

2. French is restricted to a smaller vocabulary and a stricter, narrower word-order and grammar than English.

3. French is more philosophical and metaphysical (i.e. more abstract and opaque) than English.

4. The gulf between written and spoken language is greater in French than in English. (It is partially bridged in English by phrasal verbs.)

5. The English translator tends to break up long French sentences (particularly relative clauses).

6. The more explicit the sentence, the fewer the options (possible variations) for the translator.

7. Incomplete sentences, being connotative, are the hardest to translate.

8. All language is provisional. When author meets translator, both parties change their minds, have second thoughts, are not sure or forget what they originally meant. But the word in print gives the translation a certain permanence. (*Je crois à l'imprimé*. J-L. Chevalier). In any event this apparent fluctuation, which appears to challenge the status of translation (Sarah Marsh), is greatly restricted in its scope, and should not go beyond the deficiencies of the source language text, the grammatical and lexical gaps of the target language, and the tastes of the translator.

Words You Hate to Translate

A serial column on this topic has been kindly suggested to me by a reader. I have already discussed *assurer* and *retenir*. For German, my bugbear is *Anlage*, to which the *Langenscheidt* assigns 18 senses, followed by *Leistung* (17 senses), and for French I would add *charge*, *service*, *effort* and *prestation*. My reader suggests *Belastung* (9 senses) and *verrechnen*. Many German words beginning with *ver-, ein-* (*einstellen*), *um-, auf-* (the notorious Hegelian *Aufhebung*, 'cancellation' plus 'preservation') or *ab-* come in this category, since they may have contradictory senses. As for *permettre de*, so favoured in economic texts, I tend to simply ignore, i.e. not translate it.

Redefining Translation

Redefining Translation: the Variational Approach by Lance Hewson and Jacky Martin (Routledge; London and New York 1991 ISBN 0-415-03787-5) is a solid, substantial and challenging contribution to translation theory and practice. Whilst the first part of the book is mainly theoretical (and overcharged with grecolatinisms such as 'homologon', 'aoristic' and 'surmodalising'), the second part incorporates the theory in an analysis of seven English and three French texts — literary and non-literary — and their translations.

The book's main emphasis is on the translator's choice. There is a succession of syntactic units in all texts which have to be considered intra- and extratextually, as 'homologa' (*sic*) each containing in the source and target language, 'many variations in a vast paraphrastic set'. The only example given is the following list of 'syntagms': a brave (*sic*); a hero; a man of courage; a brave/courageous man; a man who has courage; a man who knows no fear; a Hector (*sic!*), whose common formula is the relation between 'a male human individual' and 'absence of sensitivity to danger'. This common denominator serves to effect conversions, comparisons and manipulations, presumably between the source and the target language text.

For the authors, the essence of translation is paraphrase, a term which is not loosely used; in fact the rigour of its application is neatly summarised in a diagram (p. 183), which takes the reader through a process of production of homologies, cultural equations, various socio-cultural/economic parameters, up to the final selection. In practice, this is often brilliantly illustrated in the course of the analysis and translation of the ten texts, where the number of possible variations is mercifully restricted.

What is missing is a set of criteria; the authors fail to define translation or its purposes, though they dismiss virtually everything written about the subject in the literature. The theoretical part of the book is debilitated by too many banalities: 'the systematic construction of texts which translation has to account for has finally to be envisaged as being oriented towards a finality expressed in textual strategies. Both formulation and referencing as constitutive of meaning definition are finally organised in the perspective of overall strategies which gear texts to their often complete referential functions and objectives.' (p. 96) Such heavy sentences at a high level of abstraction without any examples disfigure much of the first part of the book. Further, the authors write as though no translation theorist had ever discussed the reader (Nida's pioneering contribution is ignored), the 'translation initiator' (Lefevère has written more pungently) or even translation criticism (Juliane House's *A Model for Translation Quality Assessment* is not even in the Bibliography.) Vinay and Darbelnet are scantly treated; in spite of their scorn for the *chassé-croisé* procedure, the authors make effective use of it ('clamour against'; *assaillir de leurs clameurs*, pp. 234 and 204). Moreover all cultures are stated to be 'radically different' (p. 48), and the prospect of a 'middle term' is not seriously considered.

The strength of the book lies in its subtle and sophisticated analysis of cultural and linguistic differences in the particular texts; (excellent comments on Warm Springs and Opatija (Abbazia); 'nationalise' and 'social ownership' — two of many); its rejection of final versions, if not of 'finality', which they use in the French sense of the word; its persistent 'variations' (but not enough attention to 'parasitic paraphrases') and its weight (the 'clearly' and the 'of course's' take their toll.) It's not my kind of book (I operate at a 'lower' level, though I reject the proposition that literary texts (*Lear?*) are 'subject to the same constraining norms as patents') but I respect it.

Asterix or Getafix

Since *Asterix* seems to have an unfailing fascination for translation post-graduates (Spurius, Odius Asparagus), it may be helpful to quote some of Anthea and Derek Hockridge's golden rules for translating comic strips:
1. Keep the feel of the original [Stylistic register?]
2. Don't try to translate puns literally. Make a different joke to fit the spirit of the French one. [What if Romance and English puns coincide?]
3. Make sure the English fits the drawings [and diagrams, for technical texts], particularly facial expressions [and in children's stories].
4. Have roughly the same number of jokes — knockabout and literary — even if they aren't quite in the same places as in the original strip. [Compensation, as in translations of light comedy or farce] (See *Sunday Times*, *Funday Times*, 26.1.92).

The House on the Hill Upturned

Le ministère d'État chargé des affaires sociales; not 'The Ministry for Social Affairs', but 'the Ministry (the Ministry of Labour) responsible for social questions'.

Translation Studies

The revised edition (1991) of Susan Bassnett-McGuire's *Translation Studies* (Routledge ISBN 0 415 06528 3) preserves the original text and has a new Preface and select Bibliography for 1980–1990, from which Juliane House is again regrettably omitted. The Preface, reviewing mainstream literary translation theory in the last ten years, gives rather too much emphasis on the Manipulative school and not enough on the impact of discourse analysis, but it is stimulating and modish enough. Ms Bassnett states that 'finally (*sic*) the old normative discussions have begun to die away', but she forgets that employers still have to assess translations and translators; professional translators like Paul Danaher are still seeking criteria for good translation, and even in literary translation, which is mainly what Ms Bassnett is concerned with, translations as free and inaccurate as those published earlier in this century would no longer be tolerated (as I have shown). Ms Bassnett believes that 'raising the status of the translator and the translated text will improve the quality of translations'. I see no correlation.

The Importance of the Target Language

I have previously written that accuracy and economy are the main purposes (and therefore criteria) of a good translation. I substitute 'writing well' for 'economy', economy being included within good writing. I think that the translator, the technical and general as much as the literary translator, has to write well (neatly, elegantly), both formally and informally, deploying and manipulating the full range of syntactic structures and an extensive vocabulary, as the target text typically has to be clear and agreeable to read, therefore free from the ambiguities, vogue-words and otiose jargon of so many of the (non-authoritative) texts that have to be translated. The customer has to be pleased as well as informed.

Personally, I have always found a high correlation among students between good writing and the other translation skills. When Martin and Hewson (see above) discuss 'Dissimilative Competence (DC!), presumably the ability to discriminate nicely between various TL versions of a stretch of text, do they mean much more than writing well? Of which they are hardly paradigms.

The Poetics of Imperialism

The Poetics of Imperialism: Translation and Colonization from the Tempest to Tarzan by Erich Cheyfitz (OUP 1991 ISBN 0-19-505095-9) states that American imperialism has functioned historically and still functions by continuously renewing its politics of translation; the relations between the Old World colonists or settlers and the New World colonised or natives are described in terms of literal (proper) or metaphorical translation, or of the refusal to translate (which represses the difficulties of communication). Examples are variously taken from Columbus, the confrontation between Prospero and Caliban (the 'cannibal') in *The Tempest*, the Renaissance, American imperialism, European literature from Montaigne to Fanon, and Edgar Rice Burroughs' *Tarzan of the Apes*. Translation is seen as usurpation and transportation, but also as a humanising activity. Place (*topos*, property) is seen as the 'seat' of every culture, which is based on an ideology. The analysis is severely critical, subtle and able; the (two) references to a contrasting socialism are now rather sad. It is a dualistic, confrontational book, without a hint of any third term universal values. It is also quite original and remarkable.

The Moral Responsibility of the Translator

Susan Bassnett states that 'the translator cannot be the author of the SL text, but as the author of the TL text has a clear moral responsibility to the TL readers' (*Translation Studies*, p. 23); this is incontrovertible, but to support her proposition, she adduces Neubert's view (later supported by the Russian translation theorist, A. D. Sveycer, who wants 'summer's day' replaced by 'beautiful weather' or some such), that Shakespeare's sonnet 'Shall I compare thee to a summer's day?'

cannot be 'semantically' translated into a language where summers are unpleasant. I disagree with this view, (a) because the context of the sonnet (e.g. 'darling buds of May') makes it clear to the non-anglophone reader that summers are beautiful in England (sometimes), and if necessary, this could be explained extra-textually, (b) the translator also has a moral duty to Shakespeare, (c) repeated imaginative reading will eventually induce dynamic equivalence (or dramatic illusion)! (I believe that Neubert has since withdrawn from his position.)

Enceintes de Confinement Renforcés

If in a technical (nuclear engineering) text I am unable to trace a term (appearing in a list virtually out of linguistic context), I assume that it may be spoken rather than written, or that it may be descriptive rather than a term of art. *Enceinte* is the 'shell' or 'vessel' of a reactor, and I assume that the reference is to a 'pressure-vessel' (*récipient à pression, cuve sous pression*). To play fair to the 'translation initiator' or 'translation commissioner' or 'commissioning agent' (I prefer the third term), I would translate with a descriptive term 'reinforced containment structures', and offer 'reinforced pressure vessels' as an alternative in a footnote. In the same text, *a contrario 'per contra'*, could be translated as 'on the contrary' (in the context, 'in its favour' is more appropriate), and *stockage définitif des verres* as 'final storage of the glass containers'; they illustrate typical F to E translation procedures: (a) replacing Latin by English phrases; (b) filling out an abbreviated compound.

Translation Theory

Translation Theory is mainly about what you do when you can't or don't translate literally. Usually, there's a lot to choose and decide from.

Lebensweisheit?

I was educated in the tenets that reason is superior to feeling and that perfect knowledge is useless. Long ago I rejected both tenets. I think that reason is nugatory unless it is informed by feeling which induces action, and that knowledge must always be useful. So when I write, I am never controversial for the sake of being controversial, and I usually learn more from my adversaries than from those who agree with me.

XIX
JUNE 1992

Translating Poetry

Translating Poetry: The Double Labyrinth, ed. Daniel Weissbort (Macmillan London 1989 ISBN 0 333 46056 1) is a collection of essays written at the request of Prof. Weissbort, who asked his distinguished contributors, including Ted Hughes, Michael Hamburger, Richard Wilbur, W. S. Merwin and James Kirkup, to write diaries recording the stages of their translating. Nearly all refused, and sent essays instead. The result is little insight into the process of translating poetry, which is individual and perhaps not instructive, but, in the best of these pieces, penetrating insight into some of the poems. Pound wrote that translation is the highest form of criticism (which has a certain truth), and here Keith Bosley offers an illuminating introduction to the French Baroque poet Jean de la Ceppède, who is not well known as his contemporary, Jean de Sponde. In discussing his two versions of the sonnet *Aux monarques vainqueurs*, Bosley shows how he moves from one interpretation of the second quatrain to another. John Felstiner drafts and redrafts his version of Celan's enigmatic *Einem, der vor der Tür stand*, by continually asking himself and answering, with alternatives, questions about why Celan wrote this or that word. George Kline struggles with Joseph Brodsky over several versions of a stanza in Brodsky's *Nature Morte*.

Finally, in commenting on Akhmatova's poems, Stanley Kunitz invites controversy: 'Every language reflects a set of social conventions and has its roots in the character and history of a people. In a poem that deals with human affections, it is the culture that determines how much expressiveness is tolerable in an exchange between persons. What sounds genuine and moving in one language may strike the reader in another as bombastic and insincere.' (No example is given.) I think this is at the least overstated; I think emotion that is memorably expressed is universal not cultural and penetrates the social conventions, which exist but are not all that exists.

Economic Acronyms

Les BTAN, bons du Trésor à taux annuel, de maturité à l'émission de 2 ans et de 5 ans. Normally, I would translate this snippet from *Problèmes économiques* as 'BTAN (*bons du Trésor à taux annuel*), Treasury bonds at fixed rates, maturing two and five years after date of issue', assuming an expert readership interested in the French terms, and retaining the acronym for economy, since it is several times referred to in the rest of the article. If the text were addressed to a general readership, the acronym and the French term could be omitted, and an English acronym (TBFR) reconstituted *ad hoc* for the English reader, to be repeated in the rest of the article.

Note that the *Trésor* is only a department in the French Finance Ministry, and is translated literally only by convention; in American English, 'Treasury bills' are also 'Treasury bonds'. (See *Le Nouveau Guide France* by Guy Michaud and Alain Kimmel (1990; Hachette ISBN 2 01 015387) for graphic summaries of French history and modern institutions.)

Economic Pretentiousness

La réforme du financement de l'État était consubstantielle à celle de la place toute entière. 'The reform of government financing entailed the reform of the whole money market.' The religious term *consubstantiel*, meaning 'of the same substance as' is as out of place in the English as in the French; 'was inseparable from' would be a closer translation than the above. There are normally more variations available in non-authoritative than in authoritative texts, in particular where no one-to-one equivalents are available; positives are to be preferred to negatives (except for intentional understatements) as they make for stronger contrasts.

The Peripeteias of Liberalism

Pendant la grande crise des années trente, le dogme libéral a été renversé aussi bien par l'esprit populaire ('Augmentez le pouvoir d'achat pour stimuler la consommation'), que par Keynes, qui a donné à ce principe la forme scientifique nécessaire pour la faire accepter parmi les clercs. (La Tragédie du Pouvoir. Alfred Sauvy)

Suggested translation: 'During the Crisis in the 30s, laissez-faire dogma was overturned by public (popular?) opinion ('Increase purchasing power and stimulate consumption') as well as by Keynes, who gave this principle the appropriate form to make it acceptable to the experts.' Note that it would be misleading to translate *libéral* as 'liberal'. (See Thody and Evans: *Faux Amis and Key Words*.) Acceptable variations might be: 'classical economic' or 'free market dogma'. Note also that since Benda's *La Trahison des Clercs, clercs* can be 'experts', 'scholars' or 'intellectuals'.

Translation and Foreign Language Competence

There is evidence that British industry, prodded by the Government and by the EC, is belatedly and slowly becoming aware of the importance of foreign language skills, and oral fluency in particular, in its export business. What it lacks now is an understanding of the profession and the industry of translation, which is a different concern. ('Any fool can learn a foreign language; it requires intelligence to translate'. (me)) In industry, translating is a professional and technological process, requiring legal, business and subject expertise; where it is a feature of a launch, it has to be integrated at every stage in a corporate marketing . . . strategy. Gradually the business appears to be becoming too complicated for firms and multinationals; it requires the specialised resources of multinational translation companies.

Aesthetic Truth
Aesthetic truth perhaps derives, materially at least, from the balanced and classical features of the shape and the movements of the human body (and their analogues in animal bodies and natural phenomena such as leaves, flowers and trees), and, for music in particular, from the tones and volume of the human voice (and its analogues in animal cries and the sounds of weather or nature). These are ideal and universal phenomena; but beauty is also in irregularities and deviations — 'Whatever is fickle, freckled (who knows how?)' (Hopkins) — these are the changing, particular elements, which may be cultural as well as individual, which are always present in aesthetic truth. It is the combination of these three factors — the universal, the cultural and the personal, which makes an aesthetic passage so difficult to translate. All principles of literary style and good writing derive from aesthetic truth.

The French Historic Future (The Obituary Future)
French obituaries sometimes begin with a death in the past tense and the successive stages of a life in the future. Furthermore, in many historical passages, one can only spot the historical future by comparing the date of an event in the text with the date of publication or the chronological viewpoint of the author. (Sorry, example temporarily mislaid!) A more remote 'obituary conditional' tense is also used, thus: *En 1965, la nouvelle Commission unique serait formée de 9 membres désignés par les gouvernements*; 'the new single Commission consisting of nine members appointed by their governments was (alt. 'was to be') set up in 1965.

The Independence of a Translation
Take these quotations: 'A baser meaning has been read into these characters the literal sense of which decency can safely scarcely hint . . . Evidentament he has failed as the deuce before for she is wearing none of the three.' Has a translation ever sounded so much like a translation as *Finnegans Wake*, from which these are extracts?

The Sheer Delight
Le Mariage de Figaro (Beaumarchais) . . . *Le Nozze di Figaro* (Da Ponte) . . . *Die Hochzeit des Figaro* . . . *The Marriage of Figaro* . . .

Nozze and *Hochzeit* both mean 'Wedding'. I assume Da Ponte found *Il Matrimonio* too clumsy, and the German translator followed him. (How did *Die Entführung aus dem Serail* become *The Seraglio*?)

Standards and Truth

'*It cannot be stressed enough* that the production of different translations at different times does not point to any 'betrayal' of absolute standards, but rather to the absence, *pure and simple*, of any such standards. *Such are the facts of life* in the production- and study- of translations.' (*Translation, History and Culture*, Susan Bassnett and André Lefevère. p. 5) The three bludgeoning clichés (italicised) in such a little space — when I see such clichés, (add: 'I cannot emphasise sufficiently', 'It is crucial/important/interesting to note that . . .') I usually suspect that their opposites are true — ought to be warning enough that a dubious statement is being propounded. There is rather a gap between 'absolute standards' and 'an absence of standards', which is here ignored. I think there are standards in all translations. There is plenty of evidence even in this uneven book, e.g. in the contrast made by Piotr Kuhiwozak between the distorted early 'transcultural' translation of Milan Kundera's *The Joke* and the later 'faithful' version made with Kundera's approval; or Lefevère's remark that after 1800, the 'worst excesses' of free translation (referred to as *traductio*!) came to an end.

'The concepts of norms and rules, as well as the function of the translated text, were introduced nearly a decade ago by Gideon Toury. Yet his somewhat more than hermetic [!] style . . .' (*ibid*, p. 5). Neubert discussed the various functions of translations about thirty years ago, and if 'rules' means 'methods', they have been discussed for centuries. 'With the demise of the notion of equivalence as sameness and recognition of the fact that literary conventions change continuously, the old evaluative norms of 'good' and 'bad', 'faithful' and 'unfaithful' translations are also disappearing.' (*ibid* p. 12) Another preposterous statement. 'Equivalence' never means 'sameness', and however slippery, it is an indispensable term in translation criticism and teaching; 'norms' is a weasel word here, but the implication appears to be that the values of quality and truth are foreign to translation (which is ridiculous). (It is strange that this book was given such a superficial and damning view in *Target* (3:1. 1991), which is edited by Gideon Toury and J. Lambert.)

Footnotes on Institutional Translation

1. 'The employment secretary' has to be translated as 'the Secretary of State for the Department of Employment'. And so on, for many cabinet posts.

2. The names of international organisations usually have standard

translations (unless, like Interpol, they are internationalisms), and therefore there is little point in reproducing, even in a 'couplet', the source language name in the translation.

The Future of Translation Theory

1. The production of translation theory is in spate. It is not likely to stop.

2. General translation theory leans largely on linguistics; literary translation theory on literary theory. In some cases, words feed on words; in others, social reality is implicated.

3. I see no future in new general theories of translation, each with their models, diagrams, etc. Nevertheless they will continue to pullulate. The increased and rapidly increasing requirements for translations in new fields spreads the vogue for theorising. Writers on translation will attach different values to author, language, text and tradition on the source language side; reader, language, text and tradition on the target language side; the five non-cultural forces (factual, logical, linguistic, aesthetic, moral), the translator and the commissioning agent in the middle.

4. The fundamental dichotomy pin-pointed (*précisé*) by Schleiermacher ('bring the reader to the writer' or 'bring the writer to the reader'), will always remain, but it can be modified by attention to function on each occasion.

5. Translation is not merely a dualistic process. It has to take account of five medial factors: ethics, reality, logic, 'pure language' and aesthetics, of which only aesthetics is not exclusively universal.

6. Translation theory in the future is likely to be applied rather than pure, particular rather than general; a large amount of work remains to be done in the following fields: (a) comparative linguistics, (b) terminology, (c) translation criticism, often leading to revisions of extant translations, (d) machine translation, (e) corpus-based linguistic research, (f) comparative cultural studies, (g) the sociology of translation, (h) the translating process — thinking aloud protocols, (i) comparisons of languages for special purposes, (j) principles and methods of translating dialect, puns, irony, genres of drama, legal, administrative, scientific texts, parody, humour, (k) historical reviews of the translation and reception of influential writers, in particular Ibsen, Chekhov, Strindberg, Brecht, and the French and Russian novelists, (l) the minutiae of translation: punctuation, titling, typography, spacing, capitalisation — in so far as they convey meaning.

Standard Terms and Titling

Standard terms should normally be used for the translations of textbooks, journals, etc., even if the originals use wayward terms. Thus in her description of the make-up of a balance sheet. Denise Flouzat

(*Économie contemporaine*) writes on the credit side (*À l'actif*), *Actif circulant* ('current assets'): *Il se décompose en trois postes* (Current assets consist of three items'): *Les valeurs d'exploitation qui sont les quantités de marchandises (matières premières, produits en cours de production ou produits finis) détenues à la date du bilan.*

Suggested translation: 'Stocks, consisting of the quantities of goods (raw materials, goods in course of production, or finished products) held at the date specified on the balance sheet.'

By default translation, I translate *valeurs d'exploitation*, which I could not find in my reference books, but which could mean 'assets to be used', as 'stocks' (i.e. stock in trade), (French: *stocks*) as this is the standard term. Note also that where French has a heading or title (*Actif circulant*) which becomes the subject of the first sentence (*Il se décompose* . . .), a pronoun is normally used as the cohesive term in French, whilst English normally repeats the title.

Punctuation

A series of vertical initial dashes in French are conveniently replaced by bracketed letters — (a) . . . (b) . . . (c) for a short series; bracketed numbers for a long series but they may also mean 'ditto'.

Nominalisations

I suggest that translators should not 'create' new nominalisations, particularly if the emphasis is on the modifier: thus for *la structure du bilan* 'the structure of the balance-sheet' rather than 'the balance-sheet structure'. This is close to the 'taste area'.

English Balance Sheets

Many items on the left side of a balance sheet (*biens, immobilisations, valeurs*) tend to get translated, after premodification, as 'assets'.

In Praise of Basic Glossaries

It would be useful to translators if publishers produced say 3-4000 word basic bilingual glossaries, based on key words and frequency lists, for each technology and subject field; particularly useful for translation students and translators who have to become temporary experts.

Translation Can Be Beautiful

Un électroencéphalogramme, intercritique et critique: not 'an inter-critical (semi-critical) and critical electroencephalogram', but 'an EEG both between and during (epileptic) seizures' (or 'fits'). Note that *critique* is here the adjective of *crise*, for which English has several often interchangeable 'synonyms' (seizure, fit, attack, ictus, spasm, convulsion, paroxysm), which however all have different meanings. The alternative translation, 'an ictal and an interictal EEG', is rather pale.

POCs

'Prisoner of conscience' is a technical term, and normally should be translated by its standard equivalent, which for French is *prisonnier d'opinion* not as in the Collins-Robert, *prisonnier* or *détenu politique* (nor *detenuto politico*, as in the Italian Collins-Sansoni). Where appropriate, the description has to be added: 'a person recognised by Amnesty International as detained or imprisoned for their political or religious convictions, provided they do not advocate the use of force, and adopted by Amnesty International as a prisoner of conscience.' In Germany, the standard translation is *gewaltloser politischer Gefangener* (lit. 'non-violent political prisoner'); in Austria and Switzerland, it is *Gewissensgefangener* (lit. 'prisoner of conscience'). It is not normally the translator's job to criticise standard translations that appear misguided — there are precedents, such as *Mitbestimmung* as 'co-determination'. The standard Spanish term for 'prisoner of conscience' is *preso de conciencia*, which is ambiguous, since *conciencia* also means 'awareness', in Russian it is *uznik sovesti*, which is monosemous. (Standard translations kindly provided by Amnesty International's International section).

Technical versus Descriptive

In technical translation, one is frequently tempted to replace a descriptive by a technical term; however, it is often possible to combine them: thus for *La méthode la plus simple consiste à diviser la valeur initiale du bien par sa durée d'existence*, 'the simplest method (for measuring depreciation), that is the 'straight line method', consists in dividing the initial value of the asset by its expected life.'

The Power of Music and the Weakness of Words

The concentrated longing and hope in the music of the four times repeated word *vielleicht* (the fourth repitition is a stroke of genius) in the *Magic Flute*, Act I, Scene 12 is so strong that nothing is impaired if it is sung as 'perchance', 'perhaps' or *peut-être*. Compare *geschwinde, stille, Gerechtigkeit, Weisheit* and a hundred other words, in or out of context, in the same work, provided that the stresses and the number of syllables are reproduced. (The only justification for writing about an artist is to give some fresh insight into their art; writing about their lives almost never achieves this.)

A Good Translation — Two Views

Christine Durieux, the author of the useful but verbose *Fondement didactique de la traduction technique* (Didier, Paris 1988; ISBN

2–86460–132–X), sets out her criteria for a good translation in *Qu'est-ce qu'une bonne traduction?* (Pontificia Catolica de Chile, Santiago; 1988): (1) It must faithfully reproduce the information given in the SL text; (2) Its language must be correct (right, appropriate); (3) It must take implicit factors and complementary information (*compléments cognitifs*) into account; (4) Its language must give evidence of abundance and ease of expression; (5) It must be written in the appropriate register; (6) Its language must be adapted to its readership. Ms Durieux always has technical texts in mind, but she regards her principles as valid for any type of text or translation. She admits she is not concerned with poetry (*ce n'est pas du tout ma spécialité — purtroppo*, indeed) but she wants to abolish the distinction or close the gap between the literary and the technical. Just as her mentor Danica Seleskovitch, an interpreter, wants to 'take over' translation, she, as a technical translator, wants to take over the full range of translation. Her method is 'interpretative translation', which she commends unstintingly and indiscriminately in comparison with what she calls 'contrastive' (*sic*) translation. Compare Nida's 'dynamic equivalence' with his 'formal correspondence', but Nida is a great deal subtler and wiser. For Ms Durieux, problems of untranslatability do not exist; they are simply due to the linguistic incompetence and lack of world-knowledge of the translator. Thus 'A pioneering team of doctors in Sheffield is unblocking arteries with lasers' is to be translated as *'L'équipe de Sheffield est la première à opérer le débouchage des artères à l'aide de lasers.* This is indeed a possible translation, but Ms Durieux barely recognises the loss of meaning ('pioneering', 'doctors') and emphasis. As for 'contrastive translation', I assume this refers to the work of Jacqueline Guillemin-Flescher and her team (see, for instance *Linguistique contrastive et Traduction/*T.1 ed. J. Guillemin-Flescher, 1992, Ophrys Paris), which I have always found more imaginative and useful than anything produced by the ESIT *adeptes.*

Ms Durieux is concerned with 'message' rather than 'meaning'. Message is 'performative', meaning is 'descriptive', to take up again Austin's old distinction between 'performative' and 'constative', for which he later unfortunately substituted 'illocutionary' and, for a short time 'locutionary'. Message is usually the core of meaning, but it is not all meaning; meaning is richer, subtler, larger, wider than message.

I would define a good translation as typically a translation where the meaning given to a text by its author is conveyed appropriately and as accurately as possible.

I am assuming here that the translator has grasped the degree of importance of the structure, the words and the sound of the language of the text; that the text is well written, and, if it is not, then the translation is well written, unless the form and the language of the text are important and authoritative. Further, by 'appropriately', I am referring to the occasion of the commission, which is instrumental in determining to what extent the translator has to explain or interpret the text to allow for the cultural, intellectual and linguistic limitations of the envisaged readership, if one exists. (And this is the translator's job, not some editor's or copy-editor's; at least Ms. Durieux and I are in agreement here; this is an integral part of any translation.)

Finally, a good translation is typically characterised by distinction and elegance of language, which has to be perceived instinctively, through the intuition (a combination of intelligence and feeling) of the critic.

XX
AUGUST 1992

Notes on the Translation of Three Medical Texts on Epilepsy
(with assistance from Jane Soulal, Senior Information Officer, Ciba-Geigy Pharmaceuticals, Horsham, venue of a recent Medical Translation Workshop and ITI Medical Network meeting.)
1. *Le terme, encombrant d'épilepsies liées à une localisation.* 'The term, which is rather clumsy (alt. cumbersome), "epilepsies related to a specific area".' (Note that the plurals of disease should be reproduced; also that this is a metalingual translation: the term is 'cumbersome' in both languages.
2. *La neuro-imagerie est muette.* 'The neuro-imaging does not show up.'
3. *Crises sensitivo-motrices.* 'Sensory and motor seizures.'
4. *Grandes pointes émoussées.* 'Large flattened (alt. blurred) spikes.'
5. *En bouffées sous une électrode rolandique basse.* 'in bursts appearing under an electrode in the lower part of the motor (alt. rolandic) area of the cerebral cortex.'
6. *Crises résistantes.* 'Seizures which are resistant to treatment.'
7. *États de mal non rares.* 'Fairly frequent *malaises*' (alt. periods of mild sickness.)
8. *Signes végétatifs.* 'Involuntary movements.'
9. *Genuine Epilepsien (G).* 'Idiopathic epilepsies.'
10. *Liquorzirkulationsstörung.* 'Disturbance of CSF (cerebrospinal fluid) circulation.'
11. *L'aggressività e la vischiosità anticamente riferite agli epilettici in generale.* (It) 'The aggressiveness and sluggishness generally attributed to epileptic patients in times past.' (N.B. Not 'to epileptics' (derogatory).)
12. *La casistica; les antécédents.* 'Case history'.
13. *Gêne épigastrique.* 'Epigastric discomfort' (alt. 'discomfort in the epigastrium').

An Aphorism
Translation, like art (but music to a lesser extent), like metaphor, is a form of simulation (but to a lesser extent if it is only concerned with facts).

Gombrich
'However hard it may often be to render the meaning of a sentence in another language, and however much we may have to resort to glosses and roundabout explanations, the sense can be made accessible even though it may entail a loss in neatness and elegance'. (*Topics of Our*

Time; Twentieth Century Issues in Learning and in Art by E. H. Gombrich
p.41; Phaidon, London, 1991.) Thus Gombrich, expressing his
conviction that translation can always, even with difficulty ('a
difficulty is never an impossibility') penetrate the cultural complexities
of another language, from its colour system onwards.

In fact, in this
marvellous, instructive and morally outstanding book, in which he
devotes four chapters to attacking what he calls 'cultural relativism',
Gombrich goes further: 'Art and literature are now menaced by . . .
this trend, which constitutes a threat to all aspects of scholarship
because it denies the existence of any objective standards of truth . . .
Recognising differences must not lead us to deny the unity of mankind
. . . Art is an embodiment of values' (p. 9.) 'The humanities would
atrophy and die if they attempted to become value-free' (p.55). . .'I am
sure that Michelangelo was indeed a greater artist than the English
seventeenth-century painter John Streeter.' (p. 72.)

Gombrich names some of his adversaries (Paul de Man, Jacques
Derrida, Harold Bloom, Norbert Bolz [Barthes, Greimas, Kristeva,
Foucault unaccountably missing]), but not the so often trumpeted
'value free' movements: structuralism, post-structuralism, deconstruction, reception theory, pop art, trends in post-modernism,
historicism as relativism.) With rejection of or indifference to values,
standards cannot exist.

Translation and Lexicography

Translation and Lexicography edited by Mary Snell-Hornby and
Esther Pöhl (Benjamins, Amsterdam 1989 ISBN 90 272 2063 8) has
some excellent articles. Notably the incomparable Fritz Senn in
'Beyond the Lexicographer's Reach: Literary Overdetermination'
demonstrates that in a well-written literary text (but I think this applies
to any superbly written text), where there is no 'noise', i.e. redundancy,
there are so many semantic factors to take into account apart from
mere referential meaning that one is faced with 'insolubilities' (but they
have to be solved, and that is the translator's glorious 'failure' that
excels so many slick successes where meaning is purely referential). He
illustrates this beautifully with a few examples from James Joyce, e.g.
'Do ptake some ptarmigan' (*Ulysses* 144): *Ptrenez un pteu de ptarmigan*
(Morel); *Ptrendete un pto di ptarmigan* (de Angelis); *Bitte schnehmen
Sie noch etwas Schneehuhn* (Wollschäger); *Treba nebo netreba jeste
porci tetreva* (Skoumal) — alliteration reinforced by internal rhymes;
Egy pppici ppparmezanit (Miklos), where the ptarmigan has become a
parmesan cheese; Senn's comments are just and delightful. Senn points
out that literary texts are always overdetermined and rightly, wistfully
but vainly, again appeals to 'translatology' for help.

Further, there are useful more prosaic pieces by K. and R.
Birkenhauer, Esther Pöhl and Paul Kussmaul, some of whose analyses

of English texts are controversial; e.g. in a sociology text that contrasts 'posture' with 'stance', he translates 'posture' as *feste Position* and 'stance' (the latter acceptably) as *Einstellung*. Both words show up lexical gaps in the foreign languages that I know, but I think that 'firm position' unnecessarily goes beyond the semantic range of 'posture', which is 'strained' and 'temporary', and which could be translated as *eine Position* or (to make a contrast) *eine bestimmte Position* (or *Haltung*). But Kussmaul is always challenging to read, and he accepts accuracy as an aim.

The Chronology of Literary Translation

The time-sequence of the three short story translations I quote in *Paras 8* (*Linguist* July 1990), 'anecdotal' and insufficient as they are as statistical samples does suggest that the kind of free, inaccurate, 'creative' and fanciful translations published in the thirties could no longer be perpetrated even in the sixties and seventies and later; this also applies to the more recent translations of Kafka's *The Trial*. In good translation practice, the scientific (non-cultural) factor, accuracy, at least increasingly in time reduces the hold (*emprise*) of the cultural and ideological factor, which however always operates. (*jouera.*)

Intensifiers

'I *totally* reject . . . I *profoundly* regret . . . I *completely* concur . . . you are *fully* aware . . . I *deeply* sympathise . . . I *strongly* oppose . . . I *greatly, entirely, absolutely, much, very much, warmly, wholly* (etc) . . . approve' . . . '*purely* notional' . . . '*monumental* insensitivity' . . . typically, nine times out of ten, these sentiments would be more impressive, and would sound sincere, if the intensifiers were deleted.

Lexical Gaps

When I print a word and then put a foreign language near-synonym after it in brackets, it's not to translate but to express myself instinctively, and therefore I intuit a lexical gap.

Translating: A Struggle between Sense and Naturalness

Quasi-stagnation (F) (of an economic year) . . . 'quasi-stagnation' . . . 'near-stagnation' . . . 'almost stagnating' . . . 'nearly stagnating' . . . 'quasi-stagnation' . . . 'near-standstill' . . . 'quasi-stagnation' . . . 'close to stagnation' . . . 'as though inactive' . . . 'as though stagnating' . . . 'quasi-stagnation' . . . 'semi-stagnation' (finish).

An Aphorism

Translatability is in inverse ratio to creativity in translation, viz, the less translatable the text, the more creative the translator has to be.

OR the more information he must get

Boy!

Alex Duval Smith (*Guardian* 23.4.92) has rightly excoriated some phrase books [add: for British bourgeois] for translating 'Waiter!' as *Garçon!* [instead of *Monsieur!*] (In a Madras British club, waiters are still being addressed as 'Boy!' *Das Mädchen* and *la bonne* seem similarly archaic).

Cultural Focus?

Argent, encaisse, trésorerie, numéraire, espèces, liquidités . . . did ever a language have so many technical words for 'cash' as French?

The Translation of Alliteration

1. My common sense tells me that onomatopoeia is intimately associated with the origin of language, and that Saussure's dictum that the word is an arbitrary sign is diachronically and to some extent synchronically nonsense. I suspect that alliteration, where the repeated initial sound is iconic, is a sophisticated and later form of onomatopoeia; it is also used to arrest attention (e.g. 'Hongkong Bank's global gamble' (*weltweite Wette?*)) — where however the alliteration may pass unperceived — to please, and to revive an old verse form.

2. Alliteration may be involuntary or intentional. Where it is involuntary, it should be ignored, and if obtrusive, eliminated in translation (e.g. *ganz gross*; 'quite large').

3. Where it is intentional, it is quite common in journalism (particularly in headlines and titles), advertisements and TV commercials, as well as in the literary works with which it is usually associated.

4. As a trope, alliteration appears to be more common in Celtic and Germanic languages, where it is an integral feature of the form of the earliest poetry, than in others.

5. Where it is important, and used onomatopoeically, it should be at least partially reproduced through onomatopoeia:

Pour qui sont ces serpents qui sifflent sur vos têtes? (*Andromaque*, 1.1638, Racine)

'For whom are those snakes that hiss over your head?' (tr. John Cairncross)

6. Alliteration is also a constituent of old English and German similes, but they are not usually intertranslatable (e.g. 'pretty as a picture', *bildhübsch/schön*; 'dead as a doornail', *mausetot*; 'fit as a fiddle', *kerngesund; wilder Wurm* ('savage serpent'?) Wagner should provide more examples (*Zweifel und Zwist, Speichels Schweiss*), but I doubt if more than a 'taste' of the alliteration can be reproduced.

7. Note that if the alliteration is the main point, as in Alaric Watt's immortal (?) *The Siege of Belgrade:*

An Austrian Army awfully arrayed,
Boldly, by battery, besieged Belgrade;

Cossack commanders cannonading come,
Dealing destruction's devastating doom . . .,
all the alliteration has to be reproduced in translation, and the
semantics, except for some kind of loud disaster, has to go. I don't
know if it's ever been translated into the sister-languages, Dutch or
German.
8. Assonance, the use of the same vowel sound with different
consonants or the same consonant with different vowels in successive
words or stressed syllables (time, light; mystery, mastery) is a kind of
internal alliteration within successive words. It is an attractive device,
not as powerful as rhyme unless it startles by its unusualness. It
preceded the introduction of rhyme in French 12th century poetry, and
remains in Spanish and Portuguese poetry. In English, it is in many
traditional ballads, and above all in Hopkins and Owen, and it hovers
over Isaac Rosenberg's powerful *Dead Man's Dump*. Like alliteration,
it also appears in common phrases like 'mad as a hatter' and 'high
as a kite'. Any translation of assonance depends on the usual
conflict between the degree of importance of the device and of the
meaning of the poem. There are useful hints on the translation of
alliteration, assonance and onomatopoeia in Jiri Levy's *Die literarische
Übersetzung*.

The Words in the Translation
    Albrecht Neubert's brochure, *Die Wörter im der Übersetzung*
(Akademie Verlag, Berlin, 1991, ISBN 3-05-001779-1) is a stimulating
and instructive essay on the function and meaning of words, specifically
titles, in a translation. He takes the short story *Slippage* by John
Updike (whose quality as a writer he considerably exaggerates with the
support of clichéd blurbs from American journalists ('master of
words', 'prose of solid gold', 'a straight-A student who happens to
write the most vivid prose in America'), and examines the word
'slippage' first in several monolingual English dictionaries, then
extracontextually in its German meanings, and lastly through its
various occurrences in the story. The process of arriving at his final
version of the title (*Anzeichen eines Niedergangs*) is as exciting as a
thriller, and more enlightening. Since one would not be likely to find
Niedergang as a translation of 'slippage' in any bilingual dictionary
(but it covers several of the senses of the word in the story), Neubert is
justified in warning translators to treat bilingual dictionaries with
caution; but there is a distance between this and his claim that 'The
dictionary virtually never offers the translator the word that will get
him out of his difficulty.' (In my opinion, the better and the larger the
dictionary, the more likely it is to do so.) Neubert makes a valuable
distinction between *Worte* (connected context-dependent words and
also important statements) and *Wörter* (unconnected words say

'haematology'?) in translation; like most oppositions in translation, they are on a cline and merge with each other.

Technical and Institutional Terms

One can set out general principles (I think of them as hints) on how to translate terms of art, but some have to be taken individually, since they are not typical, and simply discussed. Take the case of *allocations de solidarité*, several times mentioned in J.-M. Fahy's *Le Chômage en France* (P.U.F., 1985), but taken for granted, never described, as though the specialist French reader would be sure to understand them. Since there appears to be no standard English equivalent, what is the translator to do? First, perhaps, s/he traces it in the *Grand Dictionnaire encyclopédique* Larousse, where it is defined as a Government unemployment benefit scheme affecting (a) young applicants looking for their first jobs (*allocations d'insertion*, the latter a horrid word to translate), (b) unmarried women with children, (c) (mainly) workers who have used up (*épuisé*) their normal rights to unemployment benefit (alt. are no longer eligible for them). A portion of this information has to be included in the translation, depending not on the readership's knowledge but their interest and motivation, and preferably in a footnote at the bottom of the page. The term *allocation de solidarité* could be transferred and referred to as the '*solidarité* benefit' or 'this support benefit or scheme', at later mentions.

Pension d'invalidité should, I think, be translated as 'disability pension'. The UK 'invalidity pension' imposes special conditions.

Allocations de préretraite. Only a search of 'reality' can determine whether this means 'early retirement pension' or supplementary pension just before retirement'.

Chambres consulaires. This refers to the *tribunaux consulaires* where the *juges consulaires* hold their sessions. Translate as 'commercial courts'.

Quotations Again

In quotations, as elsewhere, ordinary language should be translated by ordinary languages. The Swedish for 'I'll read the tea-leaves to foretell your future' is 'I'll read the coffee-grounds to foretell your future', provided the quotation is a metaphor, and no tea-leaves are read. But the general principle remains that quotations must be translated closely at the author's level and not be linguistically or culturally filtered by the translator.

Further, referring back to *TL* Vol 30 No 2, p. 63 on Quotations, I now think my translation of Howard Jacobson's 'O for a beaker full of the warm south' was philistine, and I should go for something like: *O hätte ich nur einen Wein des warmen Südens voll, wie der Dichter Keats beinahe sagte!* in the hope that the German reader knows or becomes curious about Keats, possibly adding a note to help the German reader, provided there are other notes in the translation of the novel. If a novel quotes Shakespeare, the Tieck-Schlegel rather than the Erich Fried translation should be used, as it is likely to be more familiar.

Forms of Address

Forms of address, for spoken and written languages as well as for translation, are awkward in many languages. French has *Monsieur* and *Madame*, and should sooner or later drop the *Mademoiselle*; correspondingly Italian has *Signore* and *Signora*, and should drop the *Signorina*. English and German are relatively silent. Personally, I think the subservient 'Sir' should be dropped, and the gentle 'Mr' or 'Mrs' (you can't say 'Ms') plus surname should be introduced; for German, *mein Herr* and *meine Frau*, which sounds rather Dutch, for people one doesn't know. However, for English it may be necessary to keep the 'subservient' sir and the more natural 'madam' for people one doesn't know. Note the degrading tendency of hospital and social workers to call all patients by their first names or 'dear/love/darling' without expectation of reciprocity. This is two-tier NHS populism. The above is a tentative para.

Neologisms Again

In principle, all deliberate neologisms have to be recreated in the target language, provided they are likely to be enduring in the source language. Whilst in fiction they should be immediately recreated, in 'reality' texts they have to be recreated by an official translator. Before that event, a synonym/paraphrase will have to do. Thus *désétatisation* has been in French since 1967, and is defined as 'the reduction of the State's share in the management and the financing of the public sector'.

At a first mention, most of this has to be reproduced in the translation, coupled with the French term in brackets; at further mentions, the French term could be alternated with 'State disempowerment', and may have to be contrasted with 'denationalisation' and 'privatisation', if these appear in the same text.

Translation Theory

As I once nearly wrote: 'He who can, does; he who can't, writes; he who can't write, translates; he who can't translate, becomes a translatologist'. Reading the perhaps latest book on translation theory (but they pullulate every month), Rosa Rabadan's *Equivalencia y traduccion; problematica de la equivalencia translemica ingles-español* (Universidad de Leon, 1991, ISBN 84–7719–2545–5), I wonder if this is not the most parasitical, abstract, boring, most remote from reality discipline in existence. Here we have the world's most overworked word: *problemat/ical/ique/ik/ic* with an unnecessary neologism (*translemica*) straightaway in the title. It takes me back to logeme, texteme, inforeme, diatheme, classeme, glosseme, plereme and that remarkable trio, seme, sememe and semanteme and so on (the history of linguistics is strewn with these corpses, which even Austin and Peirce couldn't resist) and 'introduces' transleme — all the vain terms with which these translatologists vainly sought immortality on the analogy of the hardier 'phoneme' and 'morpheme'.

And yet this is a nice, cosy, intelligent, book, which gives evidence of immense tortured reading (a real thesis-buster) all about the difficulties of equivalence, ending with an 'inspired' quote: 'When in a great number of the compared units a certain type of translational relationship is found to be dominant, and/or a certain hierarchy of relationships recurs as a fixed pattern, these will be taken as a guidance for the establishment of the dominant type of relationships and/or the entire hierarchy for further units of the same text, unless contradicted by the actual findings concerning them (including specific translation problems) and eventually for the text as a whole." (*sic, sic, sic* — would you ever believe it?) Thus Rabadan, speaking through her master's English voice (p. 200). Throughout the book there is much intelligent discussion with few translation examples. Thus the views of various 'authorities' (even me) on the translation of metaphor appear without the illustrations that would give substances to the concepts. And there are extended commentaries on seven haphazardly chosen English texts and their (two) translations, under their heads *intencionalidad*, *aceptabilidad*, *situacionalidad*, *intertextualidad*, which show that de Beaugrande is alive and well and living in Spain.

Yet I think that translation theory, if it made human behaviour and its consequences (sometime called 'life' by Matthew Arnold, D. H. Lawrence, F. R. Leavis) its objective, and language its mediating factor, might become interesting and not so parasitic.

Synonymic Power

Given that the final mental struggles in a translation usually revolve round the complexities of the target language — the apparently bodyless sequence of meanings has to be gingerly transferred into the new language — is the translator's main asset at this stage her mastery, control, understanding of a huge range of synonyms? Is that why *Roget's Thesaurus*, with its delicate graduations of synonyms, is so useful to the anglophones, whilst so many other nationalities, like the Spanish and the Japanese don't know what they're missing?

This last stage is often a continual adjustment and readjustment, a repeated change of mind, a kaleidoscope jostling, often centred in the adjective, the quality, as a component of a collocation or a syntagm, since adjectives with their related adverbs and cognate abstract or adjectival nouns or verbs ('quiet' (adj.), 'quietly', 'quiet' (noun), ('quieten') have more arbitrary and changing components of meaning than straight nouns (objects) or verbs (actions). Adjectives in fact are the core of synonyms.

I am at present trying out a translation training exercise that calls for synonyms for descriptive words. Thus:

'It is this financing (funding) problem (issue, difficulty) that is forcing (compelling, obliging, inducing) firms (companies) to think again about (rethink) their basic (key, fundamental) strategies (procedures, aims). Japanese manufacturers (producers, industrialists) are starting (beginning, commencing) to abandon (give up, relinquish) their time-honoured (inveterate) habit (custom) of throwing (casting, putting forward) as many products (goods) as often (frequently) as possible (they can) at the market (market place). Fewer (not so many) product changes (substitutions, replacements), they reason (estimate, guess), means (signifies, amounts to) reduced (cut, decreased) marketing (selling) costs (expenditure) and a smaller (more modest) capital-spending bill (outlay on capital).'

Note that some of the synonyms, which are all bracketed, are fairly instinctive, and after a class had proposed additional synonyms, they could then be invited to grade them in respect of their semantic closeness to their 'principals'. I am rather distrustful of translator training programmes, as the best training is to translate and learn by one's mistakes, but I hope the above synonym-building exercise, which need not take more than 20–30 minutes, is of some use.

Note that technical terms can be 'synonymized' by descriptions, but artificial synonyms should not be created out of context (Japanese; Nippon).

An Emphasis Device
'There is . . . are . . . was . . . came' etc., can neatly be used as an English emphasis device. Thus, for *Aucune disposition ne restreint, ni n' a réglementé dans le passé, la faculté des résidents français de choisir la monnaie en laquelle ils s'engagent dans leurs relations avec les non-résidents. (Économie française.* Michel): 'There is no legal provision that restrains, or has ever regulated in the past, the right of French residents to choose the currency with which they engage in trading with non-residents'. This device can only be used to emphasize the subject of a sentence; when used with intransitive verbs other than 'to be', it is apt to be too dramatic for normal translation use. (Then there came . . .)

Translating Children's Literature
After a skilful and mercifully succinct summary of some translation theorists' views, *Literatura para Niños: Cultura y Traduccion*, a collective work co-ordinated by Carolina Valdivieso (Catholic University of Chile, Santiago) examines interesting examples of translation into Spanish of about a dozen French, German and English children's books.

The Leipzig School
About 18 months ago when I heard that TAS, the Section for Theoretical and Applied Linguistics at the Karl Marx University Leipzig, which for me (most visitors?) was curiously dominated by the translation section, was about to be dissolved, I made a protest and an appeal, and received no reply. TAS was an exciting place to teach and discuss at, and the publications, *Fremdsprachen* and *Übersetzungswissenschaftliche Beiträge*, were stimulating and concrete. The School was a pioneer, and hopefully Albrecht Neubert will write its history.

The Göttingen Group Again
Reading *Die literarische Übersetzung: Stand und Perspektiven ihrer Erforschung*, edited by Harald Kittel (Eich Schmidt, Berlin, 1988 ISBN 3–503–02291–0), I have the impression that this is translation history rather than translation criticism or theory (compare pre-Leavis literary 'criticism'), a series of intelligent passionless causeries on the place of translation in Renaissance France or 19th century Bohemia and Moravia, but without reference to acts of translation, or examples of translation, or the difficulties of translation. There is much recording of movements, publications and dates, but none of the interest in words and language one would expect from translators. Arnim Paul Frank, who appears to be the leader of the group and contributes three papers, enumerates a large number of norms in 'historic-descriptive translation studies', not to mention four impressive-looking diagrams whose use he fails to explain, and concludes with some pathetically isolated translation examples from the most neglected great work in dramatic literature, Z. Krasinski's *Nie Boska komedia*. His final *Rückblick und Ausblick* relating Nida to Snell-Hornby, Holmes, Toury, and the Göttingen group is as always descriptive rather than critical. Yet even here, notably in von Stackelberg's *Blüte und Niedergang der Belles Infidèles*, on the decline of fanciful translation in 18th century France, truth sometimes breaks through.

Latin Tags
I have the impression that Classical tags and phrases are more common in Romance and German than in English texts. Thus I often translate *a priori* (F or G) as 'in principle'; in a popular text, I would translate *Calvet rencontre son alter ego* as 'Calvet meets his equal'; (the English 'alter ego' meaning 'second self' or 'close friend' — the reference is to Mitterand! — would be a mistranslation); in a scholarly text (*L'économie mixte* by P. Marchat) I would translate:
Une telle démarche, caractéristique d'une affectio societatis, est classique lorsqu'elle est le fait d'entrepreneurs et de capitalistes, à la recherche du profit as:
'This attitude, which is characteristic of a favourable predisposition of

society, is typical when it is taken up by entrepreneurs and capitalists seeking profit." (Note (a) It is unfair to leave the English reader with only the Latin collocation as he (let alone a student of economics) could not be expected to understand it; (b) I was unable to trace the collocation in many Latin, legal, and Latin tag dictionaries, as well as the Webster and the *O.E.D.*; (c) I suspect that Marchat was showing off; (d) I would relegate *affectio societatis* to a footnote.

Teachers and Lecturers

If one teaches, one tries to improve — oneself, the topic, the taught. If one lectures . . .?

Translation as a Decision-Making Process

Jiří Levy, in his contribution to the Roman Jakobson six-volume *festschrift*, famously described translation as a decision-making process. Typically, the decision will lean towards the original or the translation; more delicately, it will take into account on the one hand, the source language, the author, the source language culture, the source language tradition and norms or house-style (if these exist) of the text-type; on the other hand, the readership and the corresponding target language factors; and in the middle, the translator's thinking and rethinking, reflecting his personality and ideology and her attempts to discount them, and the five truths — moral, factual, linguistic, aesthetic, logical, which I have previously defined.

Malcolm Bowie

For the second time in twenty years, Oxbridge is about to have a professor of a foreign language with powerful views on translation (Cambridge had L. W. Forster, but unfortunately he never wrote anything more after his fine essay in *Aspects of Translation*). Malcolm Bowie, the Marshal Foch Professor of French designate at Oxford, recently gave the Translating Division a rich lecture on 'Literary Translation — the case of Proust', including a critical comparison of three translations of a Proust extract, two translations of Eugenio Montale's imaginatively onomatopaeic *L'Anguilla*, and his own eleven unashamedly prescriptive golden rules of translating, beginning with accuracy, which hopefully he will publish. Whether Malcolm Bowie will be able to make Oxford, with its various more or less literary foreign language departments and degree so ripe for reconsideration translation-conscious and translation-literate remains to be seen.

SOME AFTERTHOUGHTS

Here I temporarily end my chronicle. By the time it is published, I shall have written five more chapters.

1. In the period covered by this book I have often found translation a fascinating and frustrating occupation. I bear in mind that it can also be dull and humdrum in the grey texts of staff translators with their catalogues, manuals and company reports, where the figures change but the words remain mainly the same, and they are usually already pat in the data banks. This at a time when all the world's significant and many not so significant activities have to be increasingly mirrored in translation, when the increase in international organizations is matched by a much greater increase in national languages, although, to date, South Africa is still, to its shame, only a 'bilingual country'.

2. Translation is a discipline (profession, occupation, exercise, *jeu* — it is hardly a game) that is marked by an increasing number of contradictions and paradoxes, not least in its own nature. There is no common agreement even on its definition. Though its essence remains the same, it is dynamic in its forms and channels, ranging from interlinear translation through full translation to adaptation, summary and gist, always however, as I see it, inter- rather than intralingually. It is unique in being strictly impossible yet almost everywhere essential; like writing, it is a professional's job, but practised in one form or another by most educated and many uneducated people; traditionally regarded with suspicion by multi- as well as monolingual persons and with open hostility by many foreign language teachers. Translation is to some extent the trade of an impostor pretending to be the author of the translated text. In the translation of laws, treaties and official documents, translators have to remain anonymous, since they cannot bear the responsibility for their final versions; in other cases, they should be identified, as they have that responsibility.

3. In 1988, George Steiner noted eleven newly published books about translation (see his select bibliography in *After Babel*, 2nd edition, 1992); in the '40s, they averaged two or three per year. This is some indication of the transformation of the subject.

4. It is ironical that whilst translating out of one's language of habitual use is something most professional translators mistrust, since it normally leads to mistakes of usage, it is in fact a useful and pertinent way of improving and enriching one's knowledge and fluency in the foreign language. The revered 'prose' (first citation 1901?) was once the jewel in the crown of Latin and (ancient) Greek teaching and was taken over by foreign language teachers till the '60s; it is now usually in

disrepute among foreign language teachers. Translation into the 'home' language, curiously called the 'unseen' (1879), possibly because one was not meant to look anything up in reference books — the *O.E.D.* says 'not previously read', 'an unprepared passage for translation', was always considered inferior to the 'prose'; now it is recognized as the translator's true occupation, with mandatory use of reference books, and also as a rightful constituent of foreign language learning, though arguably it teaches the translators more about their own than about the foreign language. The *thème* (1690!) and the *version* (possibly 1596), also strangely named, parallel the 'prose' and the 'unseen', but Flaubert at any rate downgraded the 'prose' when he wrote *Le thème, au collège, prouve l'application, comme la version prouve l'intelligence.*

5. As the supermarkets and the branches of the multinationals multiply, they bring with them the labels and the packaging covered with close multilingual translations; translation is as necessary in the most tragic political situations, the world of detainees, refugees, deportees and exiles, as it is, on the other hand, in every aspect of diplomacy and tourism. It is a touchstone of the way small countries and minorities are treated. When translation is equated with enlightenment and humanity, its stature will be acknowledged.

INDEX